MW01591844

Twain's

World

Essays on Hartford's Cultural Heritage by:

Barbara Beeching

Lary Bloom

Garret Condon

Tom Condon

Steve Courtney

Jim Farrell

Anne Farrow

Brendan Gill

Joan D. Hedrick

Steve Kemper

Rob Kyff

Andrew Marlatt

Colin McEnroe

James A. Miller

Susan D. Pennybacker

Sandra Wheeler

Published by
The Hartford Courant

Designed by Cummings & Good, Chester, Connecticut

Printed in the United States of America

Published by The Hartford Courant

ISBN: 0-9646638-3-X

10 9 8 7 6 5 4 3 2 1

ISBN 0-9646638-3-X

5 1 4 9 5

9 780964 663831

Contents

Acknowledgments

The editors of Twain's World wish to thank the following for their expertise, support and enthusiasm:

Dick Ahles, Claude Albert, Nancy Albert, Steve Albert, Mark Aldam, Kathy Andrews, Michael Arace, Andre Barnett, David Barrett, Arnold Berman, Deb Geigis Berry, Christine Bettencourt, Jo Blatti, John Boyer, Jane Bronfman, Anne Brouillard, Richard Buel, Ashley Burns, Fenna Calder, Jack Chatfield, Maureen Connolly, Patricia Cousins, Ed Dombroskas, Doug Evans, Wilson H. Faude, Liz Frankel, Bruce Fraser, Lou Golden, Janet Cummings Good, Peter Good, Fran Gordon, Todd Gray, Alex Guenther, Liz Gwillim, Amanda Hamann, Robb Hankins, Laura Baione Hayden, Joseph Hilliman, Bill Hoelzel, William Hosley, Jennifer Huget, Raymond Jansen, Gary Jones, Jocelyn M. Jones, Anthony Keller, Mike Kintner, Penny Knowles, H. Catherine Ladd, Joel Lang, Jeannette LeSure, Karen Lipeika, Kirsten Livingston, Sarah Lytle, Sarah Mann, Patrick McCaughey, Caroline McGuire, Diana McKain, Patricia McNerney, Richard Medeiros, Rachel Merritt, Dean Nelson, Ruth Nelson, John Ostrout, Sandy Parisky, Lori Skoglund Pattavina, Mike Peters, Debra Petke, Marty Petty, H. Scott Phelps, Gerald Price, Dona Winzler Prindle, Susan Quirk, Lalia Rach, Christine Raymond, Merl Reagle, Jane Reilly, Ronna Reynolds, Steve Rice, Ken Richters, Karen Rossi, Patricia Rowland, Alan Sagal, Dennis Schain, Ernest Shaw, Roxanne Stachelek, Bob Sudyk, Stephanie Summers, Cliff Teutsch, Brian Toolan, Korky Vann, Deborah E. Walls, Michael E. Waller, Gail Warner, Amy Weghorst, Patricia Weiss, Katie Wells, Sandy Yamarik, David Yindra.

Introduction

Describing his adopted city, Mark Twain said: "Of all the beautiful towns it has been my fortune to see, this is the chief." It was an observation from a man who by then had inspected the capitals of Europe and the frontiers of America. What Twain had found here was a city of wide, tree-lined boulevards, stately homes, and some of the earliest and most beautiful of public parks in America. He also found a center of Yankee ingenuity, the sort of place where, aside from pursuing his literary instincts, he could go on the line in other ways, investing in new technology.

It is true that his forays into technology led to his eventual financial embarrassment. And like its most famous resident author, the city itself went through a lengthy period when its fortunes where not what they once were. Some of the lovely architecture that Twain had known during his nearly two decades of residing here disappeared. There was no longer a trace of the book publishing industry that drew Twain to Hartford in the first place. As a manufacturing center, the city lost the ranking it had when Sam Colt produced his revolver in a factory with a blue dome. Even the insurance industry, which always provided strong leadership and vision for the community, discovered many other cities in which to employ workers. Most of the workers who remained lived in the suburbs. The result was that what was once America's richest city in terms of per capita income was now one of its poorest.

And yet not even a century of failing to safeguard its assets can do in a city like Hartford. Over the decades, we were reminded time and time again of urban resiliency, of vision, of the courage of citizens who worked on behalf of the community they loved. We saw how Chick Austin revitalized America's oldest public art museum, the Wadsworth Atheneum. We saw how Wilson H. Faude and other visionaries helped save Mark Twain's old house from demolition by neglect. We saw the city flourish as a center of learning and medicine. We saw the work of Wallace Stevens and Sol LeWitt and other native sons and daughters whose expressions on paper or walls became known internationally. We saw triumphs of less heralded individuals who quietly but persistently addressed social ills and made the community a better place to live. What we didn't see was the proper celebration of this remarkable heritage.

This book grew out of a major project by Northeast, the Sunday magazine of the Hartford Courant. It was our view that an appreciation for the cultural heritage of our city could go a long way to enhance its future. We had seen how the phenomenon of cultural heritage tourism had transformed so many other lesser cities — it is the fastest growing segment of the tourism business. But we saw an opportunity for more than tourism. We saw a chance for a rebirth of civic pride. From this new beginning, we thought it was possible to grow once again.

And so, in 1995, the magazine began a two-year weekly series focusing on Hartford's rich cultural heritage. We engaged many of the region's finest writers to help in our effort, from Joan Hedrick, who won a Pulitzer Prize for her biography of Harriet Beecher Stowe, to Brendan Gill, a Hartford native who wrote for the New Yorker magazine for over six decades, to James A. Miller, who at the time directed the Afro-American Studies Program at Trinity College, to a colleague of Miller's, Susan D. Pennybacker, who runs the school's Hartford Studies program. Over the period of the project, we explored the arts, manufacturing, the insurance industry, and all the forces that shaped one of America's most under-appreciated cities.

We called the series Twain's World, because it was our intent to recreate the intensity and the vision — and perhaps even the whimsy — of the time. You will see in this book some of the risk that Twain himself took as commentator, particularly in the pieces by Colin McEnroe, the author and talk show host, and Andrew Marlatt, who, by the book's end, imagines Twain as a frustrated guest on the David Letterman show.

The effort here — though based on sound historical research — is not so much to return to the past, but to make use of the past as a springboard to new ideas and celebrations.

To that end, the series naturally led to a partnership with the Mark Twain House and WFSB-TV in the effort to create Mark Twain Days, a festival to celebrate the city's cultural heritage, and to send a signal far and wide about the vibrancy of Hartford.

We wish to thank all of those authors, photographers, editors, and illustrators who contributed to the Twain's World series, to this book, and to the effort to recognize and to enhance a great American city.

— Lary Bloom, editor of Northeast

I

The Center of My Universe

Brendan Gill

Wherever I go in the world, I make a point of demonstrating that there is scarcely a single event of historic importance that has taken place anywhere in the world since the birth of Christ that I cannot successfully link to Hartford, Connecticut, and not simply to Hartford as a whole but to Prospect Avenue in particular — that still stately thoroughfare which marks the boundary between Hartford and West Hartford and also marks, as nobody will be astonished to learn, my birthplace.

It happens that the Gill family residence was on the West Hartford side of the boundary, but when I was born, some 80-odd years ago, it was mighty Hartford that mattered and to which we Gills gave our allegiance — West Hartford, as it existed anywhere beyond, let's say, Walbridge Road, amounted to a scattering of isolated and uneasy settlements, prey dragons.

Once long ago I was speaking at the J. Pierpont Morgan Library in New York City on a topic having to do with the early history of that great metropolis. I began by attempting to establish a totally fictitious connection between old J. Pierpont Morgan and me — Morgan having been born in Hartford and the Morgan Memorial wing of the Wadsworth Atheneum being located directly across Main Street from where one of my grandfathers, a well-known dry-goods merchant, had established his emporium. I went on and on with this self-important nonsense, which caused me to drift farther and farther from my assigned topic, and at last I noticed in the front row of the audience an old gentleman pounding his fist on his knee and I heard him exclaim in an all too audible voice, "For God's sake, when is he going to get out of Hartford and come down to New York?"

And the answer, obviously, then and now, is "Never!" If I happen to be visiting Biltmore House in western North Carolina and someone mentions that the grounds were laid out by the eminent landscape architect Frederick Law Olmsted, I am quick to point out that he was a Hartford boy. Similarly, if talk anywhere turns upon art, I interject that such wholly unlike artists as Frederick Church, Milton Avery, and Sol LeWitt were all born in Hartford. In the world of letters, I play one trump after another — Lydia Sigourney, Harriet Beecher Stowe, Charles Dudley Warner and Mark Twain. All Hartford! Oh, I admit that it is Twain's misfortune to have been born in a miserable little town called Hannibal, Mo., but it was his choice to live in Hartford — he was, as we say nowadays, pricing himself up when he did so, and that marvelous cranky house of his, as romantic in its way as a Mississippi riverboat, was where he was happiest.

As for the acting profession, one thinks of William Gillette, who wrote the play "Sherlock Holmes," and whose castle on the Connecticut River, now a state park, is a wonder out of some long-vanished medieval kingdom. Hartford was also the home of Sophie Tucker, billed on Broadway as "the last of the red-hot mamas," and Katharine Hepburn, not in the least a red-hot mama.

I happen to have known William Gillette, because he was a patient of my doctor-father in Hartford, and I have known the Hepburn family through three generations, but alas! I missed out on Mark Twain, who died in 1910, four years before I was born. You might think that this gap of four years would prevent me from claiming any personal intimacy with Twain, but not at all. My vanity has encouraged me to forge a close bond with him through Norfolk, where I spend my summers and where Twain spent a couple of summers many a long year ago. My wife's uncle, Arthur Knox, once offered his seat to Twain in the parlor car of a train making its way from Norfolk to New York. Uncle Arthur had a reservation and Twain didn't, and Twain gratefully accepted Uncle Arthur's offer, Uncle Arthur being obliged to ride all the way to New York seated on an unopened suitcase. If that isn't a pretty impressive connection between Mark Twain and me, I'd like to know what is.

In old age we begin to invent connections by means of memories of things that never happened. The act of memory is, in effect, the art of memory. It consists of shaping one's past ever closer to one's heart's

"The act of memory," writes Brendan Gill, "is, in effect, the art of memory."

desire — not who I was but who I had hoped to be becomes the driving force, and I sense that I am getting close to having shot pool and drunk sour-mash whiskey with Twain as the snow fell through the dark winter night and all the rest of Hartford slept. Mark and I — oh, before I die, he and I will be shoulder-to-shoulder and perhaps even arm-in-arm!

Recently, I visited Isola Bella, a delightful country retreat on an island in a lake in Salisbury, where the American School for the Deaf maintains a camp for six weeks every summer. The island, with its exotic stone towers and forest of hundred-foot-high pines rising out of the blue waters of the lake, was left to the school by its last owner, an artist named Muriel Alvord, who was a descendant of one of the old Yankee families that had gained wealth in the 18th and 19th centuries from the iron industry that then flourished in Salisbury. Does an exotic summer place called Isola Bella sound remote from Hartford, to say nothing of Prospect Avenue? So you assume that I will be able to establish no connection between them? How little confidence you have in the way fate rules our lives! For when I had put but a single question to my hosts on Isola Bella, a multiplicity of pertinent connections suddenly flooded in upon me.

It turned out that the Alvord family's winter home used to be on Prospect Avenue, that when Muriel Alvord came rather belatedly to marry she chose as her husband a neighbor on Prospect Avenue named Ferrari Ward, and when she chose to build a new studio on Isola Bella she commissioned still another neighbor on Prospect Avenue, the architect Robert Schutz, a lifelong bachelor, and kept adding room after room to her studio in order to make sure that he remained as often as possible by her side. Be that as it may, the Wards and Schutz made a happy triangle and gave many amusing parties on the island. To this day, it is remembered how tea in the late afternoon would give way little by little to beverages of a stronger nature.

Isola Bella and Prospect Avenue! Let us drink to their indissolubility.

2

Twain's Decision

Garret Condon

Editor's NOTE: *The work of Samuel L. Clemens, produced under the pen name of Mark Twain, has been analyzed in hundreds of scholarly and popular works over the last century. Far less attention has been paid in those circles to the place where he lived during the most productive period of his life, the house at 351 Farmington Ave. What was the character of the Hartford life of Sam Clemens and his family?*

To that end, Garret Condon, who has been known to cover the Twain front for The Courant, has written the following bit of historical fiction. It is based on an episode in Mark Twain's life in 1889, while he was writing "A Connecticut Yankee in King Arthur's Court" and worried about his monumental investment in the troubled Paige typesetter.

Few liberties have been taken with the known facts of the 36 hours described. But since the facts are few and sketchy, the fiction writer has had plenty of leeway. The dialogue, whenever possible, is taken from Twain's writings. (The opening episode is based on an account from Twain's maid, Katy Leary.) The journal entries are taken from his published journals.

"Oh, Mr. Clemens! The smoke!"

Clemens plucked the smoldering stub of a cigar from his mouth and examined it for defects. Finding none, he replaced it and bent to his billiards shot giving his maid, Katy Leary, a withering look. But she rushed to the window at one end of the room, hung her head out and screamed for all of Farmington Avenue to hear.

"Patrick McAleer! John O'Neill! Come upstairs! Fire! Quickly!"

Suddenly the house pounded with footsteps: McAleer with his heavy boots was first, then came O'Neill, taking two steps at a time.

Again, Clemens backed off from his shot and pulled the remains of the Havana away from his lips and, peering over the edge of the billiards table, saw the cause of Katy's alarm: the floor beneath the hearth tiles was burning. McAleer, the coachman, dashed in and made for the fireplace, quickly kneeling and prying up the stones with the pointed end of an iron file. O'Neill, the gardener, did the same with a trowel. But smoke turned to flame where they had removed the bricks.

"Blessed be!" exclaimed Leary.

Clemens twisted his bushy brows in prickly annoyance, leaned his cue against the billiards table and sauntered toward a shelf on one side of his desk, against the far wall.

"Stand back," Clemens said with his back to them. He turned around holding a round, blue-glass fire grenade, which he lobbed, with one hand, into the flames. The glass globe broke with a pop and soda sizzled across the floor, dousing the flames. Clemens opened the door to the Texas deck to vent the smoke and then strolled back to his cue and leaned again toward his shot. Now there were lighter, scuffing footsteps on the stairs: Livy's.

"Why, the house is afire," she said, entering and surveying the smoke, tiles and broken glass.

Clemens stroked his cue, banked the ball with success, and did not look up.

"Yes, I know it."

More feet ascended the stairs, and Clemens dropped his cue stick across the table in defeat. "It's a good thing I'm a tycoon and don't have to write books for a living," he growled. George Griffin, the butler, poked his head in and was silenced by the smoky gathering.

"Artillery," explained Clemens. "Katy Leary says it's the only thing for a cluttered room."

"Yes, sir, Mr. Clemens," said Griffin, now sharing a half-smile with his boss. "The colored minister from the Talcott Street church is here. He says Mr. Twichell told you that he would call."

"Oh, blazes, have you got a new church now, George?"

"No, sir, Mr. Clemens, this is the colored Congregational church, not my church. This is Reverend Wheeler."

"I am expecting Reverend Wheeler, George?"

"He thinks you are, Mr. Clemens."

"Well, if he's looking for a check, I think he should find his way back over to Joe Twichell's house, since churches are more in Joe's line, and every check I write now is for the salvation of Mr. Paige's damned typesetter, a charity which, I hope, will soon start contributing to me."

"Youth," said Livy, using her nickname for him, "see what Mr. Wheeler wants. And put on a collar and tie before you do. George, ask Mr. Wheeler to wait in the library." Livy followed George out the door. Clemens grabbed the morning's mail and a plain, leather-bound notebook from his desk and departed, leaving Katy on her knees mopping up the floor.

Unaware of the commotion on the third floor, the Rev. Robert F. Wheeler stood in the Clemens' library staring at the rubber tree and other exotic plants in the lush conservatory and past its panes to the newly-green maples and shrubs that sloped to the shallow Hog River. He forgot, for a moment, both this morning's task and his fear concerning it. But a sudden whiff of acrid smoke caused him to swivel around and find his host at arm's length, awkwardly holding a burning cigar and a handful of papers in one hand and extending the other.

Wheeler, startled to find himself greeting Hartford's most widely known citizen, forgot the order of what he had rehearsed and began rattling away at top speed: "Rev. Robert Wheeler, Mr. Clemens, sir, of the Talcott Street Congregational Church, here in the city, hoping my call is not inconvenient, as I was led to believe by Mr. Twichell that I might call on you in the late morning and make bold to ask a favor of you as a great and esteemed author and platform speaker and well-known friend of the colored race who has … "

"Mr. Wheeler," interrupted Clemens.

"… lent his support to colored institutions here and …"

"Mr. Wheeler," insisted Clemens without raising his voice.

"Yes, sir, Mr. Clemens," said Wheeler, grateful for the interruption.

"Please sit down, I have a question for you that touches on religion."

Wheeler followed Clemens to an ornate chair and perched on its edge, trying to look at ease. Twain continued to stand and smoke, tapping his ashes into an ash dish on the mantel of the huge, ornate fireplace.

"Mr. Wheeler, do you suppose God is colored?"

Wheeler, who was just beginning to regain his composure, felt hot and confused all over again, and he nervously tugged on the bottom of his vest.

"Eh, I'm not sure I follow …"

"Is the Almighty a dark-skinned African?"

Wheeler cleared his throat. "Well, theologically speaking …"

Clemens waved his cigar in front of him to cut Wheeler off.

"Grace King, she is a writer from the South and our guest here last fall, told me that she believes Providence to be dark," explained Twain. "I told her that, as for Jesus, we had had a Jew who had been satisfactory." Now Twain's eyes sparkled as he warmed to his blasphemy, half expecting Wheeler to run out the front door.

"But who could endure a French Christ?" asked Twain. Now he furrowed his brow and in an exaggerated French accent said, "Come unto me all ye who are heavy laden," and then cackled at his own burlesque.

"Think of an Irish Christ!" Now he rendered the same line in the high-pitched brogue of some musical-hall Paddy, and then laughed and then tried the line with a Chinese accent.

After a minute or two of this, Wheeler was laughing in spite of himself and delighted to have been included in Clemens' irreverent joke although the preacher kept checking furtively to make sure he and Clemens were alone in the room.

"You see? Grace King may have something," said Clemens. "At least with a colored savior, Christendom would get the singing right."

Now Wheeler saw his opportunity.

"Mr. Clemens, that is why I have called today."

"To peddle a Negro God?"

"No, sir, to ask your help in helping us purchase a suitable organ for our house of worship."

"Organ?" asked Clemens. "Organ," he repeated, answering his own question. He paced before the fireplace. "Now, Twichell's church is a place that needs its organ. When all the choir of holy speculators start in on a hymn, it sounds like so much caterwauling that one prays for the organist to pull out all the stops. White churches can't get along without one. But the jubilee songs of the colored churches are unmatched — there is no finer music in the world. An organ is just an added extravagance to that music — a mere machine."

"A skilled organist leads those voices in praising God," replied Wheeler timidly. "We've nothing now but a broken-down piano. I do not ask for your money, but only for the honor of your presence at Unity Hall on Wednesday night — that's tomorrow night."

Wheeler saw Clemens arch his eyebrows in surprise.

"I know," he continued, "that this is on very short notice. We will put on a musicale to raise funds. It was Mr. Twichell, I confess, who suggested that you might be asked to appear and say a word or two."

"Aha, that's it," Clemens exclaimed, tossing his cigar stub into the fireplace as he hiked by. "Joe Twichell has become my booking agent." He stopped and clasped his hands behind his back and faced Wheeler. "I assume that by 'musicale' you mean an evening of German music and perhaps a banjo quartet and everyone sitting quietly in his seat?"

Wheeler squirmed a bit. "The performers are donating their time," he explained. "Mr. Barker will direct the male chorus and the Charter Oak Quartet and Miss Cook will play the violin — I'm sure you've heard Miss Cook, she's very popular."

"No jubilee songs?"

"Not at Wednesday night's concert, no," said Wheeler, sensing Clemens' disappointment. "We've sold a good many tickets, but I'm sure that if I could add your name to an item in this evening's Daily Times, we could sell the entire house. Even without that, word of your appearance would help us raise funds in the coming months."

Now it was Clemens' turn to stare — at a framed reproduction of a painting depicting the mythical Medusa. On many evenings, he entertained his three girls, Jean, Clara and Susy, by spinning a tale incorporating all of the pictures and objects on and near the mantel — they insisted he go in order. He found himself trying to recall his most recent yarn and, specifically, how he had gotten the story from Medusa to the little ivory elephant that stood nearby. Did he have Medusa crossing the Alps on elephants?

Wheeler, a bit embarrassed by his own brass and feeling awkward in the lengthening silence, rose to leave.

"Mr. Clemens, sir, it has been an honor to meet you this morning — it's nearly noon — and I hope that my visit has not troubled or inconvenienced you and that ...

"Mr. Wheeler, do you know the song, 'Little David'?"

"Why, yes, Mr. Clemens."

"Yes," said Clemens absent-mindedly and still turned away from Wheeler, but now facing the conservatory. "I grew up in Missouri before the war. I learned that song and many like it from dark-skinned children who were my playmates, and the colored girl who lived with us and a remarkable old slave on my uncle's farm and others."

"I see," was all Wheeler could manage.

Clemens turned to him. "Mr. Wheeler, I am a man of heavy obligations these days." He opened his journal and silently consulted several pages. "Tomorrow evening, I must meet with my financial agent, Mr. Whitmore, regarding an important matter of finance." He closed his book. "I've also got a book to finish and many other projects too tiresome to describe."

Wheeler was chagrined. "Well, eh, God bless you, Mr. Clemens, it was a pleasure to meet you today, and I hope that I have not inconvenienced you in the least. I can find the door, I'm sure."

"This way, reverend." It was George, who had suddenly materialized at the other end of the library.

Clemens called after Wheeler: "I will speak to Pastor Twichell about this." But Wheeler was already out the door.

≥↓

"Lower the drawbridge for Sir Mark," said the Rev. Joseph Twichell, as he opened the door of his home on Woodland Street later that day.

'Yes, Sir Mark, come to skewer that black knight of humbug, Sir Joe," said Clemens, a bundle of mail and other papers under his arm as he steamed past Twichell and up the stairs to a room in the Twichells' house which he had used for the past several months to escape the visitors and telephone calls (and occasional fires) that kept him from work at his own house. Twichell knew him to be nearly done with a novel set in the days of knight-errantly. He shuffled up the stairs behind Clemens to the temporary study.

Clemens tossed his hat from the room's door so it landed in the middle of the large oak table that served as Twain's desk. He walked over and dropped his papers on a corner of the table, and then turned to face Twichell.

"I had a long talk today with your dusky colleague, Rev. Wheeler," announced Clemens, visibly perturbed. "That was after Katy Leary tried to burn the house down this morning."

Twichell raised his hand in a gesture meant to accept blame and to calm Clemens. "This is all my doing, Mark. I'm sorry. I told Wheeler he could call, but I never got to warn you beforehand." Clemens, still bristling, tossed his jacket over the back of a chair.

"You know my circumstances, Joe," said Clemens, cooling off a bit. He turned a chair so that he could sit and face Twichell, who stood in the doorway. "Everything depends on the damned machine. The minute it's in working order, Paige takes it apart again and gives me a new date, which is a lie. After that day passes, he offers another fraudulent deadline. In the meantime, I'm paying $3,000 a month to keep Paige and his co-conspirators fat, all the while trying to scare up investors before Paige scares them off. The money comes from my publishing house, which Webster has already looted, but the machine must be fed. I may end up selling some of Livy's interest in her family's business for cash poor Livy, who is nearly blind with pinkeye, as you know. And I must finish this book."

Twichell stepped into the room now, took a chair, and set it to face Clemens. He sat and put his hand on Clemens' shoulder.

"Mark, old friend, it was careless and stupid of me to add to your burdens. Wheeler has been a pastor in the city only a few years. He asked me yesterday if Mr. Clemens would help raise funds for a colored group. I told him you had twice taken the stage to further the work of Father Hawley and the city's poor, and that you had given a reading at the African church on Pearl Street."

Now Twain sat back. "What else did you tell him?"

Twichell nervously twisted one end of his mustache. "Of course, I said nothing more," he said. "What I know of your other philanthropies, Mark, the colored students you have helped at Yale and at Lincoln, I would not share with anyone. I think the public should know about your charities toward the colored race, but you have preferred to keep them quiet." Twichell felt himself beginning to sermonize, and cut it short.

"I told Wheeler that the time was late. I said you are busy and travel often, but that you would hear him out."

Clemens now fished in his jacket pocket for a fresh cigar, selected one, and ignited it with a match struck across the sole of his shoe. He paused and drew the smoke with satisfaction. He felt himself simmering down. Just being with Twichell, he thought, was a tonic for a bad mood even if Twichell was the cause of it.

"Forget about it, Joe," Clemens said, waving a window in a wall of smoke he had just created. "Why don't you go save some souls so I can get some writing done? I'll see you tonight at our house for dinner. Don't worry about dressing up," he added with a sly smile. "Just wear that shirt you always wear."

Twichell grinned broadly with the relief of a man forgiven. "Just don't say that with my wife nearby, Mark. She'll take it to heart and order me a dozen new shirts." He stood and strolled to the door. "You should have the house to yourself for a few hours."

Clemens nodded and turned his chair to the desk. He opened the inkstand, dabbed his pen in the well, and wrote a note to himself in his notebook.

ॐ

"Ladies, ladies, don't run off, George is just pouring more champagne," said Clemens, standing, as always, at the head of his table and gesturing toward the butler, who held the bottle aloft as proof that more bubbly was in the pipeline. But the three women only smiled and continued their retreat.

"If I have one more drop of champagne, I shall have to call for a stretcher," complained Harmony Twichell.

"We have a supply of stretchers on loan from the State Armory and Patrick and George have agreed to bear any unconscious guest home," said Clemens. George looked up warily as he filled neighbor Charles Dudley Warner's glass.

"We've more sober and educational pursuits," protested Livy, her eyes red and swollen, as she guided the female guests into the parlor. "Yes," added Susan Warner with a smirk as she drew the parlor doors closed, "subjects proper to the feminine sphere."

Now the richly papered dining room walls shimmered, reflecting three nearly simultaneous pillars of flame as Clemens, Twichell and Warner lit their cigars. Warner then turned to his champagne, but perhaps too eagerly — he had to mop his mustache and beard with his napkin.

"Mark," said Warner after pushing his chair back from the table, "my wife tells me that you were visited today by Mr. Wheeler of the Talcott Street Negro church. Was he canvassing the neighborhood? I'm happy to say he skipped my house."

"Not the neighborhood," replied Clemens, "he just canvassed my house, although I dare say he'll be over to see you now that I've turned him down."

"It's all my fault and I've got Mark awfully cross," confessed Twichell, sending a plume of smoke toward the ceiling."

"Joe, Joe," protested Clemens, "do you think they can't find my house without your help? Do you know how many begging letters I get every day? I could wallpaper Charlie's bedroom with one day's mail although I think it would trouble his sleep considerably."

Clemens, who had been leaning against the fireplace mantel, walked to the table and set his glass down. "If you'll excuse me for a moment, I'll show you what I mean," he said, and walked into the adjacent library, returning with a notebook stuffed with letters and envelopes which he brandished with one hand, holding it aloft as he spoke.

"Royalties from my English publisher? Investors lining up for a chance at the machine that will revolutionize publishing? No. Begging letters from my public — our public, Charlie. Those for whom an author is no better than a bottomless wishing well." Now he placed the notebook on the dining room table and thumbed through the letters.

"Well, this is typical," he said, pulling one out with a flourish and scanning it silently for a moment. "I am a young woman struggling to become a competent 'carpet designer,' " he read, and then looked up. "A woman from New York. She wants me to send her to design school in London or Paris, for which she would be 'deeply grateful.' She will pay back the tuition 'if any way could be arranged to do so.' " Clemens replaced the letter in the book and set it on the mantel.

"Others are more direct," he said. "Send me a check, build us our old-age home, endow our chair of agriculture, and so on.

"You two know me too well, so I can't pretend I've never been moved by such letters. But my time and money are all tied up these days. I know you're guilty of sending out checks, too, Charlie. As for you, Joe, Christian charity is part of your job — you get a salary for it."

Twichell grinned. "You're not expected to be the city missionary, Mark," he said. "If others here did half of what you do, there would be little work left to be done."

Clemens scowled in disapproval.

"Charity," said Warner, "can be for the worse. The laboring class is better actually and in possibility than it ever was in history. What little poverty we have accompanies human weakness and crime. Charity can make the weak weaker. Giving money to able-bodied tramps, for example, only encourages them the wrong way."

"Perhaps," said Twichell, "but too much of the misery that remains falls on Mr. Wheeler's flock and other Negroes, especially the women and children."

*For Samuel Clemens, the pertinent questions were
whether to speak, and what to say.*

The three fell silent as George entered with a tray of coffee and collected the champagne glasses and dessert dishes.

After the butler departed, Warner picked up where Twichell had left off.

"Pastor, do you now advocate equality of the races?"

But before Twichell could answer, Clemens, who had turned his back to his guests and was surveying the darkness outside through the window above the fireplace, whirled around to respond.

"It's not a matter of equality, Charlie," he said, "although, Lord knows, it would be but a small achievement to equal the white race with its barbaric popes and emperors. The black man's possibilities are few because we have been worse than stingy with him. No, we have ground the manhood out of them. The shame is ours, not theirs."

Warner was about to answer when the house suddenly rang with the lilt of Chopin, and the three men turned toward the closed drawing room doors, as if they could see through them.

"I believe my wife is performing," said Warner, making a show of cupping his hand to his ear.

"Five minutes of Susan at the piano is worth five years of our bombast," quipped Clemens, and Warner and Twichell joined their host as he quietly rolled open one of the doors and led them through the cigar-smoke haze into the drawing room.

&

"Susan played wonderfully tonight," said Livy as she combed out her hair before her mirror.

"Hmmm," replied Clemens without looking up. He was sitting up in bed in his nightshirt and scribbling with a pencil in a notebook.

Livy turned toward him. "Susan told me that tomorrow night's musicale for Mr. Wheeler's church will be quite an occasion."

Clemens now stared at the ceiling, while still scratching in his notebook and muttering softly about printing technicalities. "The World's reading page is 35,000 ems, so with the machine setting 6,000 ems an hour, that's, hmmm … the Wants page is 46,000 .."

"Youth," said Livy, in a tone sharp enough to pull him away from his figuring. "Will you speak at Unity Hall? What did you tell Mr. Wheeler? Your name was not mentioned in the newspaper notice this evening."

Clemens slid his notebook onto the night table and put his hands behind his head. "I told Mr. Wheeler that a colored church hardly needs an organ — or anything mechanical — because the singing is perfect. I have no plans to speak there. In any case, it sounds as if the musical program will be more than enough."

"Youth, dear," said Livy as she walked to her side of the bed and sat, "why would you tell Mr. Wheeler how to conduct his services? Why should his church be limited in the kind of song it offers in worship? I know you are fond of the Negro spirituals, but surely Mr. Wheeler aspires to greater works of sacred music."

"German music?" asked Clemens dryly.

"Well, yes, German, English, European — and American," said Livy, turning off the gas in the chandelier and sliding under the covers. "It's all the same to me, Youth, I can't go. The girls and I go to New York tomorrow so I may have a consultation with the specialist, Dr. Rice, suggested for my pinkeye. Did you remember that we're leaving you alone for the day and returning Thursday?"

Clemens, still sitting up, grunted in the affirmative.

From across the hall came a series of sharp, barking coughs and both Clemens and his wife cocked their heads.

"Jean," whispered Clemens. His wife nodded, waiting for another cough, as if that would be the signal to go to Jean's bedside. But all that followed was a soft, sleepy whimper from the congested eight-year-old and the rustle of bedclothes.

"Perhaps your specialist will look at Jean, too," suggested Clemens. Olivia nodded.

"Youth," she said gently as she sat up a bit. "I know your business with Mr. Paige is all very crucial right now. But even the children are caught up in it. When the nurse asked today if she could buy shoe black for the girls' shoes, Jean scolded her, saying, 'Why Marie, you mustn't ask for things now. The machine isn't done.' "

Clemens chuckled and leaned over to kiss Livy, who then turned to go to sleep. He picked up his notebook, placed it on his raised knees and, under the glow of his bedside lamp and the gaze of the carved mahogany cherub that topped his bedpost, calculated on into the night.

❧

Blam! Blam! Blam!

James W. Paige was startled from his drawings, which lay on a long table, striped by late-morning sunshine beneath the windows of a second-floor shop at Pratt & Whitney on Flower Street. The knocking sent him to the window. He pushed the bridge of his glasses up with the little finger of his right hand and surveyed the street: Sure enough, there was the familiar carriage. Ten feet from the pile of mechanical drawings was the long, four-footed contraption that occupied Paige and his crew. Charles Davis, one of Paige's assistants, lifted his head from the back of the machine, his eyebrows arched and mouth open slightly in question.

Paige wiped his hands on his apron and silently mouthed: "Clemens."

Blam!

"Paige!"

Now Paige walked briskly through the narrow shop to the bolted metal door, threw the bolt and opened the door just in time to see Clemens winding up for another knock.

"Awfully warm for ear muffs, Paige," said Clemens as he marched past Paige and toward the machine.

"It's rather noisy here, Mr. Clemens, I'm sorry …" said Paige, but a sudden, brief whining noise from the floor above made it impossible for him to finish. Clemens slowed his pace as he approached the typesetting machine, and he greeted Davis and two other crew members who were on hand. The sight of the device cheered him — it always did. He resisted making unannounced visits, believing Paige should be left to do his work. But when his anxiety reached flood tide — anxiety about the machine that had implications for his publishing house, his station in the world and his family — he had to see the thing.

Now he slowly walked around the creature — this was his habit — and the workmen's heads moved in unison as they watched him appraise it. He stopped and ran his hand gently over the keyboard. He wondered to himself why a piano or an organ couldn't have the same keyboard. It would be easier to play. Print the note on each key, with a different color for each octave. Or one-key chords on a left-hand keyboard, or pedals, perhaps. He could invent such a thing, he thought, once the typesetter made his fortune.

The silence held until Clemens' shoe struck a thin, metal rod that protruded from beneath the machine. Clemens caused it to roll across the floor with a metallic clatter.

"What's that?" he asked.

Paige ran back to where Clemens was standing and then stooped to examine the rod. "This is a piece of the frame that secures the galleys."

Clemens squatted down and saw what would have been obvious to anyone less entranced by the appliance: a large number of various-sized parts — steel wheels, copper sleeves and the slender, brass arms and rods that were part of the typesetter's justifying mechanism — were sitting in neat rows on a large rectangle of beige canvas beneath the machine.

Still squatting, Clemens brought his hand to his face, closed his eyes and squeezed his temples. Now the workers looked at each other.

"Paige," said Clemens wearily, rising to his feet. "I believe there are more parts on the floor than in the blessed machine."

The inventor wiped his hands on his apron. "Now, Mr. Clemens," he began, but it had come out too patronizing, so he started again. "Mr. Clemens, it's the same problem we have talked about as recently as last week. The keys are jamming. We are readjusting the keyboard mechanism to prevent that."

"July, Paige, you have promised July and now May is almost gone," whined Clemens. "Everything we have is right here — everything I have, I and my family. And this place looks like a hardware store after a hurricane."

Paige did not flinch. "We shall be ready for a grand demonstration in July, as scheduled. And by then, I think we shall have a surprise even for you." Paige shared a knowing smile with Davis and the others.

"What?" asked Clemens, beguiled as he glanced from Paige to Davis and back, and smiling in spite of himself.

"You have advertised this machine at the rate of 6,000 ems an hour," said Paige. "It is a certainty that we will achieve the ability to set and distribute 8,000 ems an hour and," he glanced again at Davis, "some here think a speed of 11,000 will soon be standard fare."

Clemens brightened. "My God, Paige, that's the work of a train load of compositors!" He returned his hat to his head. "I leave you men to your sacred calling. I'll see myself out." Paige, wiping his hands on his apron, followed Clemens anyway. "Soon, Paige," said Clemens softly, "our only money problem will be to work out the spending of it all."

But Clemens was not in his carriage five minutes when his exuberance left him. Paige had done it again, he thought. The man's charm and self-confidence cast a trance. What did Clemens have to show for his visit? A machine in pieces and another solemn promise — like the last dozen or so, all of which had been solemnly broken. He cursed aloud and swore he would not visit until the thing was operating again.

By the time he reached his house, his mood was dark. He was struck, upon entering, by the silence. He remembered that the house was all his this afternoon. He climbed to his billiards room, took out his manuscript and opened his ink stand. But it was no use. He was so unaccustomed to getting work done in his house that, even without the usual distractions, he could not write. He opened his notebook to his calculations regarding the speed at which the typesetter could set specific pages at particular newspapers he hoped would buy the thing. The new, faster speeds that Paige had hinted at in the morning had buoyed him. He tried to go through all of the previous night's figures with the new speed in mind, but all Clemens could think of now was the sight of the machine's guts spread all over the shop floor.

He rose from his desk, lit a cigar, and took his billiards cue. For the next several hours, he set up the most difficult and unlikely billiards predicaments he could dream up and, with very little success, tried to play his way out of them. It passed much of the afternoon, but the game didn't provide its usual solace.

Why hole himself in his billiards room with the rest of the house deserted, except for servants? He walked down the stairs and roamed the second floor, looking in on the girls' rooms and their schoolroom. He reflected with pride on the material wealth he had provided them, and he felt a stabbing apprehension when he allowed himself to remember the machine.

Clemens walked quietly down the stairs. The only sounds came from the kitchen — the slam of the oven door and Griffin's voice. In the library, Clemens ground out his cigar in an ash dish near the fireplace and then made for the drawing room. Before entering, he peered down the hallway and listened intently to make sure he was alone, then he pulled the door shut behind him. Closing the only open window, he sat at the piano and tried a few chords, softly, with his left hand.

Suddenly he pounded with both hands, rocking the stateliness of the drawing room with a honky-tonk clamor and he began to howl:

"Little David, play on yo' harp, hallelu, hallelu, little David ..." His high notes were a nasal falsetto, while he growled the low notes, and jerked about, shaking his mane of hair and rising up from the piano bench, only to return and rise again, rolling and closing his eyes and tilting his head heavenward as he sang.

"... go down into Egypt, O Lord, tell ole ..."

He could not have heard the telephone ring, but he somehow sensed that someone was outside the drawing room door and stopped in mid-verse.

"George, is that you? What is it?"

Although he was perspiring and out of breath, he tried to regain his usual demeanor. Griffin stuck his head in the door.

"I'm awfully sorry, Mr. Clemens. That was the telegraph office ringing the telephone. Mrs. Clemens sent to say she will return tomorrow on the 3:10 train — instead of the noon train — so she can shop."

Clemens snorted and smiled. "Shopping. That's the real cure for Mrs. Clemens. George, will you tell Patrick to be sure to meet her?"

"I surely will, Mr. Clemens." But instead of backing out of the room, he lingered for a moment, creating a bit of awkwardness.

Clemens looked down at the keyboard.

"George, do you know 'Little David'?"

"Yes, sir. Since I was a child."

"Well, as long as you interrupted me, you must help me finish the last verse."

Griffin grinned a conspiratorial grin and started for the piano, but stopped when Clemens pointed behind him.

"The door, George," said Clemens. "Close the door."

Griffin pulled the door shut and walked to the piano. Clemens started in again, slamming the keys, but he sat still this time and sang more quietly, allowing Griffin to fill in with his reedy tenor.

"God told Moses, O Lord! Go down into Egypt, O Lord! Tell ole Pha-ro', O Lord! Loose my people, O Lord!" Clemens pounded the final chord and he and Griffin erupted in laughter.

"I don't remember the last time you played on the piano, Mr. Clemens, sir," said George.

"I don't play it, George, I torture the thing."

"You could play at my church any Sunday," said Griffin. "You sing that song good, too. I know you learned it from old slaves."

Clemens nodded.

"Before the war." Griffin shook his head. "Those songs were everything to me before the war. During the war, too."

Griffin stepped to the door and opened it.

"George, perhaps we'll keep today's recital to ourselves," said

Clemens, rising from the piano and sweeping his hair into place with one hand.

"Of course, sir," he said.

"George," added Clemens before the butler could depart. "Does your church have an organ?"

"Yes, sir, a very fancy one, I think."

"And does your organist play 'Little David?' "

"Yes, sir. And not just jubilee songs, but some of the songs you sing at Mr. Twichell's church."

"Is that so?"

"I guess no matter what the song is, praying and singing are mostly the same thing. Most everyone gets to feeling sad and scared and wants to feel better — white folks, too, I expect. I've seen that in Mrs. Warner's face here when she performs for the ladies."

Clemens looked down at the piano, as if to picture what Griffin had just said. When he looked up, Griffin was gone. He plucked his watch from his vest, but had to walk to the window to read it in the light of dusk. Then he breezed into the hallway and started up the stairs, yelling after George in the kitchen: "George, don't put out my supper. I'll eat later. Have Patrick bring the carriage around."

He dashed to his room, replaced his damp shirt with a fresh, dry one and then rushed up to his billiards room, pulling papers out of his pigeonholes frantically until he found what he was looking for. He bent over the pages, reading and mumbling, while he replaced his collar and tie, and then flew down the stairs to the front hall. Again he called to the kitchen: "George. If Mr. Whitmore comes, give him a drink and a billiards cue. Tell him I'll be along later." He grabbed his hat and ran out the door to the waiting coach.

"Patrick, see how quickly you can reach Pratt Street without killing us," he said.

The sidewalk in front of Unity Hall was empty. For a moment, Clemens wondered if he had gotten his nights mixed up. But he pressed his ear to the front door and heard the plaintive whine of a violin solo in progress. He walked back to the sidewalk and toward an iron gate on the right side of the church. He opened the gate, made his way down an alley alongside the church to a door on the far corner of the building. He tried it gingerly, and it opened without a sound. He found himself in a narrow hallway, climbed the few steps in front of him and opened another well-oiled door to the church's vestry, where he was suddenly face-to-face with Wheeler.

"Mr. Clemens!" whispered the minister.

Clemens took Wheeler's hand, and then tossed off his hat and peered out onto the stage. "Sorry I'm late," he whispered. "I'll go on whenever you like. I can give you two speeches, but it's best if I do one now and one later."

Wheeler looked at his program, pulled a pencil out of his pocket and scratched "M.T." twice in the margins. "You can go on, eh … " The music ended and the hall erupted in applause. "Now. You can go on now, if you like. Let me make the introduction."

"Never mind, Mr. Wheeler," said Clemens, pulling his coat straight and filing for his tie. "I'll save you the trouble."

Wheeler watched as Clemens wove his way through the line of exiting musicians and made his way to center stage. The applause, which had all but died down, now exploded as Clemens was instantly recognized.

"Pastor Wheeler wanted to make an introduction for me, but I told him he'd better not. For one thing, it's easier for me to lie because I've got more practice in it than Mr. Wheeler. And, furthermore, I don't think I could stand the guilt of making a preacher lie on my behalf. Happily, my subject is lying, or, specifically, the decay of the art of lying. Observe, I do not mean to suggest the custom of lying has suffered any decay or interruption no, for the Lie, as a Virtue, a Principle, is eternal …"

3

Statesman of the Old State House

Colin McEnroe

To a person looking west toward the dormant, darkened Old State House on this gloomy afternoon, the sad face in an upper story might be that of a ghost, a forlorn Wadsworth or tubercular Huntington haunting the halls, moaning and sighing over a 200-year-old close vote.

But no, it is the House's (usually) lively and living executive director, Bill Faude, who gazes east toward the hidden river. The grim day, with its gray clouds in a raw, scudding wind, has sent Faude's thoughts down a macabre path.

"May 1, 1637 is when the Court met and declared war on the Mashantucket Pequot nation. This is the site where they … sent forth John Mason to do them in," he says.

Faude's voice is, in most weathers, the honk of a reasonably well-brought-up goose, but today a cold has him by the throat so that his every utterance is a handful of ground glass splattered on the backwall of a furnace. On the morrow, Faude (rhymes with howdy) will have to croak through a ceremony in front of the Old State House. It will be a kick-off ceremony leading up to a kick-off ceremony, a small hullaballoo starting a 50-day countdown to a big hullaballoo: the reopening of the Old State House after four years and $12 million of renovations.

"This is your building!" Faude will shout into the microphone. The cruel March wind will whip down Main Street. A high school band wearing, oddly enough, the red coats of our British oppressors, will play. A cannon will boom and confetti will fly.

An aptly Faudean event, his detractors would say. Sizzle preceding sizzle. His admirers would say that once again Faude has put noise and excitement and energy in downtown Hartford, where such things are desperately needed, where indeed the white collars and gray faces and stricken looks and furtive scuttlings make the city seem, nowadays, like a colony of some species of nearly extinct crab.

But all of that is 24 hours away.

Right now, Faude is in the grip of the dark afternoon and dark history.

He is a great one for collecting and palpating firsts, co-author, in fact, of *Connecticut Firsts*, a book claiming Connecticut gave America its first witch, first twine, first free-standing keystone archbridge (whatever that is), first cheese containers, first lollipops.

Right now he is staking a claim for first ethnic massacre, which he thinks he can trace back to a planning meeting at this location, "this square where it happened first in America, simply because people were different, simply because of the color of their skin or their race or whatever."

The Old State House did not open until 1796, but its location was, before that, the town square and the site of the city's Meeting House, allowing Faude to scoop up other juicy bits of history and claim them for his institution. His guiding principle for ancient Hartford history is: in the absence of proof that it happened somewhere else, it happened on his turf. This allows him, for instance, to claim that the Charter Oak legend starts with a confrontation at the Meeting House. He claims the Fundamental Orders, sometimes described as the world's first instance of a written constitution creating a government, as his baby because they were adopted in the Meeting House in 1639.

On this day, Faude describes his latest idea: To create a national peace park, both in memory to the Pequots, their women and children, but also to all the innocents who are the true victims of any war. We always put up a monument to the generals but what about the orphans? Where did the flamboyant, sarcastic Bill Faude go? Who is this rather vulnerable-looking middle-aged man musing hoarsely about bombed-out Serbian orphanages and the horrors of My Lai?

"...which is what really happened down in Mystic, you even read Mason's accounts, and there's no way to justify it — setting a fire at one end of a wigwam and standing at the other end with guns and sabers drawn ..."

Little by little, though, the more familiar Faude, the impresario, creeps in. The idea would be to have the cash-laden Mashantucket Pequots fund the memorial. Maybe Maya Lin, of Vietnam Memorial fame, would take the commission. And the park would be open, and there would be concerts creating the tension between the memorial and the street.

Whoa. Now we're in prime Faude territory. Creating tension. Faude has not even pulled the shiny bow off his $12 million restoration, which has required enormous amounts of good will to achieve, and will require even more good will to carry forward. And what is he doing? Ballooning into high voltage wires with the reporter's tape recorder running. Massacres, racism, hypocrisy. Just what the Daughters of the American Revolution and all the other upholders of Yankee antiquity want to hear about.

He can't help himself.

On the one hand, he is Wilson H. Faude, very much a child of Hartford's WASP establishment, a staunch Episcopalian, educated at Kingswood, Darrow and Hobart, a consumer of bow ties, member of more arts and humanities boards than you can shake an altarpiece at, and husband of the very-well-thought-of Janet Bailey Faude, herself a former Fleet bank official and the daughter of a former Aetna CEO.

On the other, Bill Faude is, with respect to that very same establishment, a toddler at Pottery Barn. Take your eye off him for one minute, and he's pulling down a whole rack of expensive sensibilities.

"He's the closest thing to Barnum we have in town," says DeRoy Pete Thomas, chairman of the Old State House board. "He seems to have a flair for doing things in a grand style."

"I like Faude," says Real Art Ways director Will K. Wilkins, who brokered a peace accord between Faude and black artist James Montford about five years ago when Faude removed a controversial Montford work from a group exhibition. "He's an iconoclast. He doesn't follow party lines, which is rare in Hartford."

"He's a delightful impresario," says lawyer Edward Lane-Reticker, who served as a trustee when Faude worked at the Mark Twain Memorial. "He's always up."

Faude's thumb prints are all over the Twain house. He was, at the tender age of 25, its first curator, his first real job after a stint in the U.S. Army. He has done two separate tours running the Old State House, with a three-year side trip to the University of Hartford. He came back to the Old State House in 1985 and balanced the budget in less than a year, erasing a $250,000 deficit.

A year later, he offered his board two choices for the 200th anniversary: "Clean it up; have a party; and get out of town. Or take a long hard look at it and really do our duty."

The latter course meant extensive restoration. Faude thought it might cost $3.4 million. The building had other plans. The Old State House was planning to keel over, dead from a disease of the feet. Its foundation had problems that were going to eat up a lot of money.

These are jobs that require finesse, diplomacy, the raising of funds, the coaxing of treasures away from clutching dowagers. It's tough to do one of those jobs if you're the type who can't walk by a chain without rattling it.

Consider Legacy/Legado, the major exhibit of contemporary Latino art that Faude has insisted on staging for the reopening of the Old State House.

If the audience is expecting George Washington Contemplating a Bust of Thomas Hooker, what it will get instead are fiberglass sculptures offering a Latino consideration of Manifest Destiny, mixed media installations with names such as "When We Die, We Take Nothing," and a performance artist's take on Puerto Rican migration to the mainland. Inexplicably, corporate sponsors did not rush forward with fistfuls of money to underwrite this, so Faude went into debt, hoping some angel would come forward later to make up the difference.

He's still waiting. "My life is on the line," he says dryly.

And it's tough to do one of those jobs if you're the type of person who, oh, I don't know, gets in a dust-up with a cop, as Faude did in a 1991 incident that resulted in his arrest. (Faude subsequently described it as a misunderstanding and got special probation. Today, he says the full story has never been told but that he considers the matter closed.)

It's tough to do one of those jobs if you're the sort of person who writes a witheringly impolitic commentary piece that stings civic organizations for mediocre efforts and lousy, inadequate work, as Faude did in 1993.

But Faude does it. And the new Old State House may be the jewel in his thorny crown. The renovated building is a creamily understated Yankee beauty, and Faude has promised to populate it with a cast of costumed guides acting the parts of historical personages.

A measure of Faude's esteem for the Old State House can be seen in the proposal he's using to solicit support for Legacy/Legado.

"It is Connecticut's single most important building," reads part of the text. Who can say this is not true? Especially if you consider

Michael McAndrews, The Hartford Courant

Bill Faude has been called "the closest thing to Barnum"
to be found in contemporary Hartford.

Foxwoods to be a separate nation? Built in 1796, the Old State House has, at various times, been the seat of both state and city government. It has been War Bond Headquarters, the Post Office, the Chamber of Commerce and concert hall for the Hartford Symphony.

Before the renovations, Faude was claiming 300,000 visitors to the House per year, a number that seems, well, counterintuitive, which is to say high. He expects the new, improved Old State House, full of bells and whistles, to attract many more than the old. Just opening the formerly closed gates on the Main Street side, he says, could double attendance.

There will be video screens humming with testimony from other Connecticut figures and a cannon booming and a carillon ringing, concerts on the lawn, a re-creation of a Hartford museum of curiosities (two-headed calves and 8-foot alligators), debates in the great halls.

Faude has arranged with some of the judges who do naturalization ceremonies to conduct them in his august building, and he is working with The Courant on a computer-equipped news center to restore the square to its old status as the place where people assembled to get the latest word.

"And all we need is one Persian Gulf crisis," Faude says dreamily. "and suddenly the bell will start tolling in the cupola and the cannon will fire and there will be a kid or kids with a canvas sack, saying 'Extra! Extra!' And you will have reinforced that whole concept of a meeting house square, but on today's terms."

Next year, the Connecticut Historical Society will install its long-awaited interactive museum permanently at the Old State House, cementing a partnership between the city's two major historical institutions.

To accomplish all this, Faude has had to charm millions in appropriations from governors and congresspersons and millions more from corporations and private donors.

"I haven't got the slightest idea of how to ask you for money," he insists.

He finds unusual ways. Faude's most famous fund-raising feat is typical of him. In the 1980s he imposed a "window tax" on the downtown offices with a view of the Old State House. Faude formed a "viewing rights" committee and ordered the parties in question to pony up $5 per window. The tax is still in place, and it's up to $10. It attracted the notice of everybody from National Geographic to The New York Times. It was creative, edgy, saucy, pure Faude. Wanna look at my beautiful building?

Gonna cost you, bub.

By contrast, Faude doesn't believe in charging admission to his building. He calls it an economic barrier and says he thinks city folk should feel free to wander in, if only to use the pay phone.

City Councilman Mike McGarry, who counts himself a supporter, likes to predict a graceful old age for Faude. "Some people hold the devil inside them, and it builds up there and gets them," he says. "Well, that's not going to be Bill's problem."

McGarry says he and Faude have been, over the years, friends and nose-to-nose shouting not-such-friends. Former City Manager Al Gatta once described Faude as wonderful, effective, competent and beneficial to the city and then added, "Sometimes I believe [city] staff would like to squeeze his neck until his bow tie leaked."

"But Bill finally got his pyramid," says McGarry, impishly describing the Old State House project. "And one that took as long to build as most pyramids. And one that, according to Bill, will have an effect comparable to the pyramids."

Indeed, when it comes to the Old State House, Faude's pride is so great that he has no pride at all. He will do almost anything to publicize the place or snap up a choice event for it. During planning sessions for the October vice-presidential debate in Hartford   which Faude had tried to steer right into his building — one wag produced a placard reading Hartford Debate 96: In honor of the Old State House's 200th Anniversary, a joking reference to Faude's insistence that the Earth and heavens revolve around his site.

And though his ego be large, Faude is also the self-sacrificing stage mother to the Old State House. His two volumes of old photographs, Hartford Images of America, are in their third and fourth printings, but the profits go to the Old State House, not Faude. At the end of a $12 million capital campaign, Faude drives an 11-year-old car.

Faude's critics and admirers are quite frequently the same people. Off the record, they call him egotistical, stubborn, attention-seeking, imperious. And then they admit these very qualities allow him to push through difficult projects in a town notorious for second-guessing and civic chronic fatigue. "I don't think you move as fast as he does without scrambling a few eggs now and then," says Thomas.

"I know I do offend people, unintentionally, just by sheer energy. Appearing to be Mr. Know-It-All which I in no way am," Faude says with a dry little laugh. "When I get into a discussion, I assume we're both staying for the entire game, and that I will passionately fight for a stand, and when the vote is taken I consider the issue done."

We see this exact principle in swing just a few nights later when Faude attends a meeting of the Greater Hartford Tourism District Board, on which he serves. The district consists of 21 towns, and, although you and I might find it hard to imagine Swedish tourists killing an afternoon by meandering through the atmospheric sections of Newington, visions of that sort weave themselves quixotically through the discourses of the board.

On this night, Faude is feverishly eager to get the board to wrap up a year's work on a new logo. A design firm has been engaged and has produced a very nice oval with the words Connecticut's Capital Country inside it.

Instead, he finds himself in a pitched battle about … stationery. Some of the people representing specific towns want all 21 towns listed down the side of the new stationery, but that, of course, will unbalance the oval.

"It's like cutting the hands off the painting, and gluing it on the other side," Faude fumes, a little bewilderingly. "You're changing the entire feeling of the logo. The concept, the sophistication."

Someone suggests accepting the logo for other purposes but sending the stationery back for redesign. That peculiar Hartford strain of mission-creep oozes into the room. Things are getting bogged down in the petty concerns of little towns.

With exasperation rising off him like steam, Faude pushes, pushes. He insists on a vote. He gets the logo approved, 9 to 8. The losers are eyeing him with unconcealed rage. A woman walks into the room, a late-arriving board member, a probable ninth vote for the opposition. Everybody gasps.

"Don't even try it!" Faude yells. "Mr. Chairman, I think it is finally to bed."

Ten minutes later, Faude is out in the hallway, sipping wine and joking with the very people who were ready to kill him during the vote.

Nobody has ever suggested that Faude was not interesting. In a city of dull plumage, Faude is a bird of paradise. He, at one time, affected a London bobby's cape, but even his watch fob and his trademark bow ties — the size of fruit bats in the 70s, more streamlined in the power-tie 80s and perhaps just a tad floppier in the Patrick McCaughey-influenced 90s — are eye-catching by Hartford standards.

The real color, though, is in what he says. Candid and brash amid the oatmeal-mouthed equivocators of Hartford, Faude is so quotable that newspaper reporters have sometimes had to make a conscious effort not to turn to him for a zinger on every imaginable subject.

So. Who is this guy?

The facts of Faude's life would surprise many people who think they know him.

Wilson Hinsdale Faude was born Feb. 20, 1946, and grew up on a dirt road in Bloomfield.

"It was wilderness, and you could track deer, and there was a brook and a gorge and a normal life where you would get your sled and soap it up ..."

"I can picture the way he'd come bombing in the room, full of fun and pep," says his second-grade teacher Natalie Dunsmoor. "I loved him. Their whole family was such a nice family."

But an unlucky family.

John Paul and Helen Hinsdale had three children, Paul, Ann and Bill. In 1954, when Bill was 8, his older brother Paul died of cancer. He was 10. In 1957, when Bill was 11, his father John Paul Faude died. He was 46.

"What that teaches you," Faude says, with what seems a studied casualness, "is if you gotta do it, do it. And yeah, there's a lot of life that isn't very nice, but that's OK." Faude men, it seems, have a way of dying young. Faude says he's lived longer than any male Faude he can find. He's 50. "Mother kept us going," Faude says.

Helen Faude, who died in 1982, appears to have done just that. Helen Faude was strong and no-nonsense, a steely buttress as opposed to a soft place to land.

"My mother used to say if you ever need a helping hand, look at the end of your arm," says Faude.

Helen Faude was not a coddler.

"My mother used to say if you're going to have a nervous breakdown, make sure you have lots of time and lots of money, because the worst thing that could happen is to have a nervous breakdown and worry about how you're going to pay for it or not have time to have a really good one."

Helen Faude was not one for emotional scenes. When she drove her son up to Hobart College in Geneva, N.Y., for the beginning of his college life, Helen Faude was, Bill noticed, fidgety. He asked what was the matter.

She said, "I've been told that this is the time I'm supposed to give you wise words. Well, all I can think of is that if you haven't learned the lessons that Daddy and I tried to teach you ... cover yourself."

In the midst of three unhappy years at Kingswood School (now Kingswood-Oxford) in West Hartford — notorious in those days for pounding many-sided pegs into perfectly square holes — Faude came into a small inheritance that allowed him to think about going away to boarding school. He chose the Darrow School in New Lebanon, N.Y.

"If you were to ask me to name somebody who got what he should out of the school, Bill is it," says Ron Emery, who both taught and befriended Faude at Darrow.

At Darrow, Emery says, Faude discovered his own energies. "I remember Bill as a renaissance boy, as well as a renaissance man," says Emery. "He'd like to have run faster, acted better, written more brilliantly than anyone else." The site of a former Shaker community, Darrow introduced Faude to the love of old buildings, turned loose his eccentricities and helped him find his talent for rallying troops to a cause.

"The Shakers were eccentric, and Bill was eccentric," Emery says. "The interesting thing was that Bill managed his eccentricities at school with a tremendous amount of grace."

When a fire destroyed the school theater building, Faude roused the rest of the drama club to action.

"He made a complete [theatrical] set out of paper — long rolls of wrapping paper," says Emery. "He has the most extraordinary way of improvising."

Faude's critics sometimes complain he is still improvising. Historians and scholars quietly grumble that his showmanship overwhelms any sense of detail. In Connecticut Firsts, they say, he will stretch a point on behalf of Connecticut rather than be historically scrupulous.

"Faude is like the kid in class waving his hand and stomping his feet to be called on," one of his counterparts told me years ago, "but he doesn't really know the answer."

Faude seems uncharacteristically wounded by that suggestion. He points to some of his scholarly articles, including one published in the intellectually tony Winterthur Portfolio.

"Why hasn't there been more of this? There hasn't been time," he says. "But I'm sure I've dropped the ball sometimes. I don't walk on water, I do swim."

Faude-watchers have noted some changes in recent years. The rather acid-tongued, impudent young man of 20 years ago, waggling a cigarette, has given way to a slightly more statesmanlike, thoughtful, nonsmoking parent of two children. The former bad boy now works out at a health club, but the eccentric renaissance boy is still very much alive. Faude's hobbies include needlepoint and painting tiles and plates.

"I didn't always get along with Bill. He was full of himself, and he was always sure he was right," says Lane-Reticker. "He was just a lot to handle. He's certainly mellowed a lot. He got married. He had kids. I think he overcame a lot of that."

On May 11, 1996 this new Faude — who will still never be mistaken for the shy, retiring type — will reopen the Old State House amid great ceremony and pomp.

When that first wave of excited people has gone home, Faude and his building will have to prove their mettle. He has rescued it from crumbling foundations and restored it to a beauty it probably never knew in all its 200 years.

People are already arranging to get married there, have major receptions there.

Faude is planning a series of apparitions: a re-creation, for example, of the Alexander Hamilton vs. Aaron Burr duel on the lawn. These will happen without warning, to deepen the impression that no one dare take his eye off the Old State House, where history is never boring.

But downtown Hartford is a tough sell these days. Can a 200-year-old hunk of Federal period architecture, albeit full of Faudean showmanship, draw bustling crowds each day? McGarry, who believes he was put on Earth at least partly to tease Faude, chuckles fiendishly.

"Bill had better remember what the pyramids were for."

On this March afternoon, with 51 days to go, there are still some scaffoldings up, and much of what Faude has described is not in place. There is space for the museum of curiosities, but no dinosaur bones or 8-foot-long alligators in that space. The question has to be asked:

" Are you going to make it?"

Faude stops and glares. It is a question for quitters, a race Faude professes to hate. After a long pause, he croaks, "If I don't get over this cold, I may not make it, but …"

He does not even finish. It's so obvious, isn't it? The building will be fine.

4

Remembering Rebecca Primus

Barbara Beeching

I'm no Alice Walker — wrong color for starters — but she and I have at least one thing in common: the discovery of a forgotten writer.

Some 20 years ago, Alice Walker discovered Zora Neale Hurston, novelist, folklorist and playwright of the Harlem Renaissance who stirred up controversy in the 1920's and '30's by writing in her own fresh voice and refusing to pose as a pitiable victim of oppression. Zora transcended the limits of race and gender by simply ignoring them. But time went on, tastes changed and she gradually disappeared from the literary scene, to die in 1960 penniless and alone. It was Alice Walker who introduced her to a new generation and led the movement to restore her reputation.

I discovered Rebecca Primus, a young black woman who left her comfortable home in Hartford after the Civil War to join thousands of other teachers traveling south to bring literacy to the newly freed slaves. Rebecca chronicled her four-year adventure in a series of letters to her family back home, letters that reveal a matter-of-fact sort of heroine going about what she considered the most important work of her time, racial uplift. As happened later with Zora, years passed and what had seemed a significant contribution was entirely forgotten. By the time Rebecca died in 1932 no one remembered that she had been the only black of the five teachers sent to the south from Hartford; that she had founded the first school for African Americans in Royal Oak, Maryland; that she had built her own schoolhouse, "larger than the white school," and held classes there for children and adults, certain that education was the key to their future.

As for the limits on race and gender, Rebecca's response evokes Harriet Beecher Stowe rather than Zora Neale Hurston.

While Rebecca rejected any notion of white superiority, she appeared to accept prevailing 19th-century views about woman's place. In speech, dress, and deportment she conformed to the prescribed decorum of her day, and yet when the chance came she was quite ready to travel alone to an unknown destination and live amid strangers in order to carry out a venture with manifest political and racial overtones.

My discovery of Rebecca Primus resulted from a windfall of disposable time. Five years ago, realizing that retirement was about to give me the luxury of choosing what to do next, I enrolled at Trinity College to complete the master's program I had abandoned some 40 years before in another time and place.

One of the first things I learned was that graduate courses now require lengthy research papers, perhaps to provoke the same level of anxiety undergraduates used to experience over final exams. That much effort, it seemed to me, should produce something of use beyond the classroom, so I took to asking local historical societies about their research needs. When I went looking for a late 19th-century subject, David White of the Connecticut Historical Commission recommended the Primus Papers, which he described as a primary black history source not yet fully explored. It didn't sound like what I had in mind, but I went to the Connecticut Historical Society to take a look.

That's where I found Rebecca, and in fact her 48 letters were only part of the story. The Primus Papers also include 120 letters written to her by her friend, Addie Brown, and 24 more from Rebecca's brother Nelson. Because the papers are kept in the archives, on that first visit I just scanned through the microfilm copy. The first reel began with Rebecca's poem, "I've Lost a Day," short but predictable, followed by an essay about a beloved poodle that died. Typical 19th-century schoolgirl efforts. But then came the letters she wrote from Maryland, the first dated Nov. 8, 1866, one day after she arrived in Baltimore, where she would be assigned to her permanent teaching post. I read for maybe two hours, watching her world unfold. Three passages in particular struck me then and still do, as clues to Rebecca. In the first letter, after one day in the South, she wrote: "I have already seen almost as many colored people as there are in the whole of Hartford."

The second quote was in a letter of the following spring:

"Although the whites are mostly secesh [secessionist] they all give colored men and women employment; the greatest difficulty is they do not pay sufficient wages and if the people will not accept their terms they

send off and and get 'contrabands' as they are here denominated
[homeless former slaves], to work for them so that it takes the labor right
out of these people's hands and they are obliged to submit. I hope there
will be justice, impartial justice, given to the colored people one of these
days …"

And finally, there was her own account of a "friendly" letter she
received in February 1867 from the Rev. Nathaniel J. Burton, pastor of
the white First Congregational Church of Hartford. Rebecca's letters
were being read at meetings of the Hartford Freedman's Society, the
group responsible for her mission South, and the pastor wrote that her
letters were "just what they need to keep up the interest in the cause."

"He adds," Rebecca quoted proudly, " 'I do not know any sort of
labor in the world more interesting just now than this teaching the
Freedman at the South.' And he wishes me all sorts of success, he says,
'At the present rate of work we shall in a few years have so many of them
taught to read, that all of the Andrew Johnsons in creation will not be
equal to the job of keeping them down in the dirt under the white man's
heel.'"

The three passages show Rebecca in turn awed by the mass of her
people, cataloguing the specific injustices they suffered, and finally
reaffirming the significance of the work she was engaged in. I was
convinced by then that I wanted to read all the letters. They seemed to
me not only important but unique, in offering access to the opinions and
daily life of this dedicated woman of another time.

So that's how I got started with Rebecca. I finished writing my
paper but still wanted to know more. When the time came to choose a
thesis topic, I had my chance. The following is some of what I have
learned.

Rebecca, born in 1836, was the first of the four Primus children.
The others, in order of birth, were Henrietta, Nelson and Isabel.
Rebecca must have been, in some sense, her parents' favorite: a bright
child, eager to please and easy to manage. I have a mental picture of her,
at age 5, entering school for the first time. Because it was an important
occasion, Holdridge Primus took time from his porter's job to walk his
daughter to the Talcott Street Church where the Rev. J.W.C. Pennington
and his wife conducted the African School. At the door Rebecca let go
her father's hand, dismissed him with a quick hug, and marched to the
classroom, dress immaculate, face shining: she already knew her letters. If
Mrs. Pennington asked a question, Rebecca's hand was in the air — the

pupil all teachers pray for. Here was a student who could herself someday become a teacher, an occupation that commanded universal respect.

Rebecca rose eagerly to the academic challenges the Penningtons offered, and along with her lessons absorbed their belief in the importance of securing justice and equality for blacks. The Rev. Pennington was a fugitive slave whose freedom was purchased by John Hooker of Hartford, husband of Isabella Beecher. A nationally known lecturer, Pennington urged his congregation to take part in the movement for racial uplift.

As a youngster, Rebecca undoubtedly heard abolition, colonization (emigration to Liberia or other states governed by blacks), and the search for justice debated in church, in school, and at home. Her response was to cultivate in herself the qualities that would demonstrate the worthiness of blacks for full citizenship.

Encouraged by her family and spurred by her own dedication, Rebecca did become a teacher, although we have no information about where she trained or where she taught. She was not listed as an instructor at either of Hartford's African Schools, but letters from her friend Addie Brown in 1861 and 1862 refer to her keeping a private school. Addie wished she was a schoolgirl again so she could attend.

By the time she was 25, then, Rebecca was a teacher. Literate, principled, well-spoken, proud, she represented the culmination of decades of hard work and determination on the part of blacks in Hartford, virtually all of whose forebears had been brought to New England in chains. Her father, Holdridge, may have been the single most important black individual in the city. Grandson of a slave who had earned his freedom by serving in the Revolutionary War, Primus arrived in Hartford from Guilford in 1827 at the age of 12 and became a servant to the Ellsworth family. He was taken along to Washington when William Ellsworth, later governor of the state, served in Congress (1829-33), but for most of his adult life he was a porter in the Humphrey and Seyms grocery store on Main Street. By 1849, Primus had saved enough money to buy a home for his young family, a two-story frame house at 20 Wadsworth St. On this score alone, he was a man of stature in the community: of the 716 black residents of Hartford in 1860, 35 owned property. From the same list of 35 came the officers in the two black churches and key members of the black Masonic Society. They were the core of Hartford's black middle class.

In the same year that he purchased his family home, Primus set out for California and the Gold Rush in the great adventure of his life. The "Humphrey" of Humphrey and Seyms had a son who wanted to join the prospecting expedition of the Hartford-based Warburton Mining and Trading Co., and his father would allow it only if Primus became a member of the party. Although it meant leaving his wife and children behind, Holdridge agreed to go as company cook. When the dreams of gold inevitably dissipated and the company collapsed, he found work with the Adams Express Co. in San Francisco. The white members of the party straggled back to Hartford poorer than when they left, and Primus returned with a gold medal from Adams Express for faithful service. He had been gone four years.

He went back to his job at the store, moonlighting as sexton at the Center Church and frequently serving as waiter and major domo at white society functions in Hartford. He acted as an employment broker, along with his wife, helping match black workers with prospective white employers. By no means well off, he nevertheless achieved a way of life unusual for blacks in his time. The probate listing made at the time of his death in 1884 shows that the family parlor, for example, contained a piano, carpet, books, a looking glass, 10 pictures, an arm chair and five small chairs. He appeared to have no cash savings, but his estate was valued at $3,924.68.

In 19th-century America, any black who managed to buy a home and maintain a middle-class standard of living, as Primus did, had to be industrious, thrifty and reasonably lucky. Highly paid, skilled jobs were not open to blacks, and job security was unknown, but Primus's personal qualities enabled him to maintain a 40-year association with the same firm. Known among blacks and whites as a wise and honest man, he held offices in the Talcott Street Congregational Church, of which he was a founding member, and the Prince Hall Masons. Energetic and ambitious, he worked extra jobs all his life. His unmarried children lived at home and no doubt contributed to the family income. His wife ran a business of her own.

Mehitable Primus, the former Mehitable Jacobs, was the daughter of the first free black man to settle in Hartford. That distinction, along with ownership of his shop, made Jeremiah Jacobs, cobbler, a respected member of the black community, and accounts for Rebecca's light-hearted reference to her mother's family in one of the letters as "venerable and famous." Mehitable was as industrious and as much admired as her husband. She cared for her children, kept chickens, raised

Within the Primus Papers, those letters of a century ago,
are stories of courage and perseverance.

flowers, vegetables and fruit, and trained domestic workers in her home. All this was aside from her dressmaking business, which extended to hiring other women to do sewing at home.

Rebecca's sisters, Henrietta and Isabel, were less gifted than she, and Henrietta, especially, seemed to feel herself in Rebecca's shadow, boarding out even in her early teens rather than living at home. Nelson, meanwhile, won prizes for drawing at an early age, and was apprenticed to a local carriage maker to learn carriage and sign painting. In 1866, at the age of 23, he moved with his wife and new baby to Boston to begin a career as an artist. His letters depict a young man accustomed to special treatment learning how hard an artist's life can be.

Although I have described the Primuses as leaders of the middle class, it was the black middle class. And indeed there was no black upper class to correspond to that of white society. The Hartford inhabited by the Primus family was not the Hartford of the Samuel Colts, the Horace Bushnells, the Calvin Stowes, or the Samuel L. Clemenses. Hartford whites at mid-century were no more open to the idea of racial equality than whites anywhere else, North or South. Some — but by no means all — condemned the practice of slavery, but virtually no one questioned white superiority. While a civil tone characterized contacts between black and white leaders, there was no social interaction between the races, and discrimination was practiced openly and without apology. The blacks of Hartford, Yankees in the sense that 90 percent of them had been born in the North, formed a separate community, with their own churches schools and civic and charitable organizations. Walking the same streets, buying the same goods, attending the same public events, worshipping the same God, blacks and whites in Hartford lived in very different and mutually exclusive worlds.

In 1865, the two separate worlds of Hartford showed signs of coming together. With the Civil War in its final phase, Congress funded the Freedmen's Bureau, to assist former slaves, and Hartford formed its own Freedmen's Aid Society.

The president of the Hartford Society was Professor Calvin Stowe, who had moved to Hartford in 1864 along with his celebrated wife, Harriet Beecher Stowe. The all-white board of directors included women of the Cheney silk dynasty, ministers and other important citizens. I found no records of the group's deliberations, but it is clear that sending teachers south was their major project.

This was the work Rebecca Primus had been preparing for for all of her 29 years. How the Hartford Freedmen's Society selected its five teachers we don't know, but by Nov. 7 she was on the train headed south. A year later her mother was named to the Freedmen's Society board, along with another prominent black woman, Mrs. L.W. Saunders: surely more evidence that the day of justice and equality was dawning.

In her first letter, Rebecca described the trip to Baltimore and her meeting with a Mr. Graham of the Baltimore Association for the Moral and Educational Improvement of the Colored People. Within a week, he had sent her on to her post at Royal Oak on Maryland's Eastern Shore. The Baltimore Association arranged for her to board with a local couple, Charles H. Thomas and his wife. Thomas, who had bought his own freedom, was a property owner, farmer, millworker, and horseman.

Because it had been illegal to teach blacks to read and write under slavery, there was no black schoolhouse in Royal Oak. Rebecca held classes in the church, teaching children in the morning and adults in the evening, with a combined total of about 75 students. She also conducted a Sunday School, and in her free time read books and newspapers devoted to history, public affairs and politics. Each month she prepared reports for the three offices that together supervised and funded her school: the Hartford Freedmen's Aid Society, the Freedmen's Bureau regional office in New York City, and the Baltimore Association. She also wrote weekly to her parents, and occasionally to Nelson in Boston. She kept up a regular correspondence with Addie Brown in Hartford, although only Addie's letters to Rebecca survive.

Addie Brown's voice is nothing like Rebecca's. Less educated, less dedicated to public causes and much less concerned with proper English, she describes Hartford in vivid and valuable detail — in what sounds like transcribed black speech.

How Addie, six years Rebecca's junior, came to live in Hartford is one of the puzzles of the letters. Her home was in New York City, but according to the letters she was working in Hartford and Waterbury in the late 1850's and early 1860's. In 1862 she severed her connection with her own family, objecting to the man her widowed mother had married. By this time she was bosom friends with Rebecca and accepted as kin by the rest of the Primus family. When Rebecca left Hartford to go south, Addie was devastated.

"How I have miss you. i have lost all; no more pleasure for me now. Aunt Emily (Emily Sands, sister of Mehitable Primus) ask me last eve if i was going to carry that (sober) face until you return. She also said if Mr.

(Joseph) Tines was to see me, think that I care more for you than I did for him. I told (her) I did love you more than I ever would him. She said I better not tell him so. It would be the truth and most else."

Judging from Addie's letters, the intense relationship between the two women appeared to conform with other same-sex attachments described in accounts of 19th-century life. Whether or not it can be characterized as sexual in nature, it was certainly intimate; yet both women eventually married. Over the four-year period that Rebecca conducted her school in Royal Oak, Addie gradually devoted less and less space in her letters to lamenting the loss of her companion, and more to accounts of her work and social life in Hartford: "I get along very nicely to the Dye House I was sewing nearly all day yesterday and all this morn we was paid last night I rec.d $19.00 you don't know how please I felt Dear Sister just look back $4.00 per month what a jump up I did not walk up."

When business fell off and she lost her job at Smith's Dye House, she wrote, "You say don't allow myself to indulge in glumly forebodings...How can I help it? I can't get any work. I have no money, and I stand to live out to service long at the time. That all I can aspire in this place."

Later on, when she was working in the home of the Rev. John T. Huntington, professor of Greek at Trinity College, she wrote, "Rebecca I have been working for nothing comparatively speaking now I have come to a decided stand that people shall pay me for my work — I don't care colored or white." Prof. Huntington did increase her wages, but in 1868 she went to Farmington to work as a cook's assistant and chambermaid at Miss Porter's School. On her own time, she did piecework sewing for Rebecca's mother.

In spite of her long days and hard work, Addie maintained an amazingly busy social life. She made daily calls on friends, kept up with local and national news, sewed for the poor, went out to dinner, attracted a series of suitors, and travelled fairly often by boat or train to New Jersey, New Haven and Middletown. Her anecdotes fill in for us the personalities of friends and relations Rebecca and Nelson mention in their letters — names like Sands, Champion, Mitchell, Asher, Freeman, Nott, Plato, Cleggett, Saunders — all members of Hartford's black middle class. She described fairs, balls, taffy pulls, concerts, and musical evenings at the Primus home. Of the many men who called on Addie, Mr. Tines of Philadelphia was the one she finally married.

Meanwhile, Rebecca the Yankee was discovering the rural South, eating possum and noticing that school attendance fell off during hog-killing week. Evidently in reply to a worried letter from home in December in 1866, she wrote: "I do not think the people ought to be alarmed for my safety here, it is very quiet all around me, and I feel as safe here as anywhere else. I do not apprehend danger. I hope they'll all lay aside their fears and feel that i am in the hands of the same Supreme Being that has the charge of us all everywhere." Although she was not effusive about it, religion was the source of her strength.

But there were dangers. Rebecca frequently mentioned sickness in the neighborhood — chills and fever, cholera, smallpox, typhoid, measles — but surely what worried her family most was not disease but racial incidents. There were many to relate. In April 1866, Rebecca wrote that a colleague, Miss Dickson, teaching at Trappe, Md., was "stoned by white children and repeatedly subjected to insults from white men.. In passing they have brushed by her so rudely she says 'as to almost dislocate her shoulders,' she says she tries to bear it patiently…The whites are very mean there. I'm told. White children take col(ore)d children's books from them & otherwise misuse & ill treat them."

In the same letter she reported another kind of threat:

"Miss Cummings writes me that two of the colored teachers, Miss Anderson & Mrs. Jackson, are having a lawsuit in Balto (Baltimore) with a fellow who put them out of the Ladies Room at the Depot, where they (were) sitting waiting for the train. It was going in their favor when the fellow plead a jury trial and she says there's no telling now which way it will go. I hope however he may get the worst of it at any rate."

Virtually all Rebecca's letters, in fact, contain reports of racial incidents. Clearly she was not writing these matters to worry her parents, but to keep them informed. The letters give the impression of a cumulative storehouse of news items not covered in white newspapers. Rebecca's letters carried information from afar that could be passed on by word of mouth in Hartford. Usually the news concerned other teachers, friends and acquaintances, but occasionally she herself was a target. In December of her second year of teaching she wrote:

"I had forgotten to tell you about the little difficulty I've had with this poor old secesh Postmaster here. It's all on account of the papers you've sent me & which he and his…wife have taken the liberty to open."

The papers she referred to were the Independent and the Communicator, both anti-slavery publications. The postmaster claimed they had been illegally mailed and wanted to charge a $20 fine for delivering them. Rebecca chose not to pay the fine, but neither did she fight the postmaster and his wife: "I do not intend to trouble with them hereafter. I wrote a note to the Post Master at Easton to take the charge of all my papers & letters hereafter & he sent word that he would." By February, the Royal Oak postmaster had changed his tune and become "considerate," offering to handle her mail once again. She wrote: "These white people want all the respect shown to them by the col(ore)d people. I give what I re(ceive) and no more."

This method of neither backing down nor picking a fight that couldn't be won appeared to be typical of Rebecca. When her mother and sister were preparing to visit her in Maryland, she sent this advice:

"The Conductor will tell you which car to take after you arrive at the Phila Depot, & if you find her puts you in the smoking car & the door of the next car is locked, watch the opportunity & as soon as the door is unlocked get up & go into that car. For you are not obliged to sit in the smoking car. I did not occupy it either time, as soon as I found out where I was I improved the opportunity & exchanged cars.

Addie informed Rebecca of incidents in Hartford in a style a good deal more blunt. In November 1865, when the all-black 29th Connecticut Volunteers returned from the Civil War, the troops were greeted by government officials and honored with speeches, a parade and ceremonial dinner. Addie's account of the day included information not available in newspaper reports: "I went up to meeting with Aunt Em every other person we met had niggur in his or her mouth.. They was so mad to think the white was compel to make a fuss over them. On our return home some of them said niggur to us."

Nelson's letters added to the storehouse his experiences in Boston. In October 1867 he wrote, 'The man that i was painting the house for did not amount to much. She thought i was going to work for nothing because i were colored. We could not come to terms, in consequence we parted."

By the time Rebecca returned to Royal Oak for her second year of teaching, she had made up her mind to build a schoolhouse of her own. This project became the major topic of her correspondence in the year that followed. She held student exhibitions and promoted church fairs in Royal Oak. She sold books and convinced Nelson, barely making a living for himself in Boston, to do the same, door to door.

In 1867, the Talcott Street Church in Hartford was the site of a gala fair that raised $200, almost half the total cost of the school. Rebecca schemed and cajoled to get the land, lumber and labor donated. In March 1867 she wrote of an encouraging development: "We've had trees given to us for all the sills for our school hose, and all of them from southern rights men, which I think shows they have no real hostile feelings towards the col(ore)d school, but are rather in favor of it."

Her efforts impressed Mr. E.C. Estes of the New York Freedmen's Bureau. Rebecca wrote home that, in his opinion, it would be "very gratifying to me to know what pleasing statement the (Baltimore) Ass(ociati)on sent them relative to my exertions to get assistance for building our schoolhouse here." She also enjoyed a less formal bit of praise: "Mr. Thomas's uncle says, if I should get up a dog fight I would do well at if for whatever I attempt everybody thinks it's all right."

The Primus Institute, measuring 34 by 24 feet and 13 feet high with a "neat whitewashed fence," built on land paid for by the New York Freedmen's Society, of lumber said to have come from a Civil War barracks, was ceremoniously dedicated, with speeches, recitals and ice cream, in September of 1867.

Rebecca's mission in the South continued only two more years. The Freedmen's Bureau, controversial from the start, was dissolved by Congress in 1869. Reluctant to continue without federal funds, the Hartford Society promptly disbanded and called its teachers home. Certainly Rebecca knew the work was unfinished; even with 3,000 teachers on the job, illiteracy still prevailed in the South. Unfortunately we have no letter recording her reaction to this news, and the silence in which she closed her school and returned to Hartford lasted the rest of her life.

If the first 29 years of Rebecca Primus' life were preparation and the four years teaching in Royal Oak were her great adventure, there followed a 63-year denouement.

Rebecca came home in 1869 to find that justice and equality continued to elude the black man — and woman — in the North as well as the South. The year before, 1868, Connecticut had done away with separate black schools, but the "integrated" schools of Hartford hired only white teachers. Rebecca could go south to teach freed slaves, but she could not pursue her career at home.

We can only piece together the rest of her life from fragments in the Primus Papers and entries in the City Directory. She went to work with her mother as a seamstress, and in 1873 married Charles N.

Thomas, who had been her landlord in Royal Oak. What happened to his first wife and how he happened to move North are more puzzles of the Primus Papers. In any case the Wadsworth Atheneum owns a dress of Rebecca's — a two-piece daytime gown of ribbed silky fabric, the color between tan and gray, with high neck and long sleeves. I believe it was her wedding dress. It is described by the curator of the costume collection as probably from the early 1870's, well-made but not high fashion. Originally there was a matching bonnet.

Rebecca and Mr. Thomas lived in various upstairs and rear apartments, not the style to which either was accustomed. Letters from the Hartford Statehouse regret that no positions were available for Mr. Thomas, who had served as a doorman during one legislative session. It appeared that he suffered an injury and became either physically disabled or mentally incompetent, and when he died in 1891 Rebecca moved back to the family home. She taught in the Talcott Street Congregational Church Sunday School, subscribed to a women's literary journal, The Cottage Hearth, and probably continued to sew for a living. Her father died in 1894 and her mother in 1899, and after the family home was sold she moved to a rooming house.

Thus the terrible waste of her later years: trained to teach, determined to help, prohibited from serving in her own hometown. And beyond her personal disappointment was the spectacle of the worsening relations between the races. She lived through periods of change and struggle that made the truth all too clear: the new day that appeared to be dawning in 1865 turned out heartbreakingly like all the days that had gone before.

What must she have thought — by the turn of the century, by the end of World War I, by the start of the Great Depression — when she looked back at the Emancipation Proclamation and the end of the War Between the States? Instead of justice and equality she had lived to see Jim Crow, the upheaval of the Great Migration, the outrages of the lynch mobs and the disappearance of the Negro Question from public debate as other issues took the nation's attention. One of the most basic of Rebecca's beliefs was that educated, middle-class blacks like those she knew in Hartford held the key to the future of the race in America. More than a century has passed and although Rebecca's view has not prevailed, it has stubbornly endured in the quiet, courageous and quite angry black middle class that whites are only beginning to recognize.

Whatever her thoughts may have been, the Rebecca of the letters, daughter of Holdridge and Mehitable, student of J.W.C. Pennington, would not have given way to despair. I think she got up and dressed every morning, smoothed the bed covers and put on water for tea. She followed the news, did her work, spent as little as possible for what she needed, attended church, visited the sick, comforted the afflicted. She regularly called on her sisters, read to her nieces when they were small; and quizzed them on their lessons. No doubt Nelson came home to visit from time to time until he left Boston for the far West. Sometimes, Rebecca thought about Addie, whose story had ended years before. Pencilled on the back of an envelope in the box that holds the Primus Papers is this note: "Addie died at her residence Phila. 7 Jan. 1870 at 11 o'clock a.m." At the end of the day Rebecca prayed for strength. That prayer was answered.

You may already know the final common ground I share with Alice Walker. She went looking for Zora Neale Hurston's grave and found the site overgrown, unmarked, forgotten. Shocked, she arranged for an engraved headstone to mark the spot and set about resurrecting Zora's literary reputation. The Primus family plot in Hartford is in Zion Hill Cemetery, a few blocks away from Trinity College. I was uncertain how to find lot No. 863, but the caretaker showed me the place. Rebecca's grave is unmarked, but I am not thinking of a headstone. It seems to me that a suitable memorial to her dedication, her strength and her dignity would be to make sure Hartford citizens know what a remarkable woman this city once produced. Rebecca Primus was a teacher. We can still learn from her.

5

Escapism at the Atheneum

Garret Condon

Hartford artist Peter Waite recalls a Wadsworth Atheneum event sponsored by Shawmut Bank, whose logo was prominently displayed in the museum's lobby. Some folks came in the front door, looked around and added it all up: the dark paneling, the uniformed security guards, the information desk and Shawmut Bank's insignia on prominent display.

"They thought they were in a bank," says Waite.

The other day, the Atheneum cleared up this problem. It installed an automatic teller machine in the lobby.

Not really. Actually, the Atheneum officially opened the Helen and Harry Gray Court, a bright, airy front entry hall that literally blows through an intermediate floor and opens to the roof of the original 1842 building.

Light pours in from almost every side, unobstructed by translucent walkways connecting the upper floors on either side of the new lobby. And by April, wild, intensely colorful and remarkably un-rectangular wall drawings by Hartford-born Sol LeWitt will dance and scramble from the tops of the ground-floor doorways to the roof line.

Architect Tai Soo Kim, who dreamed up the new court, was a young architecture student in 1961 when he first entered the Atheneum to take an evening drawing class. What especially struck him was the Avery Court, the Bauhaus atrium at the center of the Atheneum's Avery Memorial building. "I was really moved by that," he says. He hopes his own contribution to the Atheneum — a tall, luminous space — will prove to be just as moving and do justice to the building's Gothic Revival exterior. "When they go in, everybody is going to look up at the ceiling." It is designed to be uplifting.

Patrick McCaughey, the Atheneum's wry and infectiously buoyant director since 1988, paraded me through the lobby while it was still under construction, eagerly revealing the new vistas and sightlines. "It's a great sort of offering of the museum to Main Street," he says.

I'm not sure what Main Street will make of this gift. I can only describe the bizarre use I've made of the Atheneum in recent years. In that context, allow me to offer some unscholarly thoughts about what, and who, the Atheneum is for, and why the space itself, including the striking new entrance, is so important.

Four years ago, in the midst of what I guess was a career crisis, I found myself spending lunch times at the Atheneum. I did not look at the artworks, exactly, although I half pretended to. I rarely ate in the cafe. I just went there to get away from everything else. I favored two spots: the majestic Morgan Great Hall, and the cool expanse of the Avery Court. I was not seeking moments of intense concentration — just the opposite. In what had been only an art museum before, I discovered huge and glorious sites for peaceful distraction. Two years ago, after my father's death, I was at it again: nodding at the guards; moving in out of the changing light of different galleries and halls.

I am a discriminating man when it comes to museums, libraries and churches. I feel most at home in those that offer quiet, spacious freedom. And I love that they are utterly useless. I don't mean purposeless. I mean, here is major real estate that isn't making a buck for anyone. That seems perversely counter-cultural to me. On the other hand, such places are benefactions of the rich — and monuments to them, too. My place of refuge was built by J. Pierpont Morgan and his ilk.

❧

Whatever else I may feel about the wealthy, they are a great natural resource — like bauxite or something. My deeply ambiguous feelings about the very affluent are, I'm sure, equal parts socialist and would-be socialite. I suppose the rich provide such things as museums out of a mixture of generosity and a desire for chiseled-in-granite immortality. Also, high-culture charities position the well-to-do at top of the taste hierarchy (or finger-food chain). Such gifts, therefore, are a great ex-post-facto way of demonstrating that the wealthy deserve their loot and privilege. But once they turn it over to the public, well, it's ours, isn't it?

ૢ☙

Atheneum founder Daniel Wadsworth pioneered opening the door to the public, which produced mixed early results for both the museum and the public. For one thing, Wadsworth's idea of "public" was as imperfectly democratic as his new nation. By charging 25 cents per customer, he was excluding a lot of Hartfordites. (A quarter's buying power was in 1844 equivalent to $8 to $10 today, according to Eugene Gaddis, the Atheneum's archivist and a walking encyclopedia of its history.) For another, the public — not yet saturated with mass-produced images or weaned on art history — was not all that hot for Wadsworth's gallery. All those families whose names we now associate with buildings or major collections at the Atheneum — the Goodwins, Morgans, Colts and others — didn't merely add on to Wadsworth's museum. They saved its institutional bacon, beginning in the late 19th century. They turned it into a fashionable target for local philanthropy and, as a result, into a richer experience for visitors.

Like a lot of trust-fund brats, Wadsworth had money and connections. Unlike most, he was discreetly generous and spent much of his life pursuing his ideas of beauty in art and architecture. Through his wife's uncle, John Trumbull — the great painter of the Revolutionary War — Wadsworth befriended some of the leading American artists of his day. He supported Thomas Cole, father of the Hudson River School. And, thanks to Wadsworth, Hartford artist Frederic Church became Cole's student.

Wadsworth didn't invent art-as-commodity. Consider Giovanni Paolo Panini's 1749 painting, "The Picture Gallery of Cardinal Silvio Valenti Gonzaga," on view at the Atheneum. It's the "powerful guy surrounded by his possessions" genre so popular in European oil paintings of this era. (Bomb-tossing art critic John Berger has pointed out that not only did oil paintings become one of the proud possessions of the European middle class, but the works often depicted that class's other possessions.) But Wadsworth wanted to share his collection with us.

As a guy on the ground floor of America's art establishment, he foresaw, I think, the triadic shape of that establishment: the eager-to-be-enlightened public; the artist, or man of genius (usually a Caucasian male, until recently); and the man of taste and privilege, able to identify works of genius.

Among Jonathan Bruce's favorite pieces at the Atheneum is this work entitled "Negro Aroused."

૨૭

Put white guys in charge of finding the geniuses and guess who they find? Take your time, no hurry. Right, they find more white guys. Then they put them in chronological order and, poof! Art History! Anyway, that's the kind of art history I had absorbed as a college student who dutifully and uncritically genuflected before the great masterpieces of Europe during my junior year abroad and later. So when I first visited the Atheneum in 1982, I was, frankly, floored by the big names.

One expects (indeed, demands) masterpieces at the Louvre or the Vatican museums, but in Hartford? Here were remarkable Picassos, a jarring self-portrait by Van Gogh and among the Baroque treasures, Zurbaran's riveting "St. Serapion." This was, I knew, big league. I actually remember thinking: This is better than Hartford deserves.

Thankfully, I was being paid to write about the Atheneum and other city arts groups — they were all part of an arts beat I worked briefly for The Courant. (Thankfully for me, not necessarily for my readers.) I'm grateful because I got a chance to rethink my notions about tradition and masterpieces as these organizations conducted an often noisy debate about who gets to do art, and who gets to decide what art is. The key players, it seems to me, were Real Art Ways, the Community Renewal Team's Craftery Gallery, the Atheneum's MATRIX program and, later, the Charter Oak Cultural Center. Far from settling for the white-guys school of art, they insisted on a new role for women and minority artists. (The debate, of course, goes on.)

Despite its august facade, the Atheneum has not been terribly hidebound — at least not since 1927. That's the year the fat, sleepy museum, steeped in the historical and representational, hired A. Everett "Chick" Austin Jr. to be its director. Like a modernist tsunami, Austin swept over the Atheneum, filling it with Picassos and Dalis, Man Ray photographs, dance, drama and film. His Avery Memorial wing, with its theater, remains a monument to the international avant-garde and its perhaps naive hope that art and artists might infect and inspire every nook and cranny of culture.

Austin was the first in Hartford's art establishment to address the color line. He opened the museum to African-American artists, actors and dancers. But Austin's efforts didn't significantly affect the permanent collection or the museum's white-guys perspective after his departure in 1945. In the decades after the war, as the minority population of Hartford jumped (and whites became a city minority), the Atheneum struggled to respond.

Jonathan Bruce, 47, founding director of the Craftery Gallery and a pioneer among African-American curators, remembers working in the museum's Auerbach Art Library as a high school student. It was, he says, a very white place.

What has made the difference for Bruce — and many other African-Americans in the region — is the addition in 1988 of the Amistad

Foundation's 6,000-piece collection of African-American art and historical artifacts. It was a huge reckoning of accounts with black Hartford. By housing the Amistad collection (a special gallery opened in 1992) and creating the Fleet Gallery of African-American Art, comprising works from its own collection, in 1993, the Atheneum acknowledged that, from now on, the heritage of the slave must share space with the legacy of the slave-trader. The voice of the contemporary African-American artist — in a city with a large African-American community — must be clear and prominent.

"I think the museum has improved over the years," says Bruce. "It's very receptive to welcoming African-Americans now."

Not that a couple of new art galleries magically addresses the racial and economic disparity in our state. But every step away from Connecticut's de facto apartheid is worth taking. I remember being warmed and encouraged at a particularly raucous West Indian festival at the museum one summer in the early 1980s. It stands out in memory because it was one of the few big, racially mixed soirees I had attended in my partying years (read: pre-fatherhood). As a bachelor journalist, I was obliged to make the rounds, drink too many Heinekens and slam-dance near the Caravaggio. Just as the evening seemed to be winding down, a group of revelers invited any and all to the West Indian Social Club in the North End as a way to keep the party alive. I and some others took up the invitation. Needless to say, the regular clientele at the club was surprised but good-natured about the appearance of a handful of white non-regulars. One beer later — the band from the Atheneum did not appear, as promised — I left with a friend and crossed Main Street to my car. I had never before stepped into any North End club. For one evening, art and music seemed to have brought black and white Hartford together. The three kids who then robbed me at knifepoint weren't invited to the party and couldn't share my revelation. They only saw a half-drunk joker in a seersucker suit up way past his bedtime and far from home. But the evening showed me how a place like the Atheneum could bring Hartford's different hues together. (And I don't think the kids got too far on seven bucks and a triple-A card.)

In a sense, the Atheneum's challenge is to invite a lot more people to the party. In a 1994 grant application, the Atheneum claimed to attract "more than 10,000 African-Americans each year." That's less than 8.5 percent of the 160,090 people who visited the museum in the last fiscal year. (African-Americans made up 8.5 percent of the region's population and nearly 40 percent of the city's population in the 1990 census.) And though the museum produces Spanish-language brochures and museum guides, it does not have data on Latino visitors.

Mexican-born artist and musician Carlos Hernandez Chavez would be surprised if there are a lot of Atheneum regulars in the local Hispanic community. He says the Atheneum's heart is in the right place, but it must please its major donors, most of whom are white and Anglo. In addition, he doubts the museum really understands how intimidating the place can be to the uninitiated, especially those for whom English is a second language.

"I've seen virtually no works of Latin American artists in the museum," he says.

McCaughey says that there must be more Latino art in the Atheneum — as well as more works by Asian Americans. He's made diversity one of the museum's primary goals during his administration.

"If there has been one absolutely consistent theme in the Atheneum for the past eight years, it has been the desire to widen, deepen, diversify and add to the audience of the museum," he says. "There is not one, single element of the museum that does not sing from that particular hymn book."

Still, he adds, the idea is not just to find your own experience reflected in the Atheneum. "The good art museum will surprise you," he says. "Against your better judgment you will find yourself liking something you didn't know anything about — something that is outside of your experience."

≈

I think, increasingly, we are trying to avoid being surprised in any way, which is sad for two reasons: it's bad news for democracy and it makes it harder for the average citizen to have his or her mind blown.

Whether it's Route 44 or the over-hyped infobahn, we seem to be traveling toward places where people look like us. Our cable TV channels and radio stations give us only what we already know we like. And on-line computer services allow us to customize the news. I can't believe this is a hopeful trend in a culture that pays enormous lip service to the goal of integration and the virtues of diversity. The Bosnian model of multiculturalism was not, I think, what we had in mind.

So we avoid the unexpected. And yet, without it we miss out on some of life's most enriching moments. The planned-for experience reinforces our ideas about ourselves and all of our prejudices. The unplanned ambush is what changes us — and the visual arts — in a special and mysterious way. The image strikes us before the words come to mind. We may be left speechless. In any case, our usual way of thinking is short-circuited, if only for a nanosecond.

As you may know, creating such chinks in our thought-armor is a specialty of Zen Buddhism. There is a Korean Zen master named Seung Sahn, whom I admire. He has lived in Rhode Island for the last two decades or so. In an exchange recorded in his book, "Dropping Ashes on the Buddha," one of his students asks him about the relationship between Zen Buddhism and art. The Zen master simply encourages the student to "cut off all thinking" and to arrive at a place "before thinking." That is where we are when we create art, and it's the place to be to really appreciate it.

Now, I would have taken you a long way for nothing if I thought there was no value in thinking about any of this. All of the issues that go into creating a place like the Atheneum obviously must be thought and rethought. Much of what hangs on the walls there is wonderfully thought-provoking. But, I'd argue that the real impact occurs before thinking. We may appreciate Van Gogh's circa-1887 self-portrait as a work from his Paris years with brother Theo, but first we are fixed by the stare. We follow the cosmic reach of "The Lawrence Tree" before we note that it is an excellent O'Keeffe. When we look carefully at Silvia Plimack Mangold's "Big Green," its mind-bending grand illusion is revealed. (Hint: It's all paint.) Do we need to closely examine the circumstances in Jacob Lawrence's "Rain" to see people struggling against drab darkness?

I'm not suggesting that the benchmark art encounter is a crystalline moment of deep, Zenlike enlightenment. Maybe you erupt with laughter, or sob, or shrug, or leave the place ticked off. The shape and content of that response is entirely up to each of us. There is no television laugh track to prompt us. If we are willing to dismiss the taste-makers and the hype that might surround a "big" exhibition, we are free to make of it what we will. We can catch fifty paintings in our peripheral vision as we steam by, lost in our thoughts. (It might be interesting to tour the Atheneum on Rollerblades, though I think this might raise some security issues.) We might fixate on a single work — the pop-culture echoes of Warhol's "Early Colored Jackie?" We might seek out a particular gesture (reclining figures?) or maybe a single color. Perhaps a believer would be

moved to prayer before a medieval altarpiece — the very purpose of these
works before they became "art."

Which is not to say that just because H.W. Janson (the late author
of the monumental "History of Art") or McCaughey say something's a
masterpiece it automatically isn't. Maybe we find historians, critics and
curators helpful, or maybe we want to look at the art and skip the labels.
It's our call.

This freedom — and the possibility of random transformation —
should be at the heart of any sense of reverence we might feel as we enter
the Atheneum. Sherry Buckberrough, associate professor of art history at
the Hartford Art School of the University of Hartford (which needs a
more minimalist name), notes that such feelings can be a kind of
barrier — especially if our reverence is borrowed from someone else.
"One enters a museum as one enters a church," she says. "It has a certain
sacredness about it — it's very difficult to overcome it. One wants to let
people feel it's their church." Exactly.

It may well be that each of the museum's high-rolling benefactors
felt that he or she was leaving unique ideas about art for posterity.
Well, ideas come and go. Even collections change. What remains is a
space, reserved for us and maintained by a thoughtful staff. It is
consecrated to our encounter with the objects or marks human beings
make on purpose — for sake of God, or beauty, or to pay the rent.
Perhaps Daniel Wadsworth saw this from the beginning.

࿇

I have this zany notion that Tai Soo Kim and the Grays have
fulfilled Daniel Wadsworth's original fantasy for his art museum. Just
because this idea is based on thin scholarship doesn't mean it's not
plausible. (Anyway, thin scholarship can be very strong. It's currently
supporting millions of dollars worth of tenure at American universities.)

To begin with, I believe Wadsworth had his mind blown once or
twice. One does not say that lightly about the immediate descendants of
Puritans. As a child he traveled to France and Britain with his father, and
was deeply impressed by the Gothic churches and abbeys he saw there.
Imagine the impact of these vast, soaring spaces — overflowing with
intricate work in stone, wood and glass — on a Hartford boy used to the
stately meeting house. As a local arbiter of taste and an amateur architect,
Daniel Wadsworth was a champion of Gothic Revival. When he wrote in
defense of this movement (as he did in 1833), he explained that Gothic-

style buildings — Trinity Church on the Green in New Haven and Hartford's Christ Church Cathedral were his examples — could be bright and expansive inside. The quality of the space, he seemed to say, mattered.

Wadsworth wanted a Gothic art gallery. But he did not get exactly what he wanted. More practical (and less artistically inclined) burghers convinced him that a picture-and-sculpture gallery alone wouldn't attract enough donors. He deferred to their judgment and went along with the idea of an atheneum — a kind of cultural mini-mall — to include a picture gallery, a library (the forebear of the Hartford Public Library), and homes for the Connecticut Historical Society and the Natural Historical Society. (The Watkinson Library — in a separate building — and the Hartford Art School would also come and go.)

Yes, he got Gothic Revival on the outside in a big way, hiring A.J. Davis and Ithiel Town (architect of Christ and Trinity churches) to do his Atheneum in the pointed style. On the inside, it was all business: There were occupants to accommodate, and the gallery — though physically central — was not the only one.

I cannot say for sure what Gothic Revival meant to Wadsworth or if it was much more than a fancy. (Wadsworth's retreat atop Talcott Mountain was also done in this style.) Did he yearn for a Middle Ages that he imagined to be a time of deep, integrated spirituality? (The British architect A.W. Pugin, a rabid convert to Catholicism and a contemporary of Wadsworth, called Gothic buildings "Christian" — everything else was pagan.) Perhaps it suggested the mystery and loss of the rainswept ruins of the romantic writers. In any case, he might have imagined a voluminous, bright, interior — sacred in a way that would be neither heresy nor idolatry — for his gallery.

Tai Soo Kim gives Wadsworth's gallery the shining spaciousness that Wadsworth, perhaps, dreamed of, and complements the museum's other great spaces. It is a contemporary Gothic nave meant to startle and delight. May it fill us with genuine awe for the work of our fellow humans — not phony reverence for moribund traditions or dead capitalists — and propel us to those prized moments "before thinking."

6

Panini's Masterpiece

Lary Bloom

We stood facing the great canvas, the director of the Wadsworth Atheneum and I, and we waved our hands. Patrick McCaughey waved his at the remarkable detail in what we saw, as he expounded on the work of Giovanni Paulo Panini. I waved mine, which held my Papermate, in enthusiastic sweeps of an amateur appreciator. Too enthusiastic. In his deft Australian way, McCaughey said, "May I ask you to keep your pen from the painting." "Sorry," I said. It was little enough price to pay, for I had asked McCaughey to spend 30 minutes with me in front of "The Picture Gallery of Cardinal Silvio Valenti Gonzaga." I had asked him to "Tell me, please, why I adore this painting."

He used words and phrases such as "fantastic pictorial document" and "masterpiece." Panini gave us, in one work, not only his own genius but the work of Titian, Raphael and so many others. This, McCaughey said, was an indispensable catalogue, "the first CD-Rom" of the history of European art. But even that didn't account for the appeal. Other artists had painted galleries before. This, McCaughey explained, is a painting that is full of life, a work with imminence. It shows classic architecture — a timelessness — juxtaposed with "modern times." The cardinal's architects (in the left foreground), for example, hurriedly examine the blueprints, trying to find a place for the Raphael copy being pitched to the cardinal. He no doubt wants to add it to his walls — but where?

Yes, it is the amusement of it, as well as the grand scale, that draws me back. It is the buried treasure of it that draws McCaughey back. He finds something new every time he looks. This time it was the book on a little table. He studied it and was struck by its detail. In a painting nine feet wide and more than six feet tall there are wonderful little discoveries everywhere.

Here is a painter's work ethic dating back to 1749 that is fit to treasure today. And so the world does. The Boston Globe included it in its selection of the finest paintings that can be viewed in New England. Recently, a Japanese company turned the Panini into a jigsaw puzzle. And how does the world value — in dollar figures — this painting? It was bought by the museum in 1948, long before McCaughey's tenure, for $16,000. He said he wouldn't put a number on its worth today, but, "If we had to buy it now, we couldn't come within a bull's roar."

Happily for all of us, the Panini, the Caravaggio ("Ecstacy of St. Francis"), the Dali ("Apparition of Face and Fruit Dish on a Beach") and so many other masterpieces were bought in a different, more affordable era, before such purchases required the equivalent of state lottery jackpots. They are kept lovingly at the Wadsworth Atheneum — protected, well-lit, accessible, permanently awaiting your visit.

"Picture Gallery of Cardinal Silvio Valenti Gonzaga"
is nine feet wide, six feet tall, and full of surprises.

7

Rich in So Many Ways

Steve Courtney

It is Mother's Day at Asylum Hill Congregational Church. The reddish-brown spire of Connecticut stone tapers heavenward to a sharp point; the clock keeps the time, 10 minutes to 10 in the morning. Pink flowering cherry, white dogwood and deep brown-red Japanese maple brighten the church's dark Gothic buttresses.

Asylum Hill Congregational stands in a city many have abandoned. Department stores, factories, hotels and skyscraper pipe dreams have shut down, moved South, imploded and dissipated. Civic leaders anguish over the lack of center to Hartford, over how hard it is to get people downtown on the weekends.

But here it is a Sunday, and there are so many people coming to church under the flowering trees that they require an attendant wearing a vest to semaphore them toward parking spots. There's a middle-class mix of Fords and Toyotas and Voyagers; Buick Regals and Lincolns for the older folks; and the occasional glint of a Jaguar.

I am glad I put on a jacket before I left Canton to drive to the church that Mark Twain called "The Church of the Holy Speculators." People dress here. Women and little girls wear discreet patterns of tiny flowers, and you even see that now-rare sight, small boys wearing ties. This is not a poor congregation, or even the kind of middle-class one for whom informal dress is now de rigueur, whether the wearers are jogging or worshiping. There are a few seersuckers and the like — it's spring — but most of the men's jackets mainly range from gray to as close as you can get to black without being at a funeral.

Inside, the place keeps filling up. The sanctuary is lined with Gothic arcades and painted in a calm cream color. A dark-wood, intricately carved canopy overhangs the altar. A handbell choir picks out the old Puritan hymn "How Firm a Foundation" as ushers direct people to seats.

Wealth has defined Hartford's history ever since the day the Puritans founded the city. The river brought trade from Europe and the West Indies; its tributaries brought power for factories; tobacco lands in the Connecticut Valley were so rich that farmers had a lot of disposable cash to invest. Civil war brought economic health to the city, world wars kept its factories smoking, and a Cold War brought more wealth, right up to the past few years. The dream of wealth inspired practical Yankees such as Samuel Colt, James G. Batterson and Maurice Jewell, the wealthy industrial, actuarial and political leaders of the era. It inspired John Pierpont Morgan, who built a world financial empire on the Puritan principles of his Hartford forebears.

The idea of wealth both attracted and tortured Mark Twain, who was fascinated by the city's industry and inventiveness during the 20 years he lived here. He tried to take part in it. He cultivated its wealthy citizens as his friends.

When he came to write "A Connecticut Yankee in King Arthur's Court," the story of a Hartford mechanic transported to the Middle Ages, he planned it as a fable poking fun at Yankee business sense. But he gave the novel a disturbingly violent ending, a machine age Armageddon. It is as though he could see the Hartford of today, the cataclysm of a city, the machines piled away in storage, the gutted brick factories.

The third pew from the front of the Asylum Hill church has a small brass plaque attached to its arm: "THIS PEW WAS RENTED BY SAMUEL L. CLEMENS (MARK TWAIN) 1872-1891." Twain, whose skepticism about God and religion is famous, enjoyed the church and its speculators. Like many of the comfortable, middle-class literati who lived in an enclave a block away called Nook Farm, he liked to spend time with the rich. Their wealth came from things like stitching machines, railroad shares and insurance.

But even more, he liked the minister. Stained-glass windows above the altar memorialize the Rev. Joseph Hooker Twichell, pastor from 1865 to 1913. Twain counted Twichell as "first after Livy" among his friends for more than 40 years. Twichell presided at Twain's wedding, at the funeral of his children and wife, and finally at Twain's own funeral.

The Rev. James Kidd is the sixth pastor since Twichell. He has a broad face pretty much defined by his smile and an instinct for getting to the point. He knows that his parishioners do not like to talk about their wealth, and he's not sure that they would like him talking about it, either. When I visited him at his office, he solved the problem by ducking into a nearby room and finding a membership directory. "You can find them for yourself. It lists most of their occupations, so just look for CEOs and vice presidents," he explained.

There are CEOs and vice presidents from Aetna Life & Casualty Co., Loctite Corp., The Hartford Group, Shawmut Bank, United Technologies Corp., Heublein Inc., ITT Hartford, CIGNA, Kaman Corp., Phoenix Home Life. There are Superior Court judges, investment bankers, hospital directors and more lawyers and doctors than could conceivably have their souls saved by one church.

Still, Kidd told the story of a comment someone relayed to him, from one golfer to another at the Hartford Golf Club: "Asylum Hill has suffered a severe decline in socioeconomic status." He thinks he knows what the patrician golfer meant. When Kidd arrived at Asylum Hill in 1979, "there were still some of the older gentry around. There were elderly ladies who would be dropped off by their chauffeurs before church. The ushers wore morning coats when I arrived, and the ladies wore white gloves."

Attendance at the church was low when he arrived, he said. And some parishioners felt guilty about being well-off. "The Bible isn't very easy on the rich," Kidd told me.

He disabused them of this guilt about their wealth by suggesting they separate themselves from some of it. "I said, 'Hey, that's who we are, God made us this way, we should thank God we have these resources. Let's make sure to share them to serve the city.' "

His share-the-wealth message seems to have been successful. The church has grown from 700 members (only 170 of them actual churchgoers) in 1979 to nearly 1,500, of whom about half regularly attend the church's three weekend services. At one point in the '80s, like others determined to help Hartford survive, Kidd and his wife, Joann, moved into the city. "It cost me $120,000," he said. "I paid $160,000 for a condominium. They're going for $40,000 in the complex now."

In 1865, when the church opened and Twichell was hired as its first pastor, the city's poor were far from Asylum Hill. Most lived in slums on the river flats; few would venture to Asylum Avenue in any role other than servants and tradesmen. "Where are the poor in Hartford?" Twain wrote on his first visit to the city in 1868. "I confess I do not know. They are 'corralled' doubtless — corralled in some unsanctified corner of this paradise whither my feet have not yet wandered, I suppose."

But they were there. Even Hartford's Third-World infant mortality rates of today had their parallel in those days. In 1861, there were 488 deaths in Hartford; 206 of the dead were under 5. Causes of death were consumption, lung fever, scarlet fever, stillborn birth, cholera infantus, convulsions, diphtheria, drowning, typhus fever and hydrocephalus.

Far from the river flats, Asylum Hill church reflected the neighborhood, and like the church of today it reflected wealth. Officers of the church included the president of the Hartford Steam Boiler Inspection and Insurance Co., a judge of the state Supreme Court, a stockbroker who advertised a "private wire to New York," and the secretary-treasurer of the Smyth Manufacturing Co., which made bookbinding machines.

Bookbinding was necessary to the city's great subscription book publishing industry, which first brought Twain to the city on business in 1868. Twain was publishing what was to be his first best-seller, "The Innocents Abroad," with the American Publishing Co., but took time to look around the city.

"This is the center of Connecticut wealth," Twain wrote for a California newspaper. "Hartford dollars have a place in half the great moneyed enterprises of the Union. All those Phoenix and Charter Oak insurance companies, whose gorgeous chromo-lithographic show-cards it has been my delight to study in faraway cities, are located here. The Sharps' rifle factory is here; the great silk factory of this section is here; and last, and greatest, Colt's revolver manufactory is a Hartford institution."

A few years earlier, when Harriet Beecher Stowe moved to Nook Farm, she described Hartford as "fat, rich, and cosy — stocks higher than ever, business plenty — everything as tranquil as possible." By 1876, Scribner's Magazine could report that Hartford was the richest city in the United States relative to the number of its inhabitants. The zeroes rolled off the writer's pen: "Its savings banks have deposits of about $12,000,000; its banks of discount have capital and surplus of nearly $12,000,000, and deposits of more than $9,000,000; the capital of its other joint-stock companies is $18,000,000; the assets of its insurance companies are more than $113,000,000." Five railroads converged on the city, and river commerce was heavy.

Today, with Hartford one of the 10 poorest cities in the country, the idea of "regionalism" can bring a shudder to the spine of the

Workers on the production line at Billings and Spencer Co., circa 1880. The factory, in Frog Hollow, is now an apartment building.

suburbanite who pictures having to pay for urban problems. But in 1876, Scribner's makes clear that regionalism is nothing new. Wealth moved from the rich city outward: "All about it are manufacturing communities, mainly created by Hartford capital." It mentions Collinsville's axes, New Britain's hardware, Thompsonville's carpets, Rockville's woolen cloth, Willimantic's cotton and South Manchester's silk.

Samuel Colt's revolvers, repeating rifles and percussion-cap system constituted the industrial pride of Hartford, symbolized by his factory's blue dome by the river, topped by a rearing horse. Scribner's in 1876 printed engravings of Armsmear, the mansion of Colt's widow, Elizabeth, on Wethersfield Avenue, and the Church of the Good Shepherd on Wyllys Street, which she built to his memory and decorated with carvings of crossed revolvers. His weapons and those of Sharps had helped the North win the Civil War, and the factory was on Twain's 1868 tourist route.

"Some friends went with me to see the revolver establishment," he wrote to his paper. "It comprises a great range of tall brick buildings, and on every floor is a dense wilderness of strange iron machines that stretches away into remote distances and confusing perspectives — a tangled forest of rods, bars, pulleys, wheels and all the imaginable and unimaginable forms of mechanism. There are machines to cut all the various parts of a pistol, roughly, from the original steel; machines to trim them down and polish them; machines to brand and number them; machines to bore the barrels out; machines to rifle them; machines that shave them down neatly to a proper size as deftly as one would shave a candle in a lathe; machines that do everything but shave the wooden stocks and trace the ornamental work upon the barrels."

If Mark Twain were looking for these machines today, he might have to look up Dean Nelson. Nelson is curator of the Connecticut State Museum in the State Library on Capitol Avenue. The museum displays Colt arms and more humble items of Connecticut manufacture such as lathes, augers and chucks. Old chromolithographs — mass-produced colored prints — of Hartford factories hang on the walls.

But Nelson moves aside a barrier and leads me into a back room that contains a dark jumble of iron and steel arches and rods and disassembled metal parts. There are piles of aluminum castings, wooden jigs and dies. These are the tools that made the products that made wealth for Hartford.

Nelson and his colleagues pick these things up at flea markets and auctions, through word of mouth, or with the help of tool hobbyists. As factory after factory closes down or moves South, Nelson and his staff have found themselves a few steps ahead of the scrap dealers. Once they attended a machinery auction at a business that closed down in the 150th year of its existence. Employees stood around morosely at the sale, wearing company T-shirts celebrating the anniversary.

Nelson pauses by a huge machine, and holds up a little T-shaped wire loop it makes. You would fit the loop around a button on a pair of overalls. "Recognize this? Oshkosh B'Gosh," he says. Nearby is something that looks like an 8-foot-tall robot spider. It was used to jam the gunpowder into rifle shells.

Until they find a permanent display home, they will sit jumbled in the back room in the dark, skeletons and fossils from Hartford's past. The important thing is to find what to replace them with, how to make this a city that produces wealth again, and then to get that wealth to all its citizens.

Stowe's cozy, fat Hartford can be lean and cruel today. After a boom in real estate and business in the 1980s, when state surpluses filled the governmental coffers, the city is on the skids. But it's not the first time a decade of great wealth has been followed by one of great poverty.

John Boyer, director of the Mark Twain House and a percolating pot of interesting ideas, noted that the 1890s saw an American recession as well. "It's always interested me: What made money 100 years ago as opposed to today? How was the economy established in the 1880s versus the 1980s?" He has his hunches. When the 1980s boom became a 1990s collapse, the visual picture was one of a mass of paper collapsing — junk bonds, Colonial Realty investments, Reagan-era fraud and windbaggery. "The difference may be that in the 1980s, there was no 'product' there," he says.

Susan Pennybacker, a Trinity College professor who teaches a course on Hartford history, blames the city's plight on the township system. "There was no regional tax base here," she says. "In other states, what we consider suburbs are part of the cities. It doesn't mean that they don't have problems, too. But this political fact has made it really easy for corporate employers to retreat from Hartford."

In the 1880s, the products were there: firearms, silk textiles, leather belting, machine tools, books. The legend of Sam Colt inventing the revolver and starting a small empire in the South Meadows was a continuation of the myth of the shrewd and inventive Yankee trader, the one who would sell you a wooden nutmeg.

But a new spirit was abroad in the land. There was the vast insurance industry, a business based on paper if there ever was one. The "product" was a sense of security. And there was what came to be known as the entrepreneurial spirit, which sometimes, as Mark Twain loved to point out, resembled the spirit of the highwayman and pickpocket.

Take Albert A. Pope, a Boston businessman who became interested in the newfangled bicycle when he saw one at the Philadelphia Centennial Exhibition in 1876. He started importing them, but quickly realized that he could do better by making them himself. He and his associates visited England to see the factories where bicycle parts were made. Refused admission to one, they disguised themselves as workmen and went in anyway.

Pope contracted with the Weed Sewing Machine Co. in the former Sharps Rifle Co. factory on Capitol Avenue in Hartford to make the Columbia bicycle. (Pope's great-grandson, also named Albert A. Pope, spoke at a Connecticut Historical Society gathering in March and described the Columbia as a "knockoff" of the Duplex Excelsior, an English bike.) Pope could price his Columbias at $90, $22.50 less than he charged for the imported English models.

But to get started, Pope needed a bicycle patent owned half by a Boston company and half by a Vermont company. The Vermont company would sell, but the Boston company would not. Pope managed to buy a quarter-interest in the patent from the Boston company — and, after a dash on the night train to Montpelier, managed to acquire the Vermonters' interest before the Boston company could. Pope went on to develop inventive marketing practices and even switched to building electric automobiles in the 1890s. Like Colt and other Hartford industrialists, he built housing for his employees and endowed the city with a park; many Hartford parks have names from the Hartford social register of the Gilded Age.

Mark Twain bought a Columbia Expert bicycle for $142.50 in 1886 and wrote a funny speech about learning to ride it that ends: "Get a bicycle. You will not regret it, if you live."

The interest in the bicycle was typical of Twain's fascination with inventions. His mind would work as it did in the summer of 1883, while he was writing "Huckleberry Finn." He devised a game for his three daughters, Susy, Clara and Jean, which involved pegs placed along a driveway to symbolize the years from 1066 to the present. The girls would have to run past the pegs, calling out the names of the kings and queens of England as they went. The one making it to 1883 with the fewest mistakes was the winner.

"The following night, however," writes his biographer, Justin Kaplan, "Twain's demon sprang on this innocent pastime." Unable to sleep, he thought up an intricate plan whereby the educational game could be played indoors on a cribbage board with pins and cards. The idea would be a commercial success and make his fortune. He wrote to Twichell of his plan, and Twichell told The Courant — a move that infuriated Twain, who quickly patented the idea before someone else could steal it.

The game had roughly the appeal of a modern income tax form, but it displayed what Kaplan calls Twain's talent for "drowning his important goals and also his judgment in some 180-proof, hypomanic tipple of speculation." He patented a self-sticking scrapbook and a fastener for undergarments that looks exactly like a present-day three-pronged brassiere clasp, and invested in numbers of get-rich-quick schemes.

Twain could laugh at this side of his personality, once describing how he invested in an "engine or furnace or something of the kind which would get out 99 percent of all the steam that was in a pound of coal."

"I hired an inventor to build the machine on a salary of thirty-five dollars a week, I to pay all expenses," he wrote in his autobiography. "It took him a good many weeks to build the thing. He visited me every few days to report progress and I early noticed by his breath and gait that he was spending thirty-six dollars a week on whiskey, and I couldn't ever find out where he got the other dollar. Finally, when I had spent five thousand on this enterprise, the machine was finished, but it wouldn't go."

He used his love of machinery when he described his technique on the platform circuit. One of his most important skills was knowing exactly how long to make the pause before the punch line of a story.

"For one audience the pause will be short, for another a shade longer still; the performer must vary the length of the pause to suit the shades of differences between audiences. These variations of measurement are so slight, so delicate, that they may almost be compared with the shadings achieved by Pratt and Whitney's ingenious machine which measures the five-millionth part of an inch."

You can trace this fascination with Hartford machinery and the wealth it produced to Twain's original tour of the Colt factory in 1868.

He was shown a Gatling gun. "It feeds itself with cartridges, and you work it with a crank like a hand organ; you can fire it faster than four men can count. When fired rapidly the reports blend together like the clattering of a watchman's rattle. It can be discharged 400 times a minute. I liked it very much and went on grinding it as long as I could afford cartridges for the amusement which was not very long."

By the 1880s, however, the fun was over and invention and wealth had become obsessions. He invested in the Paige typesetting machine, a mechanical device to set printing type, one of which now sits next to the Mark Twain House gift shop, its cool, precise lines of cold, gray-green metal exuding the malevolence of a gun. It was a colossal, decade-long failure and a drain on Twain's finances, damaging his fortune so extensively that he had to close up the Hartford house, sell his horses, find new positions for his servants and move his family to Europe.

Almost exactly at the same time that the typesetter was wreaking its damage he was writing "The Connecticut Yankee in King Arthur's Court." The idea of a brash Yankee from the Colt factory dropping back 12 centuries to Arthurian Britain was originally intended to be all joke.

The hero would take over Britain and run it "at a modest royalty of forty percent." He would defeat Arthur's enemies with modern weapons. Nineteenth-century improvement would end with the knights of the Round Table re-established as a stock board, with a seat at the table worth $30,000.

But as the typesetter collapsed, along with a publishing company that Twain had set up in the early '80s, the end of the story got grimmer. The Yankee destroys the chivalry of England by electrocuting tens of thousand of knights, and by shooting thousands more. The weapons he and his band of loyal followers use in this slaughter are 13 Gatling guns.

One Connecticut Yankee made it to a king's court — only he was the king. You can find his name on a block of polished brown granite as big as half a bus in Cedar Hill Cemetery. At one end, in Gothic script, is the name "Morgan." A motto works its way around the tomb: "For if we have been planted together in the likeness of His death we shall be also in the likeness of His resurrection."

Those planted together here include Joseph Morgan, who lived from 1780 to 1847; his son, Junius Spencer Morgan, who lived from 1813 to 1890; and his son, John Pierpont Morgan, who lived from 1837 to 1913. Where the Popes and Battersons and Jewells made mere fortunes with their bicycles and insurance polices and belting, the Morgans amassed power in the late 19th century that can only be called baronial.

Most of J. P. Morgan's life was spent on Wall Street in New York. He is buried in Hartford because he was born in Hartford, and because his grandfather and father started out in business here.

Joseph Morgan read the Bible every day, and when he was done he started reading it again. When he came to Hartford from Massachusetts in 1817 he bought the Exchange Coffee House, a gathering place for merchants and river boat captains, and helped found the Aetna Fire Insurance Co. in 1819. Junius followed his father's business pursuits, becoming partners with an American banker in London and eventually inheriting the firm — the beginning of the Morgan banking empire.

In a photograph taken in 1903 by Edward Steichen, John Pierpont Morgan stares angrily over his large and pitted nose, grips the arm of his chair, the double-U of his watch chain set against his dark coat and vest. The watch and the pupils of his eyes glint. He was dogged at gathering wealth and manipulating the economic world of the time to his advantage. Even at Hartford Public High School, at the age of 13, he would take no nonsense from a teacher:

Miss Stevens,

I should like to enquire of you the reasons why you as a teacher and of course over me only a scholar should treat me in such an inhumane manner as to send [me] out of the class for laughing a little too loud which I can assure you I am perfectly able to control and which no punishment will cure me of ... I do not say this hastily in anger but you cannot say but what I have stood it a great while and I think that upon reflection you cannot say but what I have been treated unjustly.

J. Pierpont Morgan

Janet Cummings Good

J.P. Morgan

As an adult, he had offices on Wall Street and a mansion on Murray Hill in Manhattan. Morgan worked for more than three decades in active partnership with his father, who was based in London and had connections to the great banking houses of the Barings and Rothschilds. Drexel, Morgan and Co. became the main source of U.S. government financing in the 1870s. In the 1880s, Morgan began reorganizing and consolidating railroads that, in those boom years, had been ruining each other by competition, overbuilding and inefficiency. He was one of the world's most powerful railroad leaders by 1900.

In the 1890s he formed a syndicate to resupply the government's depleted gold reserves. Later he pieced together huge corporations out of small ones: U.S. Steel, International Harvester, International Merchant Marine. He began what a biographer called a "15-year assault on the world of art." He built a $1.4 million wing onto the Wadsworth Atheneum in memory of his father ("A merchant of Hartford," the tablet at the base of the Grand Staircase reads), amassed illuminated manuscripts, paintings, ivory, silver and majolica at his New York mansion and helped endow the Metropolitan Museum of Art.

In October 1907 a cataclysmic financial panic struck Wall Street, and the only one who could do anything about it was J.P. Morgan. By then, his financial house was the only American equivalent of a central bank like the Bank of England. Like Pope in Hartford finagling with his bicycle designs and patents, Morgan knew how to use other people's ideas to make things happen.

"I don't know what to do myself, but ... someone will come in with a plan that I know will work," he told a friend; "and then I will tell them what to do."

They came in. Ashen-faced over the loss of millions, well-dressed men passed through a crowd of reporters and entered Morgan's library on East 36th Street to plead for him to tell them what to do. They included railroad magnates Henry Clay Frick and Edward H. Harriman, and James Stillman, John D. Rockefeller's banker. Morgan sat at his desk, under walls of crimson damask from the Chigi palace in Rome, and played solitaire.

Like a monarch, he put his knights into action. Over the next two weeks, he saved trust companies, banks and brokerage houses in the midst of Wall Street mob scenes, hairbreadth escapes from ruin and risky offers of credit. He bailed out New York City and rescued the stock exchange. He had taken the Hartford drive for wealth and was using it to save the country.

The apparent limitlessness of his power scared the real government, which within a decade established a central bank and started trying to break up Morgan's power. But not before Mark Twain had a word of praise for this robber baron in one of his platform speeches. Twain said the Panic of 1907 had been caused by the brief deletion of the phrase "In God We Trust" from coins. "Sure enough, the prosperities of the whole nation went down in a heap when we ceased to trust in God in that conspicuously advertised way. I knew there would be trouble. And if Pierpont Morgan hadn't stepped in . . . ."

Twain was long gone from Hartford by then. A Standard Oil vice president, Henry H. Rogers, became his friend and finally helped Twain exercise control over his finances, steering him away from wild, Paige-like investments. His last years in New York and Redding were comfortable. He repaid his debts, made money on the lecture circuit and wrote best-sellers that are not read today.

He spent the latter part of his life with a nearly schizophrenic attitude toward wealth and the wealthy. When he wasn't praising Morgan and other malefactors of great wealth, he attacked them. He supported the newly organized Knights of Labor, protested Belgium's massacres in the Congo and advocated Russian revolution. He saw the hand of wealthy banditry in the United States' empire-building war against a guerrilla army in the Philippines.

"We have invited our clean young men to shoulder a discredited musket and do bandits' work under a flag which bandits have been accustomed to fear, not follow," he wrote, and parodied the "Battle Hymn of the Republic":

In a sordid slime harmonious Greed was born in yonder ditch;
With a longing in his bosom — for other's goods an itch;
Christ died to make them holy, let men die to make us rich;
Our god is marching on.

"Money is the supreme idea," Twain wrote Twichell. "Money-lust has always existed, but not in the history of the world was it ever a craze, a madness until your time and mine."

I asked Kidd whether Twichell's congregation would like his church if they could come and visit. He doesn't think they would. "Some of the people who were here when I arrived I would call stiff Yankees … I'm glad I didn't get here any sooner than I did," he said. "I wouldn't have lasted long."

Kidd has lasted. He has invited the neighborhood in, and he has used a combination of charm and toughness to get his parishioners to part with some of their money to help the city that surrounds the church. The church has an outreach budget of $300,000 and has spent more than $500,000 since 1988 on its "I Have A Dream" project, which helps neighborhood students go to college. Every afternoon children come to the church for tutoring or to work on computers stored in a closet for the purpose. Some learn to cook.

People who turn up at the door needing food or shelter are directed to the Loaves and Fishes ministry, a cooperative venture of all the Hartford churches that provides meals, a food pantry and vouchers for the church thrift shop.

Asylum Hill, the Church of the Holy Speculators, is only one of the city churches that serve suburbanites but also reach out to their neighborhoods. But it is probably one of the most successful.

And I wondered, as I drove back to my own suburb, if there was some sort of key here to getting the wealth back, the wealth that has flowed out of Hartford for a couple of centuries and that still flows out, every working day. Asylum Hill church's success seems to be emblematic — not of some Gingrichian, fake-Victorian idea of leaving the welfare of the poor to churches and charities, but of the way imagination and drive can bring the city and the suburbs together, can bring wealth, people who create wealth and people in dire need of wealth together. Perhaps the particular jobs that the city and the suburbs have to do can be seen as complementary parts of the same whole. Perhaps each can give to the other. Perhaps both can think about Mark Twain, who, his friend Helen Keller remembered, "would work himself into a frenzy over dull acquiescence in any evil that could be remedied."

As I drove over Avon Mountain, I thought of what a nice neighborhood church that was, and then I realized it was in my neighborhood: I work in an office at the base of its hill. But when I got to Canton, it would still be in my neighborhood.

*"Of all the beautiful towns
it has been my fortune to see,
this is the chief."*

—Twain on Hartford

The Mark Twain House
Hartford, Connecticut

8

Searching for Wallace Stevens

Steve Kemper

I went looking for traces of Wallace Stevens. They're hard to find, even though he spent 39 years in Hartford, from 1916 to his death in 1955, and is considered by many to equal Mark Twain in literary stature. Stevens won a Pulitzer Prize and two National Book Awards. But while Twain was a popular writer and public personage who left tracks all over town, Stevens' name often draws a blank — partly because he wrote sensuous philosophical poetry in a city built on legal prose, and partly because he always kept the city at arm's length, not that it showed much interest in a closer relationship. He declined most social invitations, which soon dwindled anyway, and evaded most visitors. He rarely allowed anyone beyond his doorstep at 118 Westerly Terrace, where, after reading case files all day at the Hartford Accident and Indemnity Co., he could disappear into the radiant haze of his imagination.

He was a hard-nosed attorney and insurance vice-president who excelled in the complex area of surety claims, yet in his notebooks refers to himself as "hermit of poetry." He was a prosperous burgher in appearance but wrote revolutionary verse like no one else's. His suits were all the same cut and color — steel gray — and he wore one even on his weekend walks in Elizabeth Park, yet some critics of his first book assumed from the playful elegance of his poetry that he was a frivolous dandy. He refused to act out the public's image of a flamboyant poet and disdained the romantic notion of starving in a garret for the sake of art. No, he wanted a steady income because, as he wrote one of his many correspondents, "I like Rhine wine, blue grapes, good cheese, endive and lots of books, etc., etc., etc., as much as I like supreme fiction." He also believed that poets who wrote for pay or took jobs in universities were soon corrupted by the need to please, which he avoided by making a good living in business.

Though American artists flocked to Europe in the 1920s, and though Stevens was a devoted Francophile, he never visited the Continent. In fact, aside from business trips and an annual vacation to Key West, he pretty much stayed home. He carried on no love affairs, caused no scandals, and had no stirring adventures, except for one brief scuffle with Ernest Hemingway, in which Stevens got a black eye and broke his hand on Papa's jaw. Year in and year out, Stevens went to the office and came home. But there he wrote wonderful poetry. Poetry was his love affair, his adventure, his exotic travel.

Biographer Richard Ellman once wrote, "As a biographical subject, hardly anyone offers more difficulties than Wallace Stevens ... Instead of the urge to confess or at least to confide, which, happily for biographers, most of their subjects evince, Stevens displays a counterurge to conceal and fall silent." Stevens ultimately failed at this in the wider world, where poets, readers and scholars have lavished attention on him and placed him near the top in the pantheon of 20th-century poets. Hereabouts, however, aside from a theater named after him at ITT Hartford Insurance Group, the successor to his old company; an annual poetry reading named after him at the University of Connecticut; and a mention in a humorous song by local singer/songwriter Hugh Blumenfeld, he remains largely uncelebrated. Don't ask anyone to point out "the Wallace Stevens house." Don't look for plaques or memorials or statues. Cedar Hill Cemetery doesn't even include him in the brochure that lists the notable people buried there.

In fact, don't even look for his poetry in the city's bookstores. At B. Dalton in the Civic Center you can find Susan Polis Schultz in more than half a dozen titles in pastel bindings, but no Wallace Stevens. At the Reader's Feast you can find the latest gay, lesbian, and Third World poets, but no Wallace Stevens. Venture a bit farther out, to West Hartford Center, and seek Stevens at Bookworm or Encore Books — sorry, nothing. Supply usually reflects demand, and there's little of that for Stevens around Hartford, not even for free Stevens: In the past 22 years his Collected Poems has been checked out of the Hartford Public Library just a dozen times. Even while alive Stevens didn't have to work very hard to be ignored in Hartford, and his death evidently made the job easier. The city seems content to let its buried poet lie.

But a small group of people are now working to resurrect him, or at least remind Hartford of his existence. The effort began with Dan Schnaidt, an administrator at Wesleyan University. When Schnaidt moved to Glastonbury from New York two years ago, he knew two things about the area: the Wadsworth Atheneum and Wallace Stevens. He found the museum but almost no trace of the poet. Then, a year ago, he went to an exhibit called "Painting in Poetry, Poetry in Painting: Wallace Stevens and Modern Art." The show, which featured works by Duchamp, Picasso, Klee, Dali, Claes Oldenburg, Jasper Johns, Richard Diebenkorn, David Hockney and many others, had been conceived by a professor of English at UConn-Waterbury named Glen MacLeod, author of a convincing book on the ways that painting inspired Stevens, and that Stevens inspired painters.

MacLeod tried for five years to interest a Connecticut museum in this Connecticut subject. He got turned down by the Atheneum ("They didn't think it would bring people in"), the Yale Art Gallery, and UConn's William Benton Museum of Art. The show ended up at Baruch College in New York, got reviewed favorably in the New York Times, and drew capacity crowds to several events associated with it. Last May, after attending the exhibit, Schnaidt wrote an op-ed piece for The Courant wondering why the city was ignoring its most renowned 20th-century artist.

A few people, including MacLeod, answered Schnaidt's call to action and began the hard work of resuscitating Stevens. Their first success was to convince ITT Hartford to expand the Wallace Stevens Poetry Reading — by sponsoring a reading in Hartford as well as in Storrs. This annual event, now 32 years old, has featured many of the century's most accomplished poets.

The group also approached Hartford city Councilman Mike McGarry and the city's chief librarian, Louise Blaylock, about naming a room after Stevens in the proposed renovation of the library. "Why not?" says McGarry. "He's as famous in some circles as Mark Twain."

Schnaidt's group hopes to raise funds to build a statue of Stevens. "There seems to be a lot of enthusiasm for him in his business clothes, walking, because that's when he composed his poetry," says Schnaidt. Stevens habitually walked the two miles to and from work, devising lines to the rhythm of his stride. "That would catch him in his creative moment and also capture his link to the business community."

In his op-ed piece, Schnaidt suggested a Wallace Stevens page on the World Wide Web; The Courant responded by starting one as part of its home page. Schnaidt recently started another, which includes a few poems and essays. He hopes to add a cyber-tour of some of the places associated with Stevens: his house on Westerly Terrace, ITT Hartford on Asylum Hill where he worked for 39 years; Elizabeth Park, where he walked almost every day. Schnaidt would like to link this to the Wallace Stevens Journal, which, in keeping with Hartford's relationship with Stevens, is based elsewhere and is not available at the Hartford Public Library. Nor are his papers here. In 1975 his daughter, Holly, a longtime Connecticut resident, sold them to the Huntington Library in California for $250,000.

I made my own tour of Stevens' residences. He and his wife Elsie moved into their first Hartford apartment in 1916 at 594 Prospect Ave., at the corner of Farmington. I called Gardner Ruggles Jr., who has lived in the building since 1988. Ruggles remembered reading some Stevens in high school English, "but nothing that sticks." When I told him Stevens once lived in his building, he seemed pleased. "He did? Really?" Ruggles said the building has high ceilings, marble in the bathrooms, and cut glass in the foyer. "It must have been luxurious once." Most of the residents now are new Russian immigrants.

An attorney and insurance executive, Wallace Stevens nonetheless wrote sensuous philosophical verse.

Stevens and Elsie lived there only a year before moving to a new apartment closer into town, at 210 Farmington Ave. It's an imposing U-shaped building made of yellow brick, across from the Aetna Institute. The Stevenses lived there from 1917 to 1924. It's where Stevens wrote most of the poems in Harmonium, his first book and the one that made his reputation. It was published in 1924 when he was 45 years old. The building is now filled mostly with young working people and some Section 8 families. Neither of the building's two oldest residents — Marshall Dockham, who's been there 42 years, and Charles Clark, who's been there 45 years — have ever heard of Stevens.

In 1924, after the birth of their only child, Holly, the Stevenses moved to an upstairs apartment in a two-family home at 735 Farmington Ave., not far across the West Hartford line. There Stevens suffered what he called his "lapse from grace," writing nothing for five years. Today it's the office and home of a chiropractor, Dr. Stephen J. Balkun. Balkun, 40, grew up in Hartford but had never heard of Stevens. Two months after he moved into the house someone showed up at his door and said, "I don't want you to think I'm weird, but I just did my thesis on Wallace Stevens at the University of North Carolina and he used to live here." Balkun has since developed an interest in Stevens' poetry, especially since he writes poetry himself. He writes in the same room where Stevens didn't.

The residence most associated with Stevens is an 11-room house at 118 Westerly Terrace, just off Albany Avenue near Elizabeth Park. He lived there from 1932 until his death in 1955. Before Elsie died in 1963, she sold the place to the Episcopal Church, which has used it ever since to house the provost of Christ Church Cathedral in Hartford. The Very Reverend Richard Mansfield has lived there for five years and is familiar with the house's history. Tourists, usually English professors, occasionally knock on the door. Mansfield gives them a tour.

"I had a passing acquaintance with his poetry before, but I read a lot more of it now," he says. "It's an interesting feeling, reading his poetry in the place where he wrote it. You really do feel his presence."

Stevens and Elsie had a strained, strange marriage. He once said that he married her because she was the prettiest girl in their hometown of Reading, Pa., and she does look striking in old photographs. But she and Stevens were a bad match. He had gone to Harvard and was an intellectual; she had a grammar-school education and little interest in ideas. Nor did she care for her husband's poetry, preferring Longfellow.

She hadn't wanted to leave Reading, nor did she make friends easily, so it was hard on her when Stevens moved her first to New York, then to Hartford. His frequent long business trips during his early years here made things worse. By the time Harmonium appeared they were sleeping in separate rooms. Stevens' small study/bedroom on Westerly Terrace is now used as "a sort of dressing room," says Mansfield.

Stevens liked to buy unusual plants and flowers, and both he and Elsie were avid gardeners. There are photographs of them standing amidst profusions of blossoms on Westerly, particularly in the back yard, where Stevens liked to sit on summer evenings. I wondered if Stevens' gardens still bloomed, if anyone still tended them.

"No, they're gone," says Mansfield. "The story I have on that is that my first predecessor had bad allergies, so he did away with them. We recently had another problem. Stevens planted a holly bush right in front of the house in honor of his daughter, but of course over the years it grew into a mammoth tree. It was invading the house. We finally had to take the tree down, and we heard from a number of people, both neighbors and admirers of his poetry, who were not pleased about that. They felt it was a desecration." Mansfield chuckles. "So we are reminded from time to time of the heritage we have here. We've planted another holly bush."

I mention the irony of a priest living in the house of a famous man who didn't believe in God and who tried to console himself with faith in the "supreme fiction" of poetry and art. Mansfield chuckles again. "There's a story about that. When the church was negotiating for the house with Mrs. Stevens, her asking price was more than the church could afford. Then she came back with a much lower price. The theory was that she took delight in selling it to a church because Wallace was an atheist, and this was one last way to get back at him as part of their dysfunctional relationship."

ITT Hartford has commemorated Stevens for many years through the poetry reading, and readily agreed to fund a second one. Many people at the company know that Stevens was a famous poet who worked there, but little else. The vice president who now occupies the office where Stevens worked for 34 years — east wing, fourth down from the rotunda, facing Asylum Avenue — was surprised to learn from me that her office had been his.

Eric Rennie, director of public policy communications, was once in charge of the company's collections and searched for materials associated with Stevens. "All I could find were two autographed letters, which is remarkable considering that he was here for 40 years," he says. "I got interested about why there was so little on the most famous personage from our company, and I still don't know why. I think it's partly because he kept his business life so well segregated and also because he was not well-liked. I talked to people who worked with him. He was not a beloved figure, to put it mildly. Everyone has notions of what a poet's personality is, but whatever emerged in his poetry, that was not his personality here. Herb Schoen [a young lawyer at the company during Stevens' last decade; he later became company president] once told me, 'I was one of the few in the company who could stand him, and I wanted to knock his block off half the time.' "

Stevens was intimidating in demeanor and size (6-foot-3, 220 to 250 pounds), and was notoriously brusque, with little patience for small talk or interruptions. In Peter Brazeau's fine oral biography of the poet, Parts of a World: Wallace Stevens Remembered, Schoen recounts his first meeting with Stevens: "I'd only been with the company a few weeks, and this very impressive, large gentleman came in and said, 'I'm Wallace Stevens. I am told that I should meet you. Why?' "

More than once, Stevens answered long involved letters about surety cases with a simple, devastating "No." After he died, the brass wanted to name the company's theater after him, but then decided to hold off. "A discreet amount of time was allowed for the scar tissue to heal," says Kevin Marton, who works in the company's corporate relations department and handles the company's end of the poetry reading.

Stevens never learned to drive and often compelled company employees to chauffeur him on errands. "I'd come in to work from West Simsbury," remembers William Sanderson, 77, "and he got so he could recognize my car. He'd flag me down — he would put out one finger and stop me. This was maybe once every other week. I would then take him to Eagle Empire Laundry on Woodland Street to pick up his shirts, and then I'd drive him to work. I think he got so he knew my name. He was very taciturn. There was never any of this 'It's a nice morning' sort of thing. This was in the early 1950s and he was well-known by then, so I was flattered to death to pick him up. I then had an old station wagon, and it was something to see this elegant man getting into it."

Stevens generally preferred to walk to work alone because he wanted the solitude to compose poetry. But Olcott Smith, 88, former chairman of Aetna, says Stevens sometimes made an exception. "My father, Harry Tyler Smith, lived on Belknap Road and sometimes walked to work with Stevens. Father would pick him up halfway down Asylum Hill. Stevens liked it because my father could whistle. He would whistle Wagner, and he and Stevens would walk, Stevens to the Hartford and my father to the Aetna. But at times — and this is a little embarrassing — a small company bus would come up there and in it would be Morgan and Newton Brainard, and Albert Putnam, and they would say 'Get in' to my dad but not to Stevens. I guess they didn't want him in the bus. Father never went to his house for a drink or dinner and I never saw him have Stevens into the house either. So it was a strange friendship.

"Once when I was in school I was going skiing in Switzerland and father told Stevens. Stevens asked if I would look around for an Aeolian harp, named after the god of winds. So father asked me to do it and I looked around, but not too carefully, and I kind of forgot about it. When I got home, father said, 'Did you have a good trip? And, by the way, where is Mr. Stevens' Aeolian harp?' Well, I'm my father's only son, his only child, and he was very very disappointed in me that I didn't realize Mr. Stevens deserved a closer look than I apparently gave him. Father had two or three of his poetry books but I don't know how much he read, and I don't remember him talking about the poetry. I once tried to read a little of him but I confess I found it difficult to understand. My wife knew a man from Baltimore who knew a lot about Stevens, but he was about the only man I ever ran into who did."

Stevens was asocial in Hartford, but not completely so. On Wednesdays it was his habit to collar a car-owning co-worker and take a long lunch at the Canoe Club, a businessmen's lodge on the river in East Hartford. Stevens liked the club's cold roast beef, large martinis and gruff bonhomie. But even there his aloof disposition made people uncomfortable — he applied for membership for years before finally being admitted in 1948. There's no brass marker or remembrance of any kind about Stevens at the club, says Lincoln Young, its house chairman, nor does his name come up among the men who continue the tradition of business lunches there.

Most days Stevens skipped lunch, preferring to take a walk alone. He often ended up at the Atheneum, where he was a generous annual contributor. He loved art, kept up with the newest movements and theories and was himself a modest collector. As MacLeod has written, Stevens' poetry was deeply influenced by Surrealism, Cubism and Abstractionism. Stevens was surely pleased when A. Everett "Chick"

Austin turned the Atheneum into the most exciting museum in the country during the 1930s, hosting America's first exhibition of Surrealism, the first Picasso retrospective, the world premiere of an opera by Gertrude Stein and Virgil Thomson, and visits by many important modern artists. Yet Stevens always declined Austin's invitations to parties with the guest artists, where he could have exercised his interest in modern art. For such things he always went to New York, where he spent many weekends and where he had several friends in the arts.

Nor did he ever mingle with the sociable Poetry Club of Hartford, which met regularly at a bookstore on Lewis Street and included such regional eminences as Odell Shepard, Wilbert Snow, and Robert Hillyer. One of the bookstore's employees told Peter Brazeau that though the store tried to push Stevens' poetry, it sold only three copies of the 1931 reissue of Harmonium: "You wouldn't find one in a thousand [among Hartfordites interested in the arts] who knew him by name, who he was."

Though Stevens refused to play the poet in Hartford and usually brushed off questions about his poetry, he didn't hide the fact that he wrote it. His secretary typed whatever lines he had scribbled down on his walk to work that day. He sometimes sent subordinates to the State Library to look up words in its dictionaries. Yet he was adamant about maintaining his business identity and his privacy in Hartford, even when his reputation as a poet had reached the general culture. In 1954, when the Atheneum asked him to repeat a lecture he had just given at the Museum of Modern Art, he refused. He turned down requests from Life and The New Yorker to profile him. In 1952, when Trinity College honored his fellow poet William Carlos Williams, whom Stevens knew and corresponded with, Stevens declined to attend and instead suggested that Williams stop by Westerly Terrace on his way out of town. "I want to keep Trinity at arm's length (to be plain about it)," he wrote to another correspondent, "because I want to keep everybody at arm's length in Hartford where I want nothing but the office and home as home."

In 1944, against Stevens' wishes, Holly married John Hanchak, a repairman of business machines. They had a son, Peter, in 1947, and were divorced in 1951. After her father's death from stomach cancer in 1955, Holly devoted much of her life to Stevens' legacy, editing a fine selection of his poems (The Palm at the End of the Mind) and a fascinating volume of his letters. She died in Guilford in 1992.

I found Peter Hanchak in Charlottesville, Va. Hanchak is a friendly man, but the conversation didn't go as I expected, though by this point in my search for Stevens I probably shouldn't have been surprised. "I remember completely inconsequential information," he says. "I was only 8 when he died and he wasn't the kind of grandfather you played ball with or anything. It was Sunday visits, mostly. I can't recall having any real interaction with him. The few times I was plunked in his lap, I remember playing with the fat little place between his thumb and fingers." He laughs.

I ask if he reads his grandfather's poetry. "The simple answer is no. I don't lean much toward poetry." When I bring up how Stevens turned his back on Hartford and received the same treatment in kind, Hanchak says with some force, "It's a perfect case of 'You reap what you sow.' He was very private. He was so up in his head all the time that a lot of stuff that I would consider normal, like getting to know people, wasn't a big feature of his life. He wasn't a worldly guy, he was an otherworldly guy. Look at the words he uses. My son just memorized 'The Emperor of Ice Cream' for school, and I mean, 'concupiscent'? Give me a break. How many guys use words like that?"

Hanchak is referring to the Stevens' poem that begins,

Call the roller of big cigars,
The muscular one, and bid him whip
In kitchen cups concupiscent curds.

I like the word very much just where it is. I remember the first time I read it, in high school, and how much I enjoyed the definition when I looked it up, and how pleasing the word was to pronounce. I want to quote Hanchak more of his grandfather's lines:

Words add to the senses. The words for the dazzle
Of mica, the dithering of grass,
The Arachne integument of dead trees,
Are the eye grown larger, more intense.

Instead I tell Hanchak that I've been reading his grandfather's poetry for 25 years and that it constantly moves and surprises me, though I don't always understand it. I would like to tell him how much I've learned from it about ways of seeing, how often it gives me sheer pleasure and solemn pause. But this doesn't seem like the right moment, and besides, my response is, to quote Stevens again, "Just one more truth, one more /Element in the immense disorder of truths." So I just say that I wish Hartford showed more interest in his grandfather.

"It's not like I don't appreciate the guy," says Hanchak. "He was sensitive on a scale that goes beyond. And sometimes I have thoughts about regaining the house on Westerly Terrace and turning it into a museum. So many people would just like to take the walk he took and feel a little of what he felt." That's why I read the poetry.

Stevens' final Hartford residence is Cedar Hill Cemetery. I visited on a drizzly morning dense with fog. Though I knew his address — Section 14, Lot 64 — I couldn't find him, and drove around and around, shadowed by raucous crows that swooped in and out of the fog. It seemed like a metaphor, as well as another of Stevens' evasions. I finally found the right section, off by itself, out of order, in the opposite direction that logic would suggest. It figured. Even then I couldn't find him. After tramping through the slush and drizzle for 20 minutes I finally conceded victory to Stevens and turned back toward the car. That's when I saw his marker, obliquely, out of the corner of my eye. I had passed it half a dozen times. Nothing on the modest brown-granite stone hinted that the man buried there was an acclaimed poet. As taciturn in death as in life. The drizzle suddenly turned into rain, making my notes run and sopping the paper so that finally my pen wouldn't write at all. I chuckled and ascribed it to Stevens, still carrying privacy to absurd lengths. He would hate this article.

9

The Life and Death
of Joseph Watson

Susan D. Pennybacker

D
eep summer blanketed Hartford, absorbing her sunshine in a
muggy mist and sending the rich folks to pack steam trains
headed to the shore. Slow, sluggish days on Main Street
welcomed fast nights in the pool halls, theater stalls, bars and
brothels. The frenetic evening motion left some dozing well past dawn,
so when shouts of "Murder!" and "My God, I'm murdered!" woke the
dreamers and the idle revelers from their light August sleep, the words
felt especially mad, brittle, brutal. It took many precious minutes of
disbelief to reckon where it was that the cries had come from. Trees and
brick got in the way. Besides, the Osborn brownstone at 23 Capitol Ave.
was an unlikely guess.

Henry Osborn, company secretary of a textile firm, Democratic
Party ward councilor and the city's former three-term police
commissioner, had returned home as usual the evening before, Aug. 4,
1904, to his customary if lonely bed — his wife and daughter had already
joined the seasonal exodus and left for Crescent Beach near Niantic a
week before. He penned Mrs. Osborn a letter and dozed off. A late riser,
Osborn had not even bid his more punctual son, William, the good
morning that would have been a last farewell.

Still, when his loyal troops — the Hartford Police Department's
finest — finally did choose No. 23 and rushed up the two flights to
Osborn's bedchamber and bath, the upstanding citizen and tipped-to-be
next mayor of this, one of America's richest cities, was lying in a pool of
blood, in his undervest and nightshirt, only a few feet from the unmade
bed. Dark liquid poured plentifully from four pistol wounds. The towel
basket and hamper in the nearby bathroom were "entangled."

Dumfounded and flushed with the remorse that comes with the realization that another's untimely death will endanger one's own position (and unable to hide that fear even in the face of the victim's greater agony), the cops inquired with frantic urgency as to who the perpetrator had been. In response, Osborn replied with unmistakable and chilling clarity: "Nigger Joe."

Of Hartford's almost 80,000 residents at the turn of the century, slightly more than 1,500 were African American. When the pioneering black sociologist Charles Johnson surveyed this population in 1921 for the National Urban League, he found that "many of the older Negro residents were connected in a more or less personal relationship with the older white families, either as servants in their homes or porters and attendants in their business establishments. Although at one time there were a few skilled artisans, these were gradually pushed out by the increasing competition of whites, most of whom, in these areas of economic conflict, were foreigners."

At the time of the events of this story, nearly two-thirds of employed black males in Hartford were personal domestic servants. Fully 86 percent of employed black women were in service. Johnson talked to men who had been house servants, day workers, cooks, waiters, chauffeurs, porters and janitors; and women who had been laundresses, day workers, cooks, nursemaids and housekeepers. Even after World War I, most black residents had no modern conveniences in their lodgings; no bathtubs, no gas, no electricity. Many had no indoor toilets. Most houses were in ill repair and unsanitary. Near the railroad station ran a tiny street named Huntley Place, a fragment of which remains today; it was a block from Chestnut, one of the streets most heavily populated by African Americans.

There was prejudice against hiring blacks in many white households. Johnson interviewed a "prominent club woman" who stated: "I have had no experience with Negro help in my own household… because I have four young children and did not wish to give over the care of them to any one but a high-grade, intelligent person with a knowledge of the care of children. As most white girls object to working with colored girls, my kitchen help has also been white." This kind of labor market greeted southern migrants.

Henry Osborn died on the way to Hartford Hospital, where he was pronounced dead by the house surgeon. The police rampaged through his brownstone, through the streets nearby, through the adjoining neighborhoods, through Union Station, finally blocking the possible getaway streets looking for the assailant, the accused — a young African-American black manservant recently in Osborn's employ, called, as servants were, by the derisive nickname that Osborn uttered with his last breath. But the young perpetrator, now confoundingly nowhere in sight, also had a given name, a proper name, a family name: Joseph Watson, a name not soon forgotten by anyone living in Hartford or the state. He was born in Hardville, S.C., near the Georgia line, the son of freed slaves. Both his parents were dead and he had left home at 10, occasionally living in Savannah with Louis Webber, his stepfather. Later on the newspapers would say that he was as young as 16 and as old as 26, but in the summer of 1904, he was an insouciant 17. He had come to Hartford two years before as a participant in the early migration, before the war and the crooked labor recruiters beckoned great numbers of black workers to Hartford. Watson would have claimed a certain settled status 10 years later, when so many other greener folks came up from the South. But in his own day he was still a Southerner with Northern pretensions. He was known as a fast cyclist around town and sported pedal pushers. He had come here from Georgia in order to join his aunt and uncle, a cousin, and his brother James, most recently of Huntley Place. His uncle, Henry Biggs, a 41-year-old day laborer and father of three daughters, said that Watson had come up North because he was out of work. His brother kept the lawns of manufacturer Lucius Barbour at 132 Washington St, where Barbour employed three Irish women servants and George Belden, a 56-year-old black coachman from Pennsylvania.

When Joseph Watson left Savannah in 1902, he bought a 10-year-old, .38-caliber, self-cocking Smith & Wesson pistol with five chambers in a pawnshop and carried it with him across the Mason-Dixon Line. His Southern relatives were happy to see him go, or so Savannah Police Superintendent Charles Garfinkel told the Hartford police inspectors two years later. He was no good, a hell-raiser, an orphan, someone who had already been in trouble. A youngster who had already worked on a chain gang and had threatened to kill his stepfather on two occasions, though he had no Savannah arrest record. The authorities here would later record no previous arrests or convictions in Connecticut, his new home, the place where his brother had come before him, the place where every black male unlucky enough to be on Aug. 5, 1904, was now quarantined in the summer heat, until Joe Watson could be captured.

This blockade inspired two well-dressed citizens "of the colored persuasion" to approach the downtown police headquarters and demand passes with which to leave town. They were not going to have to wait too much longer.

William Osborn, age 21, was notified of his father's death at his office in The Hartford Courant building where he worked as a bookkeeper for Dunham Hosiery, his father's firm. He left immediately for the shore, faced with the task of informing his mother, sister and paternal grandmother, Mazie Osborn, of the tragedy. A telegram would not do and he would need to escort them back to Hartford. When he lay dying, Osborn had asked that his family in Crescent Beach not be notified of the shooting, fearing the devastation that the news would cause, hoping, in the same breath, that he could be saved. But instead, the shoreline train was held back in order to allow William Osborn quick passage to his mother's station in order to break the awful news. Before he departed, William said that he did not know the last name of the former servant in question, that they had always called him Joe. But the cops resurrected one Albert Jones, 40, a former employee of the Osborns from South Carolina, now employed at Muzzy's Restaurant in Church Street, who had played pool with Watson on the preceding evening and knew his given name. Those on the force who recognized the name, who knew Watson by sight, were sent to the nearby towns to hunt him down. Police vehicles combed Zion Street, Ford and Pearl and Goodwin Park. They searched Bloomfield, New Britain, the "negro quarters" of Wethersfield, Berlin and Middletown. They staked out the young man's haunts on Barbour and Martin streets, as well as his aunt's on Huntley Place. And the police set about interviewing those who had lingered around the O'Laughlin Livery Stables in Whitman Court, near the Osborn house, and those who heard the shots from their rooms in the Hotel Capitol nearby, at the corner of Main Street. Several said that Watson had tackled a fence and set off on foot. This story persisted and grew when it was made known that a reward of $3,000 was to be offered for information leading to his arrest. When an afternoon special bulletin of the evening newspapers unleashed the news of Osborn's violent death, complete with the "Nigger Joe" statement, crowds began to form in the street downtown in front of the Hartford Times building. Like quicksilver, the cry "Lynch him" could be heard in the capital. The state's most recent lynching had occurred less than 20 years before when a white man accused of murder was hanged by his neighbors in Litchfield

County without benefit of trial or jury. The lynching of blacks in the South was an almost daily occurrence and the Hartford newspapers routinely reported the episodes throughout 1904. But without the accused being found, neither mob rule nor police rule could prevail. Angry, hot and frustrated, and just let off work for the day, the women from the nearby dry-goods stores, the clerks, factory workers and curiosity seekers milled around waiting for more news. Henry Osborn had been known to many of them and his prominence added to the plea for immediate retribution.

Osborn had not been born into wealth in Willimantic in 1847. Nor did he die one of the wealthiest men in Hartford. He left an estate valued at almost $11,000 (about $440,000 today) with shares in textile, banking, real estate and the Hudson River Power Co. Like Samuel Clemens and J.P. Morgan, his name (and clippings about his murder) graces the members' scrapbook of the Hartford Club, the elegant center of Hartford elite culture at the start of the new century. Osborn was one of them. But he had a provincial past, and like many of the newly monied was in his own way a servant of the rich. He was the secretary of the Dunham Hosiery Co. where he had worked since 1879, and served as paymaster of the Dunham mill in Naugatuck and of the Health Underwear mill in Poquonock. Osborn was not quite a captain of industry but a next-in-command to the captains of industry, whose position allowed him to run successfully for the Court of Common Council from the Third Ward in 1890, to join the establishment, to make up for the absence of personal millions by providing business acumen and civic leadership. He was comfortable and successful. He was a Democrat in a city where his party was making great headway with immigrant voters, the party that 40 years earlier had won votes by calling its Republican opponents "nigger-lovers."

He could afford the summer place at Crescent Beach, he was soon to marry off his daughter to the son of a respectable family and his three terms of service as police commissioner from 1891 had fed the growing rumors that he might be the city's next mayor. No doubt he slept soundly. His expanding income allowed him to rent a wonderful house in town in which to do so, complete with servants.

Henry Osborn's sister's husband, William Grant, had a farm outside of Hartford. Once upon a time the Connecticut farms had been worked by slaves and indentured servants. Now Italian immigrants and freed blacks and their descendants hired themselves out as agricultural workers; many had spent their lives in such labor across the rivers and across the ocean before moving to the state. Joe Watson had worked on farms in Derby and East Windsor, cleaned rooms at the Republican Club and done a stint of building work on the new Connecticut River bridge. He had also worked on Grant's farm in Bolton and when Watson had proved himself, Grant's wife, Mary, recommended him to her brother Henry Osborn for a position in town.

Albert Jones would later state that work at the Osborn house had been rough and demanding; Jones left and Watson replaced him, caring for the horses, cleaning and sometimes cooking. The Osborns hired Watson on May 1, and gave him a bed to sleep in off the basement kitchen, in a room facing Capitol Avenue. But Watson soon quarreled with the upstairs maid Nellie Bradley, 24, the daughter of Irish immigrants. He dropped a half-lit cigar on an umbrella in the upstairs parlor. Bradley complained, and Osborn took umbrage and spoke with him.

In early summer, Osborn's wife, Martha, and her daughter readied themselves for the pilgrimage to Crescent Beach. They informed Watson that he was to accompany them but he refused; he had been warned against the water as a child and feared that he would drown. He would not make the journey and wanted to stay in town. So they sent him to buy provisions for the trip and gave him pocket money with which to do so. Watson disappeared for a day or so and when he came back to 23 Capitol Ave. the shopping money was gone. Henry Osborn took immediate action and summarily "discharged him for disobedience" on July 16. He ordered Watson out and did not pay him what was owed in arrears.

The scene left unfinished business. By the etiquette of black and white, servant and master, what was owed was a bona fide debt yet to be repaid.

Watson managed. He returned to a Church Street rooming house from time to time, owned by another former white employer, Henrietta Smith, who also had a farm in East Windsor. Here Watson kept clothes, neckties and shoes, some of which had belonged to Henry Osborn, castoffs given to his manservant, as was the custom. He roamed the streets, played pool and dreamed of becoming a professional boxer. In his short-lived fighting career around town he had been known both as "The Hound" and as "Nigger Joe." He read crime stories, including Frank Merriwell's "Great Ride, or the Mystery of the Mazatzales"; "Diamond Dick Jr. at Rockwet City or Handsome Harry's Fireworks"; and "Frank

Reade Jr., and his Electric Car, or Outwitting a Desperate Gang." He cut out newspaper articles on the March 1903 pursuit and capture in Hartford of the Missouri gunfighters and murderers, Rudolph and Collins. The police had seized them and taken them to the train at Union Station. The wanted men were followed by an "adoring crowd." He also kept a photograph of a young white woman among his things, and a book entitled "The Secrets of Love." Perhaps he passed some time with his brother or his aunt in these idle days. But he did not forget the Osborns. He drew a floor plan of the Osborn brownstone. Maybe he reflected on his situation and the ways in which he might seek restitution. On the night of Aug. 4, he stopped in at the Baltimore Lunch, boxed with his second cousin, William Hescoe, and then, like so many others in Hartford, he attended the very popular Poli's Theater production of "Wife for Wife." This was a melodrama set in the old South in which a slave kills his master and his master's wife seeking revenge for the sale and death of the slave's wife. Watson sat in the balcony; blacks were not allowed to sit in the lower galleries. The police later recalled that Watson had recently been reprimanded at Poli's by an officer who caught him resting his feet on the seats; Watson had vowed revenge under his breath. That night he strolled from the theater to the Elm Saloon nearby and had some drinks, played some pool (he kept the pool checks in his pocket) and wandered down to the stone bridge at Main and Elm with a white fellow whose name he did not know, engaging in casual conversation. At 12:30 a.m. he walked to the Osborn brownstone and let himself in through the open kitchen side door. (It would emerge that he had done this before and had stolen some clothes and valuables. Watson kept an old coin collection and had used some of Osborn's missing coins to pay for drinks in town.) He was tired from the evening's activities and fell soundly to sleep in what had been his bed. Father and son were already upstairs. William recalled hearing his father come in after 10 p.m. No one stirred, and Watson made no extraordinary noise either. It was late.

The crowds downtown grew. Dozens of sightings of Watson were reported and he was said to be cycling about the open-air markets in a straw hat. The Courant issued an editorial bemoaning the fact that one could not walk in the streets without hearing the inflammatory term "nigger." The actions of one man should not be "visited on the race as a whole." The police were hysterical, each officer fearing the passage of each hour as Watson remained at large. A futile second and third search of the house was conducted, simply because each of those being stopped

turned out to be the wrong black man. Finally, in desperation, the cops
visited the basement kitchen area one more time and Sergeant Theodore
Dietrich noticed a sagging mattress. Lo and behold, when he pulled it up,
Watson's face was visible. Dietrich would later unabashedly tell the court
that he shouted to his partner, "Here's the nigger!" Watson lay in the
space between mattress and springs, in his former bed, wearing an
overcoat that had belonged to Osborn, his patent leather shoes resting on
the bed's slats. He wore a gray bicycle suit, gray hat, and a white collar.
Watson stared at the dumfounded officers as they searched him. Their
pleasure was tempered by the fact that it was now immediately apparent
that they had failed utterly to comb the house properly from the outset.
Heads would surely fall... but here was the pistol, at least, and here was
an unrepentant Negro assailant, ready and willing to be taken into the
station. Watson may then have said words that he would often repeat in
one form or another: "I had it in for him and went to his house to do him.
I don't care if I have to die for it." But the officers' muted triumph was
further compromised as the news of Watson's capture spread through
Hartford's streets. Hundreds gathered as they would continue to do for
every day of Watson's trial — the most sensational murder trial of that
era in the city — and these crowds were screaming for blood: "Lynch
him! Burn him! Kill him!"

As Watson was hauled through the streets in an open, horse-drawn
paddy wagon, they streamed around him; his face, as it would appear in
the first newspaper shots, greeted the crowds with pride and arrogance.
The papers would always differ on his physical appearance, some calling
him handsome and others ugly, or "an Ethiopian pure and simple." He
would attribute the copper color of his own skin to the Indian blood in
his family. Watson was shackled to a chair in Police Captain William F.
Gunn's office, where he confessed repeatedly without a lawyer present,
and then demanded that he be given a comb to fix his hair in order to be
photographed with his bicycle cap on. He asked that the photographs be
sent to friends of his in the South. He shook the hand of a white man
nearby, asking, "You're a reporter, ain't you?" and smiled when his hunch
proved right. In black Hartford the news traveled quickly. William B.
Edwards, acting as a spokesman for his community, issued a statement
praising Henry Osborn as a "generous friend of the race" and "whole-
souled." The Rev. Walter Gay of Union Baptist Church said: "No person
of the race can condone the awful act on the ground that crimes are
committed by other races. Now this crime is attributable directly to the

liquor saloons and the gambling houses of our city where the youth of both races can congregate and gamble and read low publications." He called Watson a "poor, deluded young man." Rev. Watkins of the Home Missionary Society of the African Methodist Episcopal Church denounced the act at a camp meeting in Curtis Grove in north Hartford. But James Watson simply said of his brother: "He always liked to say he was a fighting man and he has been in lots of trouble. We ain't got any relatives except for some aunts down in Virginia. My mother and father are dead." The Courant tittered: "In walking from the hips up he sways his body in a tough style and has a habit of clutching at his trousers and pushing them up."

But by now, Watson was asleep in the jail, having downed a chopped beefsteak and french fries, and neither the press nor the jailers had seemed to daunt his spirits. One reporter noted: "It is no stretch of the truth to say that Watson appeared to be the coolest man in the station." He slept straight through from 11:30 that night until 7 the next morning. The hundreds stewing outside on Kinsley Street would have to wait for his arraignment and his trial, though they would follow the wagon wherever it went in town during the ensuing days.

If the press tried and convicted Watson on the first day of his capture, based on his own statements, Henry Osborn's funeral tried and convicted him again. All the Connecticut establishment was there at South Congregational Church on Main Street, a few steps from the brownstone: The distraught family, former governor Morgan Bulkeley, the mill owners Samuel J. Dunham and A.H. Brokus, the city's political leaders, Professor and Mrs. John J. McCook of Trinity College, and finally, the mill workers, given a day's respite and brought down from the valley to occupy reserved pews in a church that they attended for this single afternoon of their lives. Police Chief Cornelius Ryan marched ahead of the coffin, which was borne by former mayor William Waldo Hyde, Gen. Henry C. Dwight, Mayor J. W. Cheney, Dunham and Brokus. All the power and sympathy befitting Osborn's standing and his contributions, and indeed all those who had stood with him, or stood to succeed him, were there. In the effervescent floral arrangements near the communion table given by the family, the police and the Lyceum; in the liturgy and the hymns, in the Mendelssohn quartet and in I Corinthians 15 were the inherited emblems of a sweeping Protestantism that had subdued this land in the 17th century and beyond. In this fourth year of the 20th century, Congregationalist and Episcopalian sat side by side.

The church's minister was overseas and the rector of St. John's Episcopal Church presided.

Osborn's grave in Cedar Hill Cemetery was a safe resting place. It is there now, bearing a lovely, carved floral facade. It bears witness to the changing city nearby only faintly, its dignity and propriety undisturbed. Look at the columns of the South Church and imagine the coffin being carried through, the procession travelling up Main Street. Whosoever had committed this crime would be punished, and the life that hundreds honored on that day would not be diminished, but would be further honored by a just and swift proceeding.

The funeral crowds were only exceeded by the crowds that surged to Watson's trial in the very late summer days that darkened into early autumn evenings. Never had so many attended a trial in Hartford. "A number of colored girls" were in evidence and the court officials asked that blacks be treated with "courtesy" and that special seating be reserved for them by the dock. "Stylishly" and "fashionably dressed" white women also jammed the limited public seating while hundreds kept vigil outside. Judge Alberto Roraback insisted on order in the court. At the arraignment, Watson was sullen, quiet and disinterested. His harried lawyers, Hugh O'Flaherty and Francis P. Rohrmayer, uncle and nephew, were court-appointed and no doubt dismayed by their unlucky assignment. A promising legal career could be jeopardized by having to defend such a remorseless and wicked prisoner, and Rohrmayer was only one year into practice. But at least this seemed to be an open-and-shut case. The jury selection went swimmingly and anyone with "conscientious scruples against capital punishment" was released from duty. To the question of whether they bore any "prejudice against the colored race," those selected had replied in the negative. Twelve were chosen from 100 white male citizens. The only Hartford resident to be interviewed was a broker, quickly discharged because he lived on Capitol Avenue, the crime scene. All those finally selected lived in the suburbs or nearby towns and included farmers, mechanics and engineers. They were dutifully instructed not to read the papers and to allow no one else to discuss the proceedings with them. There seemed little question of the plea, the verdict or the outcome. For a capital offense, a not guilty plea was customary; even a burglary in which a murder occurred still met the criteria for the prosecution of a capital offense. Watson had boasted to the press and his captors early on; the details of the murder itself would surely be quickly revealed. Just a lingering doubt may have festered in the defense team's minds, and that concerned the question of motive.

In truth we cannot know what happened, nor shall we ever know what happened between the boy and the man on the steamy August morning in 1904. No one then could know, either. Osborn had talked a little before dying. He had denied that Watson had reason to murder him. But Watson talked too, and as the trial progressed he talked more and more. The lawyers brought in William Osborn, who talked about his father. And the lawyers brought in witnesses who talked about Watson. And Watson began to shift in his demeanor. He asked for a Bible for the long days and nights in the Seyms Street jail. He read a love novel. He struck up a friendship with his jailers and began to debate fine points of Scripture with them. They would later refer to him as a "model prisoner," anticipating the jargon of the century that lay ahead of them. Watson sought solace from Rev. Atius A. Crooke of the AME Zion Church on Pearl Street (Samuel Colt had been one of the three original grantors of the congregation's land). Watson saw his relatives. Suddenly, he seemed to mature, to lose his sense of caprice, to take the proceedings seriously, to cry in his cell at night and finally to seek redemption. He was 17 and he was growing up. Later they would say that he had been transformed in his incarceration, that he had even exuded bravery. He "winced and bowed his head" when they spoke in the courtroom of Mr. Osborn's cries. He would say under oath, that he "liked him well enough. Yes, I am sorry. I ain't glad." And the lawyers saw that things had suddenly become more complicated. They searched for truth and they weighed the ethics of the law and the tenor of the times. They must have taken more and more long looks in the mirror. They may have thought: "But we cannot know why he did what he did what with the country, after all, hardly ripe for unorthodox rhetoric…" And we living only now, so late, really cannot even speculate. We cannot know. And the newspaper accounts are just a tad incomplete, wreaking silent havoc on the retelling. There is just enough to finish the story, not enough to know.

When Watson woke up at 8:30 a.m. on Aug. 5, he knew that William Osborn would be at work and that Henry Osborn would be sleeping. He knew by the light. He knew because it had been his job to clean up after this white family and he knew just where each one of them slept and for how long. He got up, marched up the back stairs, and called out "Mr. Osborn, Mr. Osborn," so as not to surprise his former employer in sleep's embrace. This, he thought, would have been unfair, even unmanly. Henry Osborn woke from his final night on this earth. They quarreled. Osborn tried to head for the nearby bathroom and lunged at Watson. They struggled a bit. And then Watson fired several shots at point-blank range, in part, in an effort to free himself from Osborn's hold. ("I twitched away from him and I shot him.") One of the shots pierced Osborn's skull, another tore through his abdomen, a third his chest, a fourth his liver. Watson departed quickly; he did not offer assistance, nor did he leave the house. He simply returned to his own room, got into his own bed and stayed there for nine hours, meditating on the rampaging police footsteps, the ambulance, the later footsteps, the quiet, the chase, the closer footsteps, the hand picking up the mattress, Dietrich's "Here's the nigger!" declaration, the pensive faces peering down on him at the final moment of his capture.

All of this was recounted and the trial was close to its end. Yet the question of motive became more ambiguous in the telling. Osborn owed Watson money he had not yet paid him, and this much was conceded by his son William on the witness stand. This had been the pretext for a conversation. And when Osborn fired Watson several weeks before, at his wife's behest, he had again invoked the hated expletive. It seems that Watson, arrogant young man that he was and almost purposefully unaccustomed to etiquette (he, the lit cigar-dropper), had audaciously threatened to sue Osborn! Osborn apparently had replied "Who are you, a nigger, to threaten to sue me?" or something to that effect. Yet prosecuting attorney John Ransom Buck, 68, said that malice could be inferred from the extreme cruelty of the slaying, "deliberate, premeditated killing." Of Osborn: "Here is a man working every day of his life, working in summer that his wife and daughter might go to the seashore." And of Watson: "Here is a fellow who, as he says, he is not able to get along with anybody. As he told one of the witnesses, 'I'm the kind of a fellow that gets even'... There is one thing the city has to be thankful for — if you had been in this city that morning of the murder and seen the anger aroused, you would have seen that in the South he would have been tried with short shrift and strung up on the spot." The defense lawyers must have weighed the scales of justice over and over, the beads of sweat, sweat about their own futures and Watson's future, trickling down onto their notes. In the unequal exchange between man and young man, surely a murder had occurred. And surely Watson had anticipated that possible outcome. But there were doubts in their minds about the context of the murder, about Hartford, about the South, about attitudes, about the impressionability of the young Negro, who had said weeks ago that he was "ready to die," that he had not fled the Osborn house because he had "nothing to live for," who had talked to a black assistant janitor at the jail privately after his arrest. Roosevelt Belcher had pleaded, "If you had any reason for killing him; if it can't help you... tell me as it may help the colored race. This is a terrible crime, and if you can tell me why you did it, it will help," to which Watson replied, "I went there to do him." Belcher asked, "Why?" "He called me a name," Watson replied. "If there was any other reason for killing him, tell me." "I'll never tell that," said Watson. Yet on the stand, Watson said of

At the center of a sensational murder trial almost 100 years ago was a young man derisively called "Nigger Joe."

Belcher's testimony for the prosecution: "I ain't got no confidence in him. He's a lie."

In late 1904, during the Watson days, President Teddy Roosevelt refused to commute the death penalty of a "feeble-minded" black man in Washington, D.C., who murdered a white child. The news made the front page in the Hartford papers. A white mob in Richmond lynched a 14-year-old black boy called Andrew Dudley who had attacked the children of two prominent white families. In Statesboro, Ala., a white mob seized two blacks accused of killing a white family and burned them at the stake. The Chicago packinghouse strike was on, as well as a lockout in the Hartford building trades. But the papers also carried the story of the children of union members who went on strike at their parents' bidding, in McAllister, Minn., in the mistaken belief that the school had hired a "colored" kindergarten teacher.

While Watson sat in his cell, pursuing his spiritual life, awaiting the outcome of his trial, a young French Canadian named Georges Lefebvre bludgeoned to death a young Polish-Jewish immigrant butcher called Louis Merzinter among the meat carcasses in the Katzenstein Brothers slaughterhouse up on Windsor Street in Hartford. All that night Jews gathered in front of the rabbi's house in an old and poor quarter of the city, where Constitution Plaza sits now, to wail and mourn the dead, this bright hope of their community, and to grieve with his young wife and child. The killer said he resented the "Hebrews" whose businesses had come to his neighborhood; Lefebvre's father blamed Katzenstein for the murder. Rabbi Jacob Beecher told the press that he had heard the killer say, "I'd like to shoot a few Jewish heads off." The kid was slow, the neighbors said.

Mary Collins, a black domestic, was caught in Union Station, trying to flee town with $400 of her employers' clothing — satin dresses, furs and gowns. In New London, the Gerschon Marx murder case was the occasion for riots in the Jewish districts of town; he had slain his farmhands, one by one, with his fourth wife's assistance. A Hartford police officer, James Vail, was suspended for intimidating a chicken seller and calling him a "red-haired Jew." A Sioux, Chief John Hollow Horn Bear, was arrested at the Pawnee Wild West and East show in Hartford for whipping an Irishman who played a cavalry officer in the show's pageant. Horn Bear wanted the story line of the pageant to be reversed; he wanted the management to let the Indians win for a change, and the fracas that cost him $5 in the Hartford police court ensued. He occupied a cell near Watson for a time, and they got to ride together in the paddy wagon, Horn Bear dressed in a red shirt, striped trousers and a blue blanket. The press said he had gone "on the warpath." On Aug. 9, the Pawnee show offered another skit in which a "Mexican greaser" stole a cowboy's horse and was hanged for it. For those strolling through the grounds, the show brought "an ethnographic display of Japanese, Singalese and other racial representatives of the Eastern hemisphere." Lew Dockstader, "Hartford's Own" minstrel, was in town, and his show, a "humorous, popular yet artistic treatment of negro life," featured sketches like "Happy Coons in Dixieland" and "Dusk on the Mississippi." Its grand finale depicted a tropical forest in which water lilies opened to reveal white eyes and a black face protruding from its petals. Poli's opened "Swinging from Zululand" on the day of Watson's arraignment while "Queen of the White Slaves," a melodrama about a New York child labor ring, followed.

There had been seven murders in the past six months in Hartford and Osborn's was the last straw for the city fathers. Cornelius Ryan, until now known for his arrest of one Joe Coburn, the "Central Row colored pugilist," resigned as police chief after Osborn's funeral and police Capt. William F. Gunn was promoted to replace him. It had simply taken too long to find Watson and there were still murderers at large, including one Rooney, who had slit his wife's throat "from ear to ear" and eluded Ryan's force. Watson must have known a great deal of this; reporters, jailers and visitors shot the breeze. And so did his lawyers and the jury. These were the stories of their times.

On Sept. 20, Judge Roraback instructed the jury to consider revenge as the motive for the murder and noted that items had been stolen from Osborn's wardrobe, constituting a possible case of burglary and murder, still a capital offense in Connecticut, requiring less malice aforethought. Osborn's use of an "opprobrious name" and the unpaid debt were the ostensible provocations, but, Roraback said, "Words do not reduce homicide to manslaughter."

"If blood could cool," he said, referring to the passage of time between the July confrontation between Osborn and Watson and the murder, then there was no immediate provocation, no violence in the first heat of the argument, no demonstrated absence of premeditation.

But the defense was yet to rest. Rohrmayer, 23, a graduate of Trinity College and the Yale Law School, rose to make his maiden speech in a jury trial, which he qualified by stating from the outset that he was there "not from choice, but in the course of duty... The bar of justice knows no race prejudice."

"What kind of boy is this? Eighteen years of age, below the average of intelligence, born in the South where a negro is looked on as little better than a dog, his life has been a sad one... He lost his father when he was two years old and his mother not long after... 'Who are you that you should sue me?' said Mr. Osborn. That excited fear in the boy's heart. He conceived the idea of having a talk with Mr. Osborn in order not to live in constant fear, and went to the house that night. It was unfortunate that he had a revolver with him. But you heard what the officer called him at the time of the capture. That was the treatment Watson, brought up in the South, was accustomed to, and led to his carrying the weapon. If he intended to shoot Mr. Osborn, why didn't he shoot him in bed? Why didn't he go to the victim's bed at midnight, the most favorable time? The law gives you liberty if these counts against the prisoner fail to find him guilty of murder in the second degree. You need not let him go free, you can send him to prison for life."

Hugh O'Flaherty mounted what the press called "an impassioned plea" for Watson's life, insisting that he had lied to the police at the time of his capture: "Can't we do something with this boy rather than break his neck?... do not pass the sentence of death as on a dog, for the warning of the community... to rob what? A pair of shoes — the life of a man against a pair of shoes?... He had a right to demand the money due him. If the money were not due, Mrs. Osborn could have taken the stand and stamped the prisoner's story as a lie."

But State's Attorney Arthur F. Eggleston of the prosecution replied to the defense: "He is not here as a negro, he is here as a subject amenable to law." He added that it was not the job of the jury "to prove the motive but to prove the crime."

The jury deliberated for just 28 minutes and handed down a unanimous verdict of guilty, murder in the first degree, to a hushed and cleared courtroom. Only a few women onlookers had been admitted on this last day, Sept. 30, 1904. An incident had been feared, but surely the outcome rendered that unlikely. Roraback declared: "You have been tried by a jury of intelligent and fair-minded men. You have been found guilty of killing a highly respected citizen of this city with express malice, under circumstances clearly indicating that you possess a wicked, depraved and malignant spirit." The decision admitted of "no circumstances of mitigation, extenuation or excuse." There had been nothing presented "to excuse or justify it." No stay of execution was requested. Roraback duly informed Watson that he was to be removed to Wethersfield state prison in mid-November, and that "before sunrise, within an enclosure to be hanged by the neck until you are dead." Watson did not break as it was read and was asked if he wished to make a statement. He "smiled nervously" and replied: "I ain't got any power at all. You-alls got it. I ain't got it. Even if I say anything, what's the use?" He thanked his lawyers. He was then transported back to Seyms Street jail where he said of the judge, "I guess he must want to get rid of me; he did not give me very long," and cried bitterly in his cell through the night.

The press was jubilant, praising the Connecticut system over Southern lynch law, though a reader wrote to The Courant protesting its interest in the case: "Why should the acts or words of this beast be given publicity?"

The Hartford Times editorial, entitled "Law and Order," stated that there was no cause for apology: "Infinitely better is the Connecticut way than the way of the lyncher is." The weekly Hartford Globe took a more cerebral view: "Who is responsible for this member of society who cannot comprehend the sacredness of human life?... A study of his character does not develop a strain of depravity, but rather a dormant intellect. Watson is not immoral; he is unmoral... he only sees the spectacular side of it... we must not whine but assume much of the personal responsibility." Booker T. Washington, after all, had identified "so many closed avenues" for blacks in the North.

Watson was kept at Seyms Street jail until a month before his execution, and then moved to Wethersfield, to a special execution cell in which he waited for his hanging. On his last night in Hartford, he was brought into the jailers' dining room, where his keepers offered him a steak dinner and again remarked on his progress, calling him "one of the best prisoners" ever held at the jail. He was, to them, no longer as he had appeared to be when he was captured. In the weeks that remained, Watson was visited repeatedly by his family and by members of the black clergy who had taken him in. As the day approached, he asked that several messages be issued from him "to the people of his race in Hartford," which concerned "the mistakes of his life." In his last visit he begged his brother James to lead a Christian life.

Watson fasted the night before his hanging, saw his relatives and took communion with the Rev. Atius Crooke before he walked the short distance from the death cell to the gallows. He told Crooke that he been saved and whether Osborn would forgive him, and said, "Pray for me. I want to meet you in heaven." His last words were these: "I will meet my death bravely, but humbly, like a Christian." It was Nov. 17, 1904, 56 days after the verdict, shortly after midnight. It took nine full minutes for Watson to die; he was young and strong. There had been 11 hangings at Wethersfield in the last decade, mostly of immigrants, but "not since the execution of Charles Boinay," a press observer commented, "has a similar exhibition of the oozing of vitality been so conspicuous." The Courant headline read, "Brave in the Face of Death": "The execution was an example of Connecticut's speedy and orderly way of administering justice... He was of strong vitality and although death came in the usual number of minutes after the falling of the weight, there was much muscular action."

Joseph Watson's grave lies unmarked in Spring Grove Cemetery, on Main Street in North Hartford. It is not as shielded from the roadway as Osborn's grave in Cedar Hill. Still, it is there somewhere within the wrought iron, and the city is there beside it, and you can walk from there to Capitol Avenue in a short hour and up Main Street past South Church and on up the blocks on an incline to Fairfield Avenue and into the grounds where Osborn was laid to rest, the former police commissioner who died just three months earlier than his younger fellow citizen. Osborn's headstone is still here in the same city where the young man's grave lies hidden. And it is has been so for almost a century now, though we have had some cooler summers.

10

Insurance for Sale

Garret Condon

Ed Stivender pulled his shenanigans at The Travelers head-quarters on the morning of Aug. 4, 1977. Stivender disguised himself in the uniform — a dark suit and tie and a tomato-red Travelers pouch under the arm — so the security guard at the main entrance waved him by.

As a bit of one-man guerrilla theater, Stivender, a performance artist and humorist, prowled various floors at The Travelers that morning (before the security staff caught up with him) asking a single, Socratic question:

"Excuse me, where do they keep the insurance?"

(Keep in mind that these were Hartford's boom days, when there was money even for zany, iconoclastic performance art — and the city was buoyant enough to enjoy some of it.)

Stivender, who has lived in New York and his native Philadelphia since 1978, recalls that most of those he asked were either mildly puzzled or downright stunned. One employee asked him if he wanted a "cert," shop talk for a certificate of insurance. Stivender just happened to have a roll of Certs ("It's a breath mint; it's a candy mint.") in his pocket. So he showed his Certs and declined the "cert." But on one floor, he made his way to a space with dozens of small desks crowded together — all empty before lunch but for an older man on the far end of the room. "He was old enough to be a supervisor," says Stivender, "but he didn't have a good desk."

"Excuse me, where do they keep the insurance?" Stivender asked.

The older gent looked up and pointed at himself — at his heart, to be exact — and said: "Right here. They keep it right here."

It is a question worthy of a Zen master: Where is the insurance? There are nearly 75,000 in central Connecticut who work in insurance, finance and real estate. That means that thousands of our neighbors can point to their hearts and say "right here." For that matter, what is the insurance? Our capital city's most famous product is a pretty abstract affair. New Britain is the Hardware City — a moniker that gets down to brass tacks. New Haven must still have an unblighted elm tree or two. But the Insurance City. It's like being the Love City. But insurance isn't love, even if we keep it in our hearts. Maybe Hartford should be called the City of Promises — "Policy" is from the Italian word for promise or proof.

We are Hartford. We promise to help you when the bad thing happens. (This promise subject to limitations and exceptions, as evidenced by the history of said industry in said city. The reader, identified henceforth as "the reader," agrees to read on.)

Now, bad things have been part of human life since Adam and Eve's ill-advised snack in the Garden of Eden. Insurance is about sharing the catastrophe. The human impulse to spread risk is ancient, as any freshman insurance major knows. Said underclassman is routinely led back through the patchy fog of time to some classic example of early "insurance," including these:

1. Yangtze River traders in central China would spread their goods among several trading vessels, so that the loss of one would not ruin any one merchant.

2. Merchants in North Africa formed caravans to cross the desert to reduce the risk to any single trader.

3. Many citizens of ancient Rome were members of burial societies which paid members' funeral costs out of monthly dues.

4. "Bottomry" contracts were used in the ancient world to protect and encourage ocean-going commerce. A group of investors extended a loan to a ship owner. If the ship completes its voyage, the investors are paid with interest. If said boat sinks, the owner is not obliged to repay the loan. Marine coverage is the oldest form of insurance. Formal written contracts date back to 14th-century Italy.

But the march of time in the developed world has also been a march of ever-increasing risk. There get to be more of us, we create bigger, faster and more dangerous machines, travel farther afield and live together in ever more densely populated cities or places subject to fires, floods or earthquakes. Nothing focuses the mind on risk as does a total calamity. The disaster that created the modern era of insurance was the Great Fire of London of 1666, which gutted the city. Talk about a plug for fire insurance: the modern insurance age began. Not that you had oxcart drivers carrying no-fault insurance cards, obviously. In this era, most risk was shared the old fashioned way: people took care of one another. So that Archibald Welsh, in his 1935 pamphlet on the history of insurance in Connecticut could write of the 1636 settlement of Hartford:

"When Thomas Hooker and his little band of early settlers first erected their huts, stockades, and meetinghouse, each man knew that he could depend on all the others in the settlement to guard him from hostile Indians; to care for him if he were disabled; to help rebuild his home if it were burned; and to care for his dependent family if he should die. It was the most complete insurance coverage that one could have, and yet not a single contract was written and probably not a verbal promise was given."

The colonists' ideal of caring for one's family and neighbors was the only insurance required by early colonists. (Alas, Indians were not covered by this policy. Thanks to the English, the Indians became very bad risks, indeed.) The tradition of maritime insurance was taken from the old world to the new and ocean gateway Connecticut towns such as Hartford, New Haven and New London, were steeped in it. Handwritten, ad-hoc contracts provided fire and property insurance in similar fashion on a case-by-case basis. One of the first printed policies in Connecticut dates to 1794, written for a year's worth of fire insurance on the Hartford home of William Imlay. Apparently, there was no fire.

We now come to the dawn of Hartford's prominence as an insurance capital. We cue the orchestra, which starts in on the stirring opening movement of Aaron Copland's "Fanfare for the Common Man," and commence a slow close-up of an aged lithograph of Hartford, circa 1800. With the music faded to background, the voice of actor Sam Waterston begins: "That so small a city could produce so great an industry is a tribute to Hartford's men of vision and their considerable wealth."

Wait, wait. Sorry. That was from Ken Burn's abandoned PBS miniseries, "Insurance." But that is the company (or companies') line. It all gets very heroic at this point. For example:

& There was Eliphalet Terry, mushing by sleigh to New York in sub-
   zero weather, to honor the young Hartford Fire Insurance
   Company's claims after a massive New York fire in December,
   1835. Terry, president of the company, pledged his personal fortune
   and got the Hartford Bank — allied with his company — to honor
   all company drafts. While many a New York insurer had gone belly
   up, Terry promised astonished New Yorkers that The Hartford was
   as good as its word. It paid all claims in full — $84,973.34 worth.
   You can't buy advertising like that. The jump in new business more
   than paid for the New York losses.

& Eleven years later, a second fire broke out in New York. Although
   not as devastating as the first fire, it affected lots of property
   covered by the Aetna Insurance Co. The directors of the Aetna,
   formed in 1819 and allied with the Phoenix Bank, met in
   emergency session. In a scene right out of Frank Capra, Aetna
   president Thomas K. Brace told the board that the losses in New
   York would probably exhaust the firm's resources, and placed
   Aetna's stock and bond certificates on the table.
       "What are you going to do, Mr. Brace?" asked a director,
   according to author Woodward.
       "Do?" Brace replied. "I am going to New York to pay all our
   losses, if it takes every dollar there (he pointed to the securities) and
   my own fortune as well." Luckily for Brace, his fortune stayed
   intact, and his Aetna flourished, spawning the Aetna Life Insurance
   Co. in 1853, which became Aetna Life & Casualty Co.

& Finally, there came the Great Chicago Fire, Oct. 8-10, 1871. Mrs.
   O'Leary's cow was bad news for the Windy City — 90,000 were left
   homeless, $200 million in property was lost — but the "Insurance
   City" rose in its ashes. Even before the smoke had cleared, former
   Connecticut Gov. Marshall Jewell, a director of the Phoenix
   Insurance Company (established in 1854), was on the lakefront.
   Jewell found himself amid "a surging, half-crazed, despairing
   crowd, which seemed to feel that even the foundations of the earth
   were crumbling with the destruction of their fortunes." He
   mounted a dry-goods box and announced that the Phoenix would
   pay all losses and he offered to write checks on the spot. Woodward

describes the city's reaction: "Immediately the Tribune dropped from its window a huge placard, announcing that the Phoenix of Hartford, had begun to pay its losses in full. As the news spread from one to another, the multitude cheered, and cried, and laughed by turns."

The vignettes above show that the early historians of insurance in Hartford subscribe wholeheartedly to the "great men" theory of history — now unaccountably out of favor in the academy. The founders and early leaders are painted as giants, from Terry and Brace to such polymaths as classicist-stone mason-turned-insurance czar James G. Batterson, who created the country's first accident insurance company, The Travelers Insurance Co., in 1863. Not to denigrate the skill and intelligence of these men, but it took something more than a steady hand on the tiller. By the 19th century, America was ripe for insurance, and Hartford was just the place to sell it. Among the assets Hartford possessed were:

Wealth — Insurance fit the bill for central Connecticut's well-to-do merchant traders and farmers. For starters, you've got to have wealth to want to protect it. Insurance was (and still is, to some extent) a luxury item. For another, there had to be effective ways to pool capital so those with cash could make some more, and to pay for the growth and industrialization that was transforming Hartford and all of New England. Insurance (along with banks and stocks and bonds) provided a capital market. Gerald Gunderson, Shelby Collum Davis Professor of American Business and Economic History at Trinity College, notes that the 19th century also created markets for insurance: "People started buying things sold regionally and nationally instead of just bartering with neighbors."

Size — Gunderson suggests that Hartford's relatively small size may have helped its early success. One has to spread risk — you don't want all of your eggs (policies) in one basket (city). Because if some cow knocks over a lantern and all of your policies are nearby, you've got a problem. Nascent insurers could hardly have made a go of it in Hartford alone, which had only 6,000 residents in 1810. Thus, the Hartford companies quickly created far-flung networks of agents.

Dumb Luck — This muddies the "men of vision" concept a bit, "but it's an inescapable factor," says Lewis Mandell, a former University of Connecticut dean and finance professor, now dean of the College of Business Administration at Marquette University in Milwaukee. Hartford never burned to the ground, for instance. The Aetna hadn't sold any insurance in New York previous to the 1835 fire. (It entered New York the next year.) The surviving companies get to own the history, so the failed companies are branded as moral or management failures.

In fact, the "science" of insurance — of assessing risk, setting appropriate rates and setting aside reserves — was not well and widely understood until the second half of the century. Of the eleven Connecticut companies that insured Chicago property, only four survived the 1871 fire with the ability to pay losses in full. We don't hear too much about The City Fire, The Merchant's and the other hard-luck cases.

Coffee — At least two world-renowned insurance companies began in coffee houses: Lloyd's of London, which originated as a coffee house; and Aetna, whose original directors first met in Morgan's Coffee House in Hartford. It is possible that financial risk is best tackled after a serious jolt of java? Probably not. Let's forget about this one and move on to the biggest factor:

Puritanism — OK, let's get all the no-fire-insurance-for-witches jokes out of the way right up front. Whether we New Englanders like it or not, many of our common values — including a pile of civic virtues of which we used to be proud — descend directly from the Puritans. Most widely known in the popular mind for persecuting sorcerers, monogramming harlots, and giving short shrift (and smallpox) to the Indians, the Puritans nonetheless turned barren, rocky New England into a remarkably affluent colony in no time. They possessed, it seemed, an almost supernatural entrepreneurial sense and capacity for labor. Let us recall that New England — and Hartford itself —began as religious experiments. The whole idea behind the Mayflower and Thomas Hooker's pilgrimage here was to make a better world in a specific way. Insurance — though driven by profit, not salvation — had a similar impulse.

Some will cavil at the thought of insurance as a Puritan enterprise. It's true that anything that smacked of usury was frowned upon by the Hooker band. (And, boy, could they frown.) Stephen Innes, a history professor at the University of Virginia and author of the recent "Creating the Commonwealth," a fresh look at Puritan New England, notes that the Puritans encouraged an honest return, but discouraged money-lending at unreasonable interest. And it's true that the emergence of life insurance in the early 19th century was a particularly thorny theological issue for some Congregationalist clergy — a certain Elder Swan preached against life insurance.

But the Puritan "saints" were replaced by increasingly worldly generations who hewed to the saintly virtues as best they could to ensure continued order and prosperity. For them, the idea of augmenting Providence with actuarial tables was far from sinful. In 1897 Woodward could write: "The act condemned by the good elder as a sin is now classed with the duties."

Religion — at least as a social phenomenon — is tied to the early history of insurance in Hartford. Harry Keiner, associate archivist and historian at CIGNA Corp. in Bloomfield, notes that the Hartford Bank and the Hartford Fire Insurance Co. were very much part and parcel of the Congregationalist "standing order" in Connecticut. The Phoenix Bank and the original Aetna crowd, by contrast, were prominent Episcopalians who helped dismantle the Congregational theocracy in Connecticut. Even more than a century later, the crowned heads of the local insurance dynasties would be nicknamed "the bishops."

Some of the bedrock truths of insurance can evoke the Rock of Ages. One is a kind of earthly predestination: the law of large numbers. It says that loss can be predicted and that accuracy in prediction increases as the number of insureds increases. (Also, doesn't "law of large numbers" sounds like it's straight out of the Old Testament?) Insurers separate the wheat from the chaff: a set of potential customers is predictable when it is homogeneous. Thus, the elect qualify for policies, and are able to fulfill their worldly duties. Innes notes that the Puritan's primary responsibility was to his family. Life insurance offers a chance to be responsible to one's kin beyond the grave. It's a way to settle the afterlife in the here-and-now.

In a utopia under God, such as Hartford was to be, the ideal mode of business was to do well by doing good. Here was insurance, providing cash rewards for virtues, such as thrift and foresight, that used to be their own rewards. Among the pioneers of insurance, we hear the voice of the social worker, the philanthropist and the preacher. The theme is never just profit — a vulgar, sinful topic — but social progress.

Ah, progress, the proverbial rising tide. And if bottom lines rise, too, so much the better. The explosive growth of group insurance in our century spread the gospel of insurance to the working class. Its proponents had an almost religious fervor about it. Robert W. Huntington was president of Connecticut General when that company was an early innovator in group life. In 1930 he said: "Anybody who is effectively helping to distribute the benefits of life insurance to that part of the population with which he can come into contact need never ask himself whether he is playing a useful part... Large or small, there never was one [claim] paid yet that didn't help somebody who needed help."

Like the Puritans, who hoped to create a kind of heaven-on-earth in New England, the insurance industry has always had a strong utopian impulse. A safer world is a better world, right? It is certainly a more profitable world for insurers.

In his book, Innes writes of the Puritan "culture of discipline," the famous ethic that shaped individual, family and community life. Keeping to the straight and narrow — or to the path of least risk — has been a guiding principle of insurance, too. The company now called Phoenix Home Life began as the American Temperance Life Insurance Co. in 1854. It would reward the booze-free lifestyle. It wrote policies for teetotalers only — at about 10 percent less than the contemporary rates. Despite its saintly goals, the company found that such a product was, in Woodward's words, "counter to the inclinations of human nature" and went off the wagon in 1861. The insurance industry helped create standards for building codes, fire protection and the safe use of electricity. The dangers of steam power prompted the creation of the Hartford Steam Boiler Inspection & Insurance Co. in 1866, dedicated to the application of scientific accident prevention.

Sometimes the Insurance City goes for the grand, utopian gesture:

> In 1962, under the leadership of visionary chairman Frazar B. Wilde, Connecticut General Life Insurance Co. (now CIGNA) invested heavily in a "planned community" — a town created from scratch between Washington and Baltimore by another visionary: builder James Rouse. Everything from housing design to income groups was to be planned in advance in Columbia, Md. (One of several "new towns" of the era.) It was meant to be a model

community. Today, Columbia, with a population of about 80,000, remains racially diverse. But it doesn't have the hoped-for economic diversity. Larry Madaras, a Columbia historian, calls it "a yuppie community."

 An organization called Greater Hartford Process planned to build a model, mixed-income community of 20,000 in northwest Coventry in the early 1970s. Process was heavily backed by local banks and insurers, but opposition in Coventry scotched the plan.

 Constitution Plaza, which opened to great fanfare in the early 1960s, was often called "a city within a city." Of course, a rather organic, though blighted, city neighborhood was razed to make way for the sterile plaza. The planned-for network of adjoining skywalks never fully materialized.

These projects have something to say about the strengths and weaknesses of insurance as a social force. There is tremendous idealism in all of this. In these and hundreds of less-dramatic ways, Hartford insurers have been involved in this and other communities. It is clear that the Puritan idea of civic responsibility has remained close to their corporate hearts — if one can use such a term. (For the Puritans, there was no boundary between church and state, so the "civic" arena was wide. Insurance, too, has recognized a large civic space. As late as 1891, Gov. Morgan G. Bulkeley, also Aetna Life's president, tapped an estimated $300,000 in Aetna loans to meet state expenses during a legislative stand-off.)

But there is an underside to such dreamy schemes. Insurance says that humans, by and large, are predictable. Predictably, such an industry will lean heavily on professional planning and social engineering and move forward with an autocratic, home-office approach. (The Coventry land, for example, was bought quietly before the plans were disclosed.)

And there is the element of stratification. In Constitution Plaza, there was the physical separation of the suits (in the skywalks) and the street folks (on the sidewalks). Stratification is part of how insurance works: Everyone must be equally subject to the accidental bad thing. Those likely to encounter more bad things must pay more for insurance. In the early days of insurance, Hartford (and most of America) was a pretty homogeneous place. If you were an upstanding guy and known to the upstanding guys of the insurance outfit, you could score a policy. But even as emancipation and immigration changed the U.S., insurers remained wary of non-whites.

The April, 1920 edition of "Rules and Instructions for Life Agents of the Aetna Life Insurance Company, Hartford, Conn." includes the following instructions under Section 4., Doubtful and Uninsurable, paragraph j.: "Agents are directed not to write the applications of negroes, mulattoes, or those having any considerable proportion of African blood, for the reason that their mortality is believed to be considerably higher than that of the white race." The next paragraph adds: "Until further notice applications for insurance on the lives of Japanese and Chinese should not be written, for the reason that the company has no reliable mortality experience of these two races."

Though such guidelines are ancient history for modern insurers, the problem persists: one person's sound underwriting can be redlining. Our contemporary ideas about diversity and fairness don't always jibe with the way insurance works. If you live in a poor neighborhood, you are probably living with more crime than someone in an affluent suburb. The poverty and the crime are not necessarily your fault, but you may be paying more for insurance. Perhaps your pre-existing health problems aren't your fault. Yet, they could price you out of coverage. (The great equalizer — making insurance available to "bad risks" in the inner city, flood-prone areas and to unskilled drivers — has been government.) Basically, those with the fewest resources and the most risks aren't likely to find great solace in insurance.

Some prefer to keep it simple, and doubt that elaborate third-party schemes have improved on Thomas Hooker's original insurance: taking

Aetna Corporate Archives

care of one another. The Amish, who are arguably the largest group of Americans (about 140,000) still building something akin to the original Puritans' paradise, don't have any insurance policies, though they do have a kind of mutual-aid fire fund. According to Amish expert John Hostetler, emeritus professor of anthropology and sociology at Temple University in Philadelphia, life insurance and other kinds of coverage are taboo.

"People themselves come to the aid of a person in distress," he says. "The Bible says to help each other, and if you don't do it, you're an atheist."

Funny, but David Ivry, emeritus professor of insurance at the universities of Connecticut and Hartford, goes to the same Bible to speak of the "nobility" of insurance, quoting from St. Paul: "Bear ye one another's burdens" (Galatians, 6:2). Ivry and others certainly take issue with the Amish. They view insurance not as a hindrance but as a way to carry out the biblical injunction in a complicated world. After all, you crack up your Toyota, it's not like the neighbors can come over and build you a new one.

Insurance is usually seen as following society's trends, but it can contribute to social changes, too. "Whatever follows, fosters," observes Mandell. So insurance helped make 19th-century industrialization possible by providing security to city-dwelling laborers who could not always depend on an extended family for help in time of crisis. In its way, it can loosen bonds of charity and responsibility — and that may be exactly what customers want.

"If parents have nursing home insurance, it almost guarantees

Above: *At Aetna, and other Hartford institutions, business has been built around the premise that things will go wrong.*

they'll end up in a nursing home," says Mandell. Yet Mandell says that the point can be taken too far. People don't want the event they're insuring against.

In this century, we're insuring against events and outcomes which the insurance pioneers could not have foreseen: automobile coverage; aircraft liability insurance; health insurance; and pooling risk for such high-risk ventures as space exploration and nuclear power plants. We have seen insurance marketed in totally new ways — packaged for specific consumers ("homeowner's insurance") and businesses, for example. And insurance benefits have become part of the way businesses pay employees. Above all, Americans began throwing around the term "insurance" to describe ways to invest and redistribute wealth to accomplish specific social goals: comprehensive health care or income security for the elderly and others. (Insurance purists insist that Social Security, health maintenance organizations and other such schemes are not "real" insurance.)

Poet Wallace Stevens, whose day job was vice president at The Hartford Accident and Indemnity Co., (now ITT Hartford Insurance Group), could write in a 1937 agents' newsletter of insurance as being so vital a social activity that it had been nationalized by fascist and communist governments in Europe. "The objective of all of us is to live in a world in which nothing unpleasant can happen," he wrote. "Our prime instinct is to go on indefinitely like the wax flowers on the mantelpiece. Insurance is the most easily understood geometry for calculating how to bring the thing about." Though he admits that we will never live in a world "in which insurance is made perfect," he seems to say that private insurance measures up to the schemes of the fascists and communists. But he has to remind his agents to dig in. He has to remind his readers that the key to avoiding the fate of insurance companies in Italy and Germany and Russia is profit.

No wonder he had to remind them. It all seemed so automatic. It's as if the practice of thrift, prudence, honesty and fairness, coupled with sound actuarial science, would naturally lead to profitability. (Just as these traits were marks of sanctity.) It seemed to work. One did not have to talk about it. After all, these were companies whose founders had risked personal ruin to make good on claims. There was a Hartford way of doing insurance, epitomized in the early years by Col. Jacob Greene, a Civil War hero and Gen. Custer's chief of staff, who was president of Connecticut Mutual from 1878 to 1905 and campaigned against scam policies pushed by big New York companies.

Hartford companies for years enjoyed a reputation for such Puritanical integrity failures — in the early years these were ascribed to moral turpitude. (Not that they have been untouched by scandal or accusations since.) Writer and New York Congressman Bruce Barton (who died in 1967) once said of Hartford: "I like to think of Hartford as a city that has been built upon faith... Hartford receives millions of dollars of savings, but it does not stop there. It returns, every day, countless marvelous streams of blessings to those in need."

The insurance industry's first blessing was to its original utopia: Hartford. Though many early insurance jobs were low-paying, they were secure. In exchange for assessing distant risks, insurance workers got to live low-risk lives in the city with solid, lifelong jobs, benefits, clubs, picnics — a whole world. Hartford — home of the first automobile speed limit — reflected the conservatism of its patron industry. After World War II, competition, increasing poverty in Hartford, troubled investments and, yes, greed, conspired to put the bottom line on top. Local insurers merged: Connecticut General took over the Aetna Insurance Co. ("Little Aetna") in 1962; The Travelers merged with The Phoenix in 1966; The Hartford Fire Insurance Co. became a subsidiary of ITT Corp. in 1969, and is now to be spun off; Industrial Risk Insurers was born in 1975 of the union between the Factory Insurance Association and the Oil Insurance Association; Connecticut General Corp and INA merged to become CIGNA in 1982; and Travelers and Primerica merged in 1993.

Aetna Life and Casualty Co. archivist Paul Lasewicz says the myth of steady work in insurance is just that. Though Aetna layoffs in the past few years have been huge and company-wide, office consolidation of field offices in the late 1950s and streamlining in the 70s resulted in some layoffs.

But in the late 80s and 90s, industry downsizing has been brutal: nearly 10,000 insurance jobs lost in the state since 1988.

Nothing articulated the new era better than news in 1993 that Sanford I. Weill, the chairman of the newly-merged Travelers, would receive a year's pay of $53 million — the same year that Travelers was in the process of erasing 5,000 jobs nationwide. The numbers were, let's face it, heart-breaking. As long as we're facing it, let's acknowledge that the Insurance City was never a Puritan paradise-on-earth and it is surely no "city upon a hill" now. Despite the benefactions of its insurers,

Hartford seems as far from perfection now as ever. It is sharply divided on class lines — part office park, part crumbling urban center — at odds with its more affluent and whiter suburbs.

Sandy Weill's paycheck and other recent revelations have torn the pin-striped trappings of gentility from the body corporate. It may have imagined itself as a special and especially-anointed enterprise, but it turned out to be only a business, alas. And business is business.

Still, the "re-engineered," stripped-down giants, with eyes on quarterly earnings reports and no illusions about assured survival, hum along. More interestingly, the entrepreneurial spark that brought forth Hartford's original companies, is still alive. In and around the city, there are start-up insurance and reinsurance companies, tapping some of the laid-off talent that remains and focusing on newly-perceived risks that are ignored or underserved by the multi-line monoliths.

Dick Shima, a former Traveler's executive, is a consultant and is chairman of Environmental Warranty Inc. of West Hartford, one such start-up. Environmental Warranty sells assessment insurance designed to protect lenders, cities and businesses against the costs of cleaning up undiscovered contamination. Shima predicts that the Hartford area will see more small, start-up insurers that are tightly focused on specific, narrowly-defined products and markets.

Which is to say that even if insurance is no longer a sacred trust, it is still a binding promise. If it ever was in our hearts, it isn't there any more. It must now live in the hard heads of the corporate survivors and the venture capitalists. It is not, as it turns out, a world, but a day's work and every employee for herself.

Yet here it remains, flowering in odd cracks, still sending its streams of calculated blessings through the world

11

Together at the Temple

....

Lary Bloom

Beneath the layers

In the autumn of 1982, John Canning, a man of a hundred old churches, stumbled upon his first old synagogue — or what was once a synagogue. He was working on a project in the neighborhood when he saw a building of Romanesque, Gothic and Moorish features. Not much of that left in Hartford, he thought. And so he wiped his work boots, poked his head in and asked in his Scottish lilt, "What is this beautiful place?"

In the autumn of 1982, John Canning was not alone in that question. Once, this beautiful place was the marvel of Hartford, where the mere laying of the cornerstone drew 10,000 or more people who came in their carriages as a gesture of good will, and where a very crucial principle about freedom was demonstrated.

But in the autumn of 1982, it was just another old building on Charter Oak Avenue, if indeed its survival as such had been remarkable in itself.

Canning learned that, like so many other historic Hartford places, it had been slated for demolition. It was saved, however, by preservationists and turned into a community center of art exhibits and dance and programs to enrich a neighborhood and a constituency sorely in need of enrichment. It was enough, wasn't it, that such a place existed these days, that substantial money was raised to replace its ancient plumbing and electrical systems and roof?

But Canning's curiosity focused beyond structural basics to the unseen: what he imagined was beneath the painted walls. He told Lynn Traiger, who oversaw the restoration and fund-raising of what was now called The Charter Oak Temple Cultural Center, about himself and what he did: that he owned John Canning & Co. Ltd.; that he had devoted his professional life — since the days of his apprenticeship in Glasgow — to restoration and ornamental painting; that he was presently restoring the lovely houses around the corner that had once been owned by the city's captains of industry, and finding design riches in the process. And he said to Traiger, "I suspect that [underneath the paint here] there is an abundance of decoration."

The point seemed moot. There was no money to restore the interior. As it was, Canning felt as if he had come on rather strongly, pointing out that architects of the Victorian period always paid as much attention to the inside as the outside, and that restored inside decoration would add a dimension to the building that would be dramatic and wonderful. He came on, he recalls, "like a maniac." But his earnestness, professionalism and his lingering accent (he refers, for example, to "refer" as "refair") were irresistible.

Canning asked for and received permission to spend time at his own expense to undertake preliminary research. And so, just to the left of the front doors, he applied solvents, and carefully and slowly circled his way through a synagogue's history.

Over the course of the next two days, the paint gave way to another layer, then another, and another and another. More than a dozen in all. In his circular motion, he created "craters," which allowed him, with the aid of a magnifying glass, to examine cross-sections. So many applications of paint were evident, he began to wonder if his prediction had been right. That's when he came across a pattern in silver, a stencil design from a period in the early 20th Century when aluminum leaf was often used. Canning was ecstatic. He wanted to announce his discovery, to accost people in the downtown streets with his news. But there was more work to do. His crater indicated more paint beneath it — perhaps there was another design. Indeed, Canning found stenciling featuring an Arabesque motif, with patterns in salmon, turquoise, gray and white. But this wasn't the original, either. Beneath this, he was thrilled to find the pattern employed when the synagogue first opened its doors: "classical complimentary colors, of orange, blue, yellow, green, maroon. A wonderful harmony of these colors."

For John Canning, this was a research jackpot. But in terms of spiritual value, even Canning, who spends his professional life in former centuries, was unaware of the full measure of richness, and of the metaphors for today, that he had uncovered.

"A Christian heritage"

We live, we like to think, in a sophisticated, civilized state. And so it is jarring to learn that according to Connecticut's Constitution, revised in 1818, only Protestants (and not Methodists, at that) were explicitly allowed to assemble publicly for worship. There were no provisions for Catholics. Nor were there for Jews or Muslims, partly because, the legislators asked, why would such people come here?

Well, Jews did come here, seeking greater opportunity and religious freedom, from Russia and England and Germany and other countries. Some settled in Colchester on farms, and some in Hartford, where many became merchants, and where they tried to carry on their traditions but prayed in people's homes because they could not legally pray anywhere else.

In the early 1840s Hartford was a city of about 15,000, and already it had a lot to recommend it as a center of commerce and culture. Charles Dickens visited during his American tour. Noah Webster, born in Hartford, had contributed mightily with his new dictionary to the literacy of millions of immigrants. Washington College, later renamed Trinity College, stood on what is now the site of the Capitol. Hartford had been a venue for the trial of rebellious slaves that had been transported to America aboard The Amistad, slaves who were ultimately freed.

So what if, among the general populace, a certain thoroughfare in town was known as "Jew Street?" Or that, down at the Capitol (now the Old State House), where eloquent arguments were made on behalf of slaves shipped to this country in chains, there were arguments against those who would practice religious rites outside the Christian mainstream?

In 1843, Lewis Rothschild, a member of the Jewish community, petitioned the Legislature's Judiciary Committee to amend the Constitution to allow public worship. The debate that followed was not recorded, but, based on what was known at the time, legal scholar Margaret Richards, at the request of the Charter Oak Cultural Center, recreated the arguments in opposition as they were likely to have been presented:

Origen S. Seymour (Litchfield): "I remind you it was we native Americans, we Yankees, who began this nation, fought and won its battles in the Revolution and in Mr. Madison's War and have held its republican, Christian principles ever since... By ratifying the Constitution with the specific designation Christian, it was clear that this is indeed to be a Christian state then and now. Therefore, we are duty-bound to use our power and authority to guard that great heritage ... In 1818 it was said there were no Jews, Mohammedans or Turks in Connecticut. Since that time we have seen some come, but they are different from us Americans. They speak another language; they don't look like us; they separate themselves into their own enclaves; and now they want to build their own places to practice their own religions and bury their dead in the sacred soil for which our forefathers gave their lives ..."

Scarborough Osgood (Pomfret): "As our Puritan forefathers said, it is a 'city set upon a hill' and 'a light to all men.' People from other countries must have wanted to be like us, or they would not have left their homelands to come here.... I hear now that Jews don't even keep our Sabbath laws. I'm told they close their doors on Saturdays but all are wide open for business on Sundays — the Lord's Day. That is against the law!... Perhaps most of them will not stay here, but will return whence they came. And for those who do decide to stay, they certainly have the privilege of joining our Christian churches."

A long time ago, yes, but such exclusionary attitudes are certainly imaginable when you consider that even as recently as November 1995, Gov. John G. Rowland stressed the connection between Thanksgiving and our state's "Christian heritage."

Those who argued in the 1840s that the federal government outlawed discrimination on the grounds of religion were reminded that the state's constitution took precedence. But in the end, tolerant views prevailed — arguments on behalf of equal treatment, and accounts by those legislators who averred that they had heard of or known Jews who were industrious. It is possible, too, that someone may have pointed out the enlightenment just across the border in Rhode Island, where as early as the 1600s Roger Williams had urged freedom of expression for all people and where the Touro Synagogue had been established in Newport.

Although the Connecticut Legislature did not amend the Constitution, it enacted a new law permitting Jews to pray in public. And so in succeeding years in Hartford the new congregation met in a renovated church called Touro Hall until, with a membership of 78 families, its members had the resources to build a place of their own.

Board meeting minutes from that era are kept in the archives at Temple Beth Israel in West Hartford, which, with the need for more space for religious education for children, is where the congregation moved in 1935, selling the old temple to a Baptist congregation. These minutes reveal the large and small questions that had to be answered, from the branch of Judaism to practice (Reform), to the prayer books to be used (which caused an emotional split in the congregation), to the donation of several hundred dollars to the victims of the Chicago Fire, to the finances of a new building, to simply paying ordinary bills.

From the yearly congregation meeting, held April 25, 1875:

"Several sites for building a synagogue were presented and it was unanimously decided to recommend purchasing the following piece: The site is on the south side of 150 Charter Oak Street ... The price is $125 per foot with the privilege to buy 100 feet of it ..."

Also from that day's minutes:

"A letter from Mr. M. Oppenheimer was read asking to give him a $50 raise as organist, which had been promised last year. It was decided to set the salary of Mr. Oppenheimer at $200 per year. Then five members were nominated as Trustees: Jos. Schwab, Isaak Goldschmidt, Abr. Hollander, Tobias Kohn, G. Fox." (The latter was Gershon Fox, founder of a dry goods store on Main Street that would become a Hartford institution over the next century.)

Other minutes reflect the board's decision to hire George Keller, the Hartford architect (who also designed the Soldiers and Sailors Monument and buildings at what is now called the Institute of Living).

In September, 1875, at the laying of the Congregation Beth Israel's cornerstone, thousands of Hartford residents came by to wish the new synagogue well. Mayor Sprague said, "Here is to arise a monument reminding all who behold it of the religious freedom which is our country's pride ..." One year later, the inaugural service was held in the first sanctuary in Connecticut built specifically as a place where The Torah — containing the five books of Moses, hand-written in Hebrew — could be chanted, discussed, and celebrated.

The meaning of "Spic"

John Canning's excitement over his discovery of the original designs at the Charter Oak Cultural Center remained a private affair for many years. His daughter, Jackie Riccio, who works with him, remembers that drawings and plans for the restoration, developed with the help of a small stipend from Charter Oak, were kept in the basement of the house, and that her father hoped that one day he would be able to restore the interior to the splendor of the opening day.

But the effort to simply keep the building and its community programs afloat was the primary concern of the directors of Charter Oak: Vivian Zoe, Davis Fox, and, for the last several years, Anthony Keller. Even ordinary maintenance required aggressive fund-raising, although the center did benefit from an endowment provided by the Auerbach Foundation (begun by Beatrice Fox Auerbach, who for 35 years ran the department store her grandfather started).

Still, as the years passed, a clear vision emerged. Charter Oak would provide a meeting ground for people of many cultures to learn about each other's traditions and aspirations. And to learn about their own.

A few years ago, Anthony Keller, who aside from his directorship has been a board member since the early days, suggested modifying the name by dropping the word "Temple," which he argued was misleading — some people still thought it was a Jewish institution. With that, and with aggressive programs and campaigns for community awareness, the center's popularity has grown.

Over the past few years it has been a place where blacks and Latin Americans have been able to find programs pertinent to their own lives, and where they have learned to embrace their art and literature. It is where they have been inspired to overcome bigoted attitudes and disheartening conditions.

It is the place where last spring the Hartford artist Carlos Hernandez Chavez created a mural to honor the city's nearly 200 homicide victims from 1989 to 1995. The "Wall of Forgiveness" displayed their names. Soon after it was created, relatives of the victims were invited to whitewash the mural, as a way to symbolically address their pain and move on.

The center (along with Real Art Ways) helped bring to Hartford the Mexican-American author and community activist Louis J. Rodriguez. The former gang member told his Bulkeley High audience that, in the hopeless streets of Los Angeles, "I was willing to die for very little," and how, through his writing, he was able to turn his life around. One student asked Rodriguez, "Did you ever kill anyone?" to which he replied, "If I did, I didn't know it," which indicated to the kids that

Rodriguez had indeed pulled a trigger. Anthony Keller remembers, "He got so close to [the students'] own raw nerves. They could see him as a sensitive guy who got embroiled in gang life, that there was not only a value in expressing himself in poetry, but that it saved his life. And it inspired them to write their own poetry."

One recent night, poet Tino Villanueva read his poem, "Scene From The Movie GIANT," in which, as a child, he felt greatly diminished by the bigotry evident on the screen when three Mexicans walked into the bar to accompanying scowls; that night at Charter Oak, the offending scene was shown. At a Puerto Rican cultural affirmation conference there, the distinguished poet Martin Espada said that, growing up in New York, "I heard the word 'spic' more often than my own name." He said that Puerto Ricans often find it hard identifying with American culture because of so many negative images, and he offered suggestions on how to focus on things that are positive.

The center has hosted a Haitian "voudun" (voodoo) exhibit, and many memorable dance performances and art exhibitions. It displayed the photographs of Juan Fuentes-Vizcarrando, who has so well documented Hartford's Puerto Rican community. It sponsors a monthly poetry group, and has published the group's collection. In March, it will unveil (with the Connecticut Historical Society as its co-sponsor) the Hartford Black History Project, an ambitious retrospective of a community whose people and contributions have never been suitably portrayed.

Anthony Keller says the center demonstrates the continuing struggle of the disenfranchised: "What's remarkable to me is that the Jewish past, and the respect for tradition of freedom of expression, is completely compatible with the present-day use, and the people who come here are well aware of that.

"Our restoration and the development of the Hartford Black History Project comes from the same impetus: to provide the people in metropolitan Hartford with opportunities to hear the narratives that make this community a community.

"Sometimes we give tours in Spanish. We ask our kids if they know what a synagogue is. They say no. We ask if they know what a Jew is, and they will say no. So this place opens a dialogue, and the interest and respect become very strong. A lot of people look at the stenciling going on, and they have an elementary feeling of connection with the designs ... and care that a tradition is being preserved. Many people are trying to relate to traditions that have disappeared in their own lives. The center serves a metaphoric purpose, whether you are Jewish or not. The people who come here have increasing respect for the original builders and their struggle for recognition and the acknowledgement of the legitimacy of their system of beliefs. They understand if somebody else made a breakthrough, they can feel hopeful that it will happen to them, despite the racism and intolerance they suffer in their contemporary life."

The center wants to establish the building as a state and national historic site and educational center that will attract visitors drawn to such places as the Touro Synagogue in Newport or Ellis Island. It also wants to strengthen its program of multiculturalism.

Such worthwhile work does not always translate into great financial support. Traditionally, the arts in Hartford have been supported well, but in a way that reinforces the influence of European culture. Most of the money granted over the years by The Greater Hartford Arts Council, for example, has been to the "big six" — the Hartford Ballet, the Bushnell, the Connecticut Opera, the Hartford Symphony, Hartford Stage, the Wadsworth Atheneum. This has left dozens of smaller organizations, including places such as the Charter Oak Cultural Center that focus on the city's growing diversity and which create programs and exhibits designed to challenge conventional thinking, to compete for a small portion of the funds.

The undrab Victorians

As Charter Oak programs were planned and produced, John Canning waited patiently to return, and in the meantime plied his restoration trade at Connecticut's State Capitol, and the San Francisco Opera House, and the Court House in Little Rock, Ark., among other places.

In 1992, Charter Oak sponsored an exhibition called "Building an American Identity: Hartford Jews, 1843-1899." For that exhibit, Canning removed the paint from a small section of wall and created a remarkable visual demonstration of the layers of stenciled design beneath it, and of the rare opportunity to fully restore one of Hartfords historic institutions.

By then, of course, Canning had been able to find out something about what he had uncovered years before. In the last years of the 19th century, the synagogue, with its membership growing quickly, was expanded and rededicated, which accounts for the second layer of stenciling. It was easy to imagine the splendor of the place in those days

— perhaps at the 1899 Purim carnival, where the children were served popcorn and ice cream, and where the men smoked cigars.

And then there was the third layer of stenciling — the aluminum leaf — which turned out to be the work of no less than Louis Comfort Tiffany, who, among many other memorable things, had worked on the interiors of Mark Twain's house on Farmington Avenue.

But returning the temple to its Victorian majesty appeared to be merely a dream until two years after the "American Identity" exhibit. Then, at the urging of representative Edward Garcia, in whose 4th District the old temple stands, the state Legislature passed a bond issue and granted $200,000 for interior restoration (another $500,000 must be raised to finish the job). A contract to create stained-glass windows was given to the William Cummings Studio in North Adams, Mass. John Canning was hired, and with his crew, including his daughter Jackie, began the interior restoration.

The hardest part was the completion of the research. Canning is nothing if not meticulous, so he investigated the sanctuary for evidence of the complete design, sometimes foiled by materials that were faded or by walls damaged by moisture in the bema, the area where the congregation's rabbis had held forth. It was hard to verify the sequences of design. Still, Canning uncovered nuances and surprises, demonstrations of what once was. He found floral patterns in rich colors that were typically Victorian. He says, "Everyone thinks of the 'drab' Victorian period — but they had a wonderful sense of color that doesn't exist in the present day." The whole process required great attention to detail, not to mention (in the case of Jackie, who did all the actual stencil work) a steady hand and climbing to great heights on scaffolding.

And when this first stage was done, by late December, it created a new and highly spiritual aura for the old place.

The eyes have it

In the last stages of the restoration project, children from the city and the suburbs were invited to learn about the art of stenciling. And so, under the tutelage of Jackie Riccio and Susan Hoffman Fishman, Charter Oak's Jewish Heritage consultant, they spent two days on a special project.

Whitey Jenkins, the artist and sports historian and man of a thousand urban ideas, collaborated with Fishman on his mural project for the new Connecticut Childrens Medical Center. The stencil designs of the restoration seemed to suggest an idea for the hospital. And so

Hartford Courant file photo

*Beneath layers of paint, Jackie Riccio found evidence
of a rich and vibrant legacy.*

children from Betances School, across the street from Charter Oak, and
from Solomon Schecter Day School, a private Jewish school in West
Hartford, were asked to base their design on the image of an eye,
because, Fishman said, "the eye is an ancient symbol for warding off evil,
and the eye is the window of the world."

Jackie Riccio says, "The workshop let the children know the
history of the building and what architects do, and what painters and
carpenters do. And the kids had a chance to create their own childrens
hospital, be their own architects." They had a chance to find out, too,
about each other, and when it was over, these 10 children — Jewish
children from the suburbs and Hispanic and African-American children
from the city — hugged each other.

And they nodded their proud approval when they were told the
new hospital would indeed reflect their work, and when they were
advised to keep their copies of their stencil patterns "forever" because
one day, "People may come to you to ask how the hospital was designed.
And you will know."

Our little synagogue

I stand in the partially restored sanctuary of the Charter Oak Cultural Center and I am reminded of the charming little place in Deep River where I attend services on Friday nights.

In order to accommodate a growing congregation, we know we must build a new place. To do it, we are not obliged, like those who preceded us, to petition the state legislature for the right to do it. We simply must raise the money. And must demonstrate the taste and commitment of the early Jews of Connecticut. Whatever we build, I think that, as a tribute to freedom and to courage, our Congregation Beth Shalom should contain a hint of the beautiful design commissioned so long ago by the people of Congregation Beth Israel.

At the flower garden

On the night of Dec. 29, 1995, the Charter Oak neighborhood was invited to celebrate the first stage of the sanctuary rehabilitation. Volunteers served popcorn and apple juice. In the aisles, clowns juggled and made kids laugh. On the stage — or the refurbished bima — bands played Latin music and jazz. A rap singer performed. And jazz musician Alvin Carter Sr. (whose African name is "Abubakar") looked out over the audience and said that it was great to see "a flower garden of people."

These people noticed not only the festivities but the remarkable design that had been restored. They noticed, too, the beautiful stained-glass windows, even if they didn't necessarily notice the bottoms where the names of the donors are engraved (among them, the Ladies Deborah Society of Temple Beth Israel, and the State of Connecticut — on behalf of the Judiciary Committee of the Legislature in 1843).

This was a night for John Canning as well. After all that work, he was surprised by the uplifted feeling he had, a result of the brightness and the rich colors. He imagined that it was a feeling close to what the congregation must have felt on the first night of prayers. For him, there will be new projects in celebration of the old — he has been one of the few invited to bid on the restoration of the curved ceiling at Grand Central Station. But for now, he looked up at this work that he and his daughter had done and he beamed, for he had recovered a part of Hartford's history, a part that belongs not just to antiquarians or to Jews or the neighborhood's African-Americans and Puerto Ricans, but to everyone.

12

Clubbing

....

Colin McEnroe

Here is a January night, drizzly and warm. Out of the mist, the Volvos and Legends roll past the porte cochere of the Town and County Club on Hartford's Woodland Street and into the parking lot.

By ones and twos the members of the Twilight Club disembark and enter the Town and County's library. There is Hugh Macgill, dean of the University of Connecticut Law School, and Jim English, former chairman of Connecticut Bank and Trust and former president of Trinity College. There is writer-historian Ellsworth Grant, for years the "convenor" or leader of the club, and there is Charlie Todd, headmaster of Watkinson School and Grant's hand-picked successor when he quits his convenorship at the end of the year.

The Twilight Club assembles for drinks at 6 p.m., an early hour apparently established years ago when the group met at the Hartford Club and Bishop Walter Gray was a member. Some of the clubmen liked to drift into the downstairs bar to fortify themselves for the meeting, but Gray, who believed the leader of the state's Episcopalians could not afford to be seen downing bourbon in even a semi-public context, waited for the others in a private dining room.

The men in the bar began drifting upstairs to keep the bishop company, and the Twilight Club group cocktail hour was established.

So let's look in on one:

Dr. Robert Massey (retired dean of the University of Connecticut Medical School) talks to Dr. T. Stewart Hamilton (retired president of Hartford Hospital).

Humphrey Tonkin, president of the University of Hartford, talks to attorney Coleman Casey, who will later deliver a paper to the club on how Shostakovich, Bartok, Britten and other composers responded to World War II.

Jim Bowers, a lawyer with Aetna Life & Casualty, talks to John Springer (another former Hartford Hospital president).

At dinner, attorney Daniel "Put" Brown raises the likelihood that Patrick McCaughey (who is absent) will quit the club when he leaves his post as director of the Wadsworth Atheneum. Brown disingenuously offers to yield his spot in the lecturing rotation to McCaughey, so the club can squeeze one more paper out of him.

Members of the Twilight Club are, you see, required to present scholarly papers, on a complex rotation system that boils down to giving two papers every three years. McCaughey was recently scheduled to give one and rose with the sun that day to begin, with a deadbeat's desperation, last-minute preparations. He was rescued when a snowstorm plunged down on the city in the late afternoon.

Todd breaks in to suggest that McCaughey be persuaded instead to host the Twilight Club in the fall at the Yale Museum of British Art, the directorship of which is what lured McCaughey out of Hartford. We'll travel down in a small chartered bus, Todd says, perhaps having our cocktail hour en route.

Macgill and Tonkin become obsessed with the phrase "to cock a snook" (meaning to thumb one's nose) and where it came from. Macgill tours the rim of each dining table, asking if anybody knows. Nobody does.

As you might imagine, what "Waiting to Exhale" was for middle-class black women, the three recent screen adaptations of Jane Austen are for this group, so there is quite a lot of talk about that.

Oh! And here is another member of the club, a woman who, in power and prestige, outstrips any two or three other Twilight clubbers in combination. But she has asked that her presence in the club be kept secret, and I am going to honor her request because I have to live with these people long after you have put aside this magazine and moved on to other concerns. Unless, that is, they cut out my heart for revealing the secrets of the inner temple. You see, I, too, am a member of the Twilight Club.

"What?" you splutter. "What the heck is the Twilight Club, some kind of elitist self-massaging highbrow clique?"

Yes, as a matter of fact, it is. You got a problem with that?

Would you be surprised to know that Twilight is not the only elitist self-massaging highbrow club of its kind, that they sort of percolate through the city? There is also the all-white, all-male Monday Evening Club, whose members wear black tie to all meetings. For women, there are the Saturday Morning Club (which meets on Fridays — it's a long story, dearie), the Friday Club, the Thursday Club and the Monday Club.

McCaughey claims there is also something called Les Femmes de la Vie, and that every year, in some kind of charity event, they win a private, McCaughey-guided tour of the Atheneum, but nobody else has ever heard of them or seen them, giving rise to the suspicion that they are his Brigadoonish invention.

Won't you join us? The Twilight Club, at its 100th anniversary celebration, in 1986.

Most of these clubs formed and started spitting out papers during the first 25 years after the Civil War, and they have churned along for a century or so with few major changes at all save one, that being the massive aging of their memberships. I am a blushing, sprightly lad of 41, a typical age for a club member back in the 1890s, but I am the youngest, cutest Twilighter. The median age is probably somewhere north of 60.

Perhaps it's not fair to say there were no other major changes or reactions to the slow crawl of history. The Saturday Morning Club, for example, shut down for an entire year during World War I. And from what I can determine, the Monday Evening Club changed its blackballing policy in 1957 so that it took two blackballs to kill off a prospective candidacy. There's radical reform for you.

The Twilight Club was founded in 1886, a newcomer contrasted to the Monday Evening Club, founded in 1869.

The Monday Evening Club does not divulge its membership roll, but it includes United Technologies CEO George David, Fleet vice-chairman Joel Alvord, Robinson and Cole attorney Robert Smith and former Aetna chairman Olcott Smith. The Monday Evening Club meets in the homes of its members, who, as I said, wear black tie to dinner. (The Twilight Club dines at the Town and County, and the dress code has relaxed so much that hiking boots and gum shoes dominate during the winter months, and well-pressed jeans with a jacket and tie are not unthinkable. On the other hand, you've never seen so many bowties in your life.)

Mark Twain was a member of the Monday Evening Club, as were the Rev. Horace Bushnell and Charles Dudley Warner. William Gillette was in the Twilight Club. Twain also took it upon himself to act as mentor to the Saturday Morning Club, which was composed of lissome young women just out of secondary school when it was founded in 1876. Today its membership skews more toward women who read Ensure advertisements with a sense of acute personal interest.

What do these clubs do?

Well, they believe themselves to be "literary clubs," descendants of a self-massaging highbrow club founded by Samuel Johnson in 1764 and known (well before the age of auto theft) as "The Club."

These literary clubs actually require their members to present papers of a more or less scholarly nature. At the meetings of the Twilight and Monday Evening Clubs, the papers follow large quantities of food and spirits, which is perhaps why the Monday Evening Club limits papers to 20 minutes in length (which makes one wonder if, for example, Francis Watkinson Cole's 1961 paper "Chaucer" could have charted new territory on the subject).

The Twilight Club has no such time limit, but the person who discourses for an hour on, say, "The Decorative Arts of Belgium" risks addressing some of his or her later remarks to lolling heads. "At no time during any paper is every member of the Twilight Club awake," McCaughey is fond of telling outsiders.

What the clubs do not do, in any obvious way, is provide members with a quiet opportunity for mutually enriching transactions. Businesslike talk is mostly frowned upon, unless it's immensely entertaining.

"What I like is the fact that nobody's trying to get anything out of it," says writer and Twilighter Mally Cox-Chapman.

In fact, there is no surer way of screwing up one's chances for membership in a club than to appear to want it. The literary clubs seem to prefer — when possible — new members who have never even heard of the club until the moment they're asked.

"The first thing that piqued my interest was that I couldn't go to a meeting before I made my decision," said Lisa Johnson, a Farmington curator and museum consultant who was asked to join the Saturday Morning Club four years ago.

She joined. Johnson has given papers to the group on Samuel Colt's paternalism and on the Victorian craze for summer cottages.

Members of the literary clubs swear up and down that they are not snobbish or elitist. On the other hand, the whole point of any club — from the guys in Billy's tree house to the Council on Foreign Relations — is to allow a certain people to gather together at arm's length from Everybody Else, right?

I'll show you how right.

Here is a letter that bleeds anguish for the rotting state of the American mind.

Because of the circumstances under which I obtained this letter, I am not going to tell you the name of its author. You would, however, recognize the name if you had followed the affairs of Hartford's oligarchy for a couple of decades.

The letter was written in 1987 when the letter-writer had just received and reviewed a list of names of men under consideration for membership in the Monday Evening Club.

Our letter-writer has been asked to check off the names of five men on the list who would be worthy of further discussion. He cannot find the heart to do so.

"I do not think this will result in getting acceptable members," he complains, "since the list contains many names of agreeable gentlemen who would be acceptable members of a country club, a bath and tennis club, a Chamber of Commerce and such but not in my opinion the Monday Evening Club."

The agreeable men, he says, are not of a sufficiently literary disposition. He quotes Twain, who described (possibly with a twitch of playfulness missed by the letter-writer) the founders of the club as "men of large intellectual calibre and more or less distinction, local and national."

He mentions also Samuel Johnson's club (home to Sir Walter Scott, Alfred Lord Tennyson and Rudyard Kipling, among others).

"I fear that many of those listed ... are witnesses to the fact that those who suggested their names did not have a clear understanding of the type of person suitable for election," the letter bemoans. Ain't life a bitch?

Whatever happened to the great Hartford man of yesteryear, who could run an insurance company all day, then slip into a tux, show up to the monthly meeting, down a bit of champagne with his snipe, and then, if it was his turn, deliver a smashingly apt paper on the later odes of Horace?

Those men represent a certain amount of wishful thinking. The Hartford men who slurped turtle soup and claret at Monday Evening tables down through the years often bore such profitable names as Robinson, Cole, Day, Shipman, Brainard, Alsop and Cheney. They were well-born and well-to-do, but they were not necessarily scholars who would have passed Dr. Johnson's muster.

Yes, it is true that Austin Cornelius Dunham, who owned a hosiery company and was president of Hartford Electric Light, illuminated the Monday Evening Club on such topics as "Sir Thomas More and Utopia" (1880), "The Genesis and History of Death" (1900) and "Swedenborg and the Emperor William" (1916, his final undertaking).

It is also true, however, that members of the club have spoken on such profound literary matters as "Shall Government Control the Railroads?" (Henry Robinson, 1891), "Filtration of City Water Supplies" (Edward Root, 1909) and "The Art of Beagling" (Ostrom Enders, 1948).

Still, the letter gets at some more basic, savage truth about clubs.

With the act of welcoming in a chosen few to sit by the fire, a club leaves others to blink woefully in the darkness.

When farmer-writer-politician Roger Eddy was asked to join the Monday Evening Club in 1964, his father's reaction was not unalloyed joy. The senior Eddy, who had spent years feeling that his best efforts as a Hartford stockbroker were somewhat thwarted, was momentarily choked with a mixture of pride and envy upon hearing that his son would be entering an inner circle of privilege.

In a strangled voice, Eddy recalls, his father said: "I used to compete against those guys."

Eddy is now retired from the Monday Evening Club. No active member would speak with me for this article, and, indeed, the club is roughly as comfortable with publicity as the average Thuggee cult. It is so prestigious and exclusive that most people don't even know there's something prestigious they're excluded from. But the shifting politics of the times have cost the club some of its clout. Indeed, notable Hartford men have, in recent years, rebuffed overtures from the club because it is determinedly all-male (to say nothing of all-white).

One candidate, when he asked if the wife in whose house a meeting was held would at least be allowed to join in, was told, "No, but we think they usually sit on the stairs and listen to the papers." This turns out to be a received tradition. According to a 1970 private history written by Francis Goodwin II, from the earliest days it was customary for the wife to ask several friends to sit with her, "usually in the hall or on the stairs."

Which means in November of 1966, some lucky woman or women, clutching the banister in rapture, may have heard Ostrom Enders discourse for 20 minutes on "Management As An Honored Profession."

For a century or so, the members of the Twilight Club also were white and male to a man, as it were, but after a decade of social upheaval, the group has become a veritable Pepsi commercial of inclusiveness.

Alice DeLana broke the 103-year-old barrier in 1989, and she was perfectly suited for the job. She was, not insignificantly, the widow of Twilight Club member William DeLana and was herself for years a member of the Saturday Morning Club. After decades of teaching English and history of art at Miss Porter's School, DeLana had all the necessary intellectual credentials, more connections than an IBM mainframe and a blithe and bubbly spirit that glides over bumpy social situations.

It doesn't hurt that her papers are often quite stunning. Last spring she teased the club with a title, announced in advance, "Bring Back the Bishops." Most of the members assumed this referred to the baronial circle of business executives who guided the city as its uncrowned kings in the 1970s.

Because the very concept is as defunct as Buffalo Bill and because at least one bishop is still in the club, the paper promised to be both boring and uncomfortable.

It was instead a dazzling study of the parallel lives of the painter Isabel Bishop and the poet Elizabeth Bishop, who lived at the same time, weren't related, didn't know each other, yet shared coincidental passions. DeLana had discovered that, rather eerily, both women had turned, for ongoing inspiration, to the exact same line from Gerard Manley Hopkins: "Send my roots rain."

In the midst of her paper, DeLana coaxed Tonkin into an unplanned reading of the entire Hopkins sonnet, and the university president blew the room away.

When DeLana was voted in, a few of the club's grumpier old men made noises about spending their dying days in exile from the club but drifted back after a period of wound-licking. Three other women have subsequently been admitted, and last year Bowers became the club's first African-American member.

What am I doing in the Twilight Club?

McCaughey, the club's chief trouble-maker, asked me precisely that at my first meeting.

"McEnroe," he whispered conspiratorially, "what the hell are you doing in this antediluvian group?"

I don't know.

I like the Twilight Club.

It's the only club I've ever been asked to join, and I probably, on egalitarian grounds, should have refused the offer. But I was weak.

Lisa Johnson, speaking of the Saturday Morningers, says, "These women grow on you."

So it is with the Twilighters. One thing we do a lot is ask each other questions. Bowers is forever explaining complicated economic matters to me, and architect Jared Edwards has educated me on matters of design.

The dinner table is often a place of interesting arguments. McCaughey vs. Tonkin on Shakespeare. McCaughey vs. Macgill on Gladstone. McCaughey vs. Grant on whether sherry should be served with the soup course.

The papers are often quite startling, whether it is Massey on the cultural and medical history of tuberculosis or Brown on his own archaeological expedition to Alaska.

Cox-Chapman's paper on "Near-Death Experiences" touched off a spirited argument between her and McCaughey (are you noticing a repeated motif here?) about whether or not there is any convincing proof that heaven exists.

I missed Bowers' presentation on the history of black education in America, interlacing his own family's occasionally searing personal experiences. I am told I missed one of the best ever.

If none of the above sounds exactly like pulse-pounding excitement, all I can say is that, by the standards of the Preppy Establishment, this stuff is "The Silence of the Lambs."

Small Hartford literary clubs are so deep and dotty a topic as to warrant the sole consideration of this article, but I should mention a few of their equally peculiar cousins: The Acorn Club (which publishes small-scale works of historical interest), the Twentieth Century Club (a larger lecture-and-discussion group formed in 1892 as an outgrowth of the Twilight Club), and the 117-year-old Canoe Club, whose pursuits of river sport, beverage alcohol and card-playing are resolutely non-literary. As an especially delicious irony the only major literary figure to tarry in Hartford during this century, Wallace Stevens, belonged to the Canoe Club and no other. He apparently liked to sit on the porch of its East Hartford building and investigate new ways of looking at blackbirds with the aid of enormous containers of martinis.

But the Monday Evening and Twilight clubs, with 20 members each, are tiny organisms on the Hartford intellectual landscape compared with the four womens clubs, each of them 30 to 35 members strong, with commitments to scholarship that make their all- or mostly male counterparts look fainthearted.

Here is a pin, gold with an enamel spray of lilies.

It is the symbol of the Saturday Morning Club, and Mark Twain is said to have designed it.

When Twain wasn't palling around with the middle-aged men of the Monday Evening Club, he was, it appears, palling around with the young women of the Saturday Morning Club.

The club was founded in 1876, and Twain addressed it no fewer than 15 times. He was made an honorary member. His final return visit to Hartford after moving away was to speak to the Saturday Morning

Club on "Reading" in April of 1907.

The Saturday Morning Club spawned imitators, so that, after a decade or two, there were (and still are) the Friday Club, the Thursday Club and the Monday Club.

Further confusing matters, the Saturday Morning Club changed its meeting time, in the 1950s, to Friday mornings. According to DeLana, who wrote a short history of the club, some of the pressure on Saturday mornings came from husbands who complained Saturday meetings interfered with their getting off to an early start for Ivy League football games.

The women's literary clubs differ from the men's in several respects. While the men's clubs favor an odd mixture of genial anarchy and received traditions, the women's clubs have strictly adhered-to constitutions and bylaws. The Saturday Morning Club, for example, forbids the serving of any food at its Friday morning meetings. This, says its president Mary Dodd, keeps the women's appetites whetted for scholarship and staves off any thought of Martha Stewarty baking competitions.

"Sometimes women call and say: Can't I just serve muffins?" says Lisa Johnson.

None of this 20-minute paper stuff either. The women's papers are more typically twice that length and often require months of research.

"It is a serious intellectual group. They take it seriously, and there are no excuses," says Johnson. "The audience is quite critical, even more so than some of the academic groups I've been involved with. If you're writing about a Hartford subject, you really had better have your facts right. On matters of architectural style, I've been corrected by a person who knew the architect personally."

"We write two papers each year, a 40-minute and a 20-minute," says Katharine McLane of the Friday Club. "We're a little bit smug about that because the other clubs only write one."

The women's clubs also typically build each year around a theme, but it's very hip to respond creatively to the theme. For instance, the Thursday Club's theme this year is "Points of the Compass," but members have done papers on Benjamin West and "East of Eden."

The women's groups do not let eating, drinking or any other form of revelry get in the way of paper-writing, a nod to their roots. In Twain's day, when even well-born young women didn't often go to college, these clubs represented desperately needed oases in a landscape that was not designed with the intellectual stimulation of these women as one of its big priorities.

In their own way, in that long-ago day, the clubs were progressive. Now they seem just a trifle archaic. They continue to meet in the morning (except for the Monday Club, which has a luncheon meeting) in defiance of the fact that, for the past 25 years or so, a lot of women are working then.

They meet often, too, either twice a month or once a week in most cases. The result has been that the clubs, founded for women just beginning their adult lives, have become more comfortable places for women in their 60s and 70s.

"People come into the club at a later age," says McLane, a member of the Friday Club since 1944.

Some, like Johnson, join when their children are babies, as a way of keeping their minds alive in the welter of diapers and bottles, but the new generation seems to find some of the club traditions trying. "A Survival Guide for SMC Members," written a few years ago by some of the younger women, notes that the custom of having the person who is giving a paper also host the meeting "originated at a time when cleaning ladies and nursemaids were more ubiquitous and certainly cheaper than they are now."

Here is something for you to consider. McCaughey is almost certainly leaving the Twilight Club.

On some future night, not long hence, Grant will look around the table and ask if anyone has a name to put in nomination. If I mentioned yours, you'd wind up on a ballot along with a bunch of notables and semi-notables. We'd vote on you by mail, using a complicated system of first, second and third choices, which only Grant understands and which usually results in our picking somebody he likes.

If we voted you in, then every three weeks or so, roughly from October to May, you'd wander out into the night to hear somebody talk about the economic theories of Schumpeter or the architecture of Saarinen, and you'd increase your roast-beef intake, drink some red wine and grow ever more accustomed to the way tweed smells when its wet.

You should, naturally, tell us to take our highbrow, elitist, self-massaging club, fold it four ways and stick it where the moon don't shine.

And that's exactly what you'd do, right?

I said, right?

13

To The Tower

....

Steve Courtney

The journals were packed in a neatly labeled cardboard box. When I drew them out — there were 13, each of them blue, each the size of a paperback, each tied up with string secured with a delicate bowtie knot — it was like being in a stranger's attic, picking through the kind of private things people write down and pass on to their children, things perhaps unexamined for several generations.

It was as quiet as an attic, but the reading room was below ground level; a few scholars sat at tables broad enough to hold a whole spread of manuscripts and books. One wall of the room was glass, looking onto a sunken courtyard with a pyramid, with a huge marble Life Saver set on edge. What the writer of these journals, the captain of the Yale crew, Class of 1859, would have said about Yale's Beinecke Rare Book and Manuscript Library, I can't imagine. His rotund, delicate Victorian penmanship displays the aesthetics of a different era.

The journals had been filled daily and carefully over more than 40 years by the Rev. Joseph H. Twichell, who was pastor of the Asylum Hill Congregational Church in Hartford from 1865 to 1912. Twichell has a permanent corner in literary history as Mark Twain's best friend. They met when Twain was on a visit to the city in 1868. Twichell married Samuel Clemens to Olivia Langdon in Elmira, N.Y., in 1870; he performed their daughter Clara's wedding ceremony in 1909. He presided over the funerals of three of the Clemens children, then over Olivia Clemens' funeral, and finally over Twain's own.

I was looking through the journals for references to the walk the two men took as a regular Saturday outing during the 25 years Twain lived in the city. They walked from Farmington Avenue, where the Mark

Twain House is a museum today (Twichell lived just up Woodland Street at No. 125), to the top of Talcott Mountain in Simsbury, where Heublein Tower now stands, a distance of about 8 miles.

Heublein Tower is a 1913 newcomer, but in the 1870s there was a tower there, too: a wooden one kept as a tourist attraction by one Matthew H. Bartlett. Twain and Twichell would rest there, perhaps have a drink and a meal at the saloon Bartlett kept, and walk home again. If time was short, they would walk the couple of miles to Bloomfield and catch one of the frequent trains to the city.

And they would talk. "Mark Twain says he and Mr. Twichell always return to Hartford after one of these jaunts with the jaw ache, but never footsore," reads an 1874 newspaper account.

Why not get a few people together and retrace the walk? When I told Lisa Johnson, the curator of Heublein Tower — which is still a popular goal of shorter autumn sightseeing walks — about this idea, she liked it. "Sometimes we think Mark Twain just stayed in the Mark Twain House all the time," she said. And so it was that on an October morning John Boyer, Jim Kidd and I set out from the humorist's fantastic brick house on Farmington Avenue on our way to Talcott Mountain and the Tower.

> *I have always practiced doubtful things on*
> *Twichell from the beginning.*
> Mark Twain, Autobiography

Why did Mark Twain, the blasphemer, the author of "Letters from the Earth" and other dark books in which he took God to task for his cruelty, have a minister for his best friend?

"It seems a strange association, perhaps, the fellowship of that violent dissenter with that fervent soul dedicated to church and creed," wrote Twain's first biographer, Albert Bigelow Paine, in 1912; "but the root of their friendship lay in that frankness with which each man delivered his dogmas and respected those of his companion."

In the winter of 1868-69, Twain was in Hartford to work on the manuscript of "The Innocents Abroad" with his publisher. According to Paine, the young, relatively unknown humorist was attending a reception where conversation turned to the fashionable new church, where many of the Hartford's financial movers and shakers preened and worshiped.

"The Church of the Holy Speculators," Twain loudly dubbed it. His hostess whispered that the church's minister was standing behind him, and tried to patch things up by introducing them.

Twain was invited to Twichell's after the party, politely rose to leave at 9:30, and stayed until 11.

"He enjoyed not only Clemens' humor but also his bawdiness and profanity," writes Justin Kaplan, Twain's best modern biographer, "and in return [Twichell] preached to him a kind of muscular and nondoctrinal Christianity." Twichell had learned this approach as chaplain to a New York regiment during the Civil War and in the fires of reform in the Congregational Church, a movement led by Hartford's Horace Bushnell.

Twain later put Twichell, under the name Harris, into his travel book "A Tramp Abroad," and the novelist Russell Banks recently drew parallels in the New York Times Book Review between the two men's friendship and Huckleberry Finn's friendship with the slave Jim. Banks, who is married to Twichell's great-grand-daughter, wrote that they were all "American males clearly blessed with the gift of friendship, of giving it and receiving it and holding onto it."

Twain took refuge from his busy Hartford social life at Twichell's house on Woodland Street in the 1880s, even when the house was full of children (Twichell and his wife Harmony had nine) and carpenters. "It's like a boiler factory for racket," he wrote while at work on "A Connecticut Yankee in King Arthurs Court," "and in nailing a wooden ceiling on to the room under me the hammering tickles my feet amazingly sometimes and jars my table a good deal, but I never am conscious of the racket at all, and I move my feet into positions of relief without knowing when I do it."

There are cognitive psychologists who believe that the parts of the brain that control the creation of language are the parts that our ape ancestors used to grab bananas with their hands and feet. If Twain's colossal powers of storytelling — "The perfect art of a certain kind of story telling will die with him," Twichell wrote in his journal after a dinner party — could be improved by such foot-tickling, then what would an 8-mile walk do?

> *With M.T. to Bloomfield by rail, thence afoot to the Tower,*
> *and back afoot home to this house to dine at 6 1/2 o'clock.*
> *Splendid exercise and lots of pleasant talk.*
> Twichell's Journal, Oct. 26, 1874

If people find it hard to picture Mark Twain outside his house, it is certain that John Boyer spends too much time there. Or so he said, phoning his wife to see if he could take off an October Saturday when he was supposed to help paint the kitchen.

"It's OK," he told her. "I can take a weekday off and paint then. This is work. I always say I have to get out more."

Boyer is the director of the Mark Twain House, and has put his institution firmly into the community — keeping the place humming with activity, be it Roy Blount Jr. on Southern humor or a recent symposium for teachers on the racial issues raised by "The Adventures of Huckleberry Finn." Almost every time I call him, he's in a meeting.

When I invited him to join the walk, he said he had always wanted to do it. Whether his wife grudged him the lost Saturday of painting is not clear, but she did suggest that we invite Jim Kidd.

There would be some real symmetry in that. Kidd is the present-day pastor of the Asylum Hill Congregational Church, and another exponent of a muscular and non-doctrinal Christianity. Since 1979 his church has been a force for aid to the city's poor — as it was in Twichell's day — and has increased in attendance fourfold. It's Boyer's church, too. Though Boyer and I wondered: We're in our 40s; Kidd, we figured, was in his 50s. Would it be too much for him? Could he keep up?

"I've always wanted to do it," Kidd said on the telephone a couple of days later. He has been interested in the friendship of writer and minister and once preached a sermon called "Twixt Twain and Twichell." He warned me that he had to get back in time to officiate at the church's Saturday evening service. I suggested an alternate day. "No, just assume I'll be there," he said.

Nobody seemed to have any idea how long it would take to walk from the Mark Twain House to Heublein Tower in Talcott Mountain State Park. It's just not a route people walk anymore. The park personnel had bets going, Johnson, the Heublein curator, told us as the date approached: The shortest time estimate was five hours.

But first we had to figure out what route to take. Did they walk up what's now Route 44, and then along the ridge of Talcott Mountain? Or was there a route through the woods, long lost?

A clue came from a reference to the walks in Paine's 1912 biography: "Sometimes they took the train as far as Bloomfield, a little station on the way, and walked the rest of the distance, or they took the train from Bloomfield home." That put the route to Bartlett's tower roughly the same as the route one would take to Heublein Tower today: out of town along Albany Avenue, to Bloomfield Avenue, and then along

Route 185 up the mountain to the park entrance. From there, Johnson said, the footpath to the summit and the tower follows the carriage road Bartlett put in for excursionists.

> *For Mr. Bartlett, who has robbed the historical command*
> *Away with him to the Tower! of all its terrors.*
> Mark Twain, inscribed in a book presented to Matthew H. Bartlett

Bartlett erected his tower in 1867 because of the healthful air — he had lung problems — and the magnificent view available from the Talcott Mountain ridge. "The Farmington River Valley lies before one in all its extent," a Philadelphia traveler wrote in the 1870s, "the white churches and farm-houses in pleasing contrast with the darker colors of the trees and meadows — the fields, some covered with their treasures of waving grain, others from which the summer's harvest has already been reaped and housed, now displaying all the various shades of green and

Hartford Courant file photo

The Heublein Tower has been rebuilt, but it's still a
long walk from Hartford.

yellow, with here or there one just tinged with brown." To the east was Hartford, "its towers and graceful spires rising among the beautiful elms and maples which shade its streets."

Omnibus parties from Hartford would drive to the tower, or whole towns of walkers, or the girls from Miss Sarah Porter's school in Farmington. Buffalo Bill Cody visited, and Harriet Beecher Stowe.

Jim Kidd and John Boyer found themselves in the footsteps of Twain and Twichell.

Clemens and Twichell were among "my most faithful and frequent visitors," Bartlett wrote many years later. It was an age when people could walk long distances without having to call it "hiking."

"The middle-aged and the elderly walked constantly, for pleasure and health, and the boys tackled marathon distances," wrote Kenneth Andrews in "Nook Farm: Mark Twain's Hartford Circle." Twain and Twichell started on a walk to Boston in November 1874, but Twain's feet gave out and they ended up taking the train. (Twichell, however, walked nine miles from Boston the next morning to preach a sermon in Newton Highlands.) Twain was a celebrity by then, and his walk was well-covered in the press.

"It has long been the custom of these two gentlemen to take walks of about ten miles in the vicinity of Hartford for the purpose of enjoying a social chat and exchanging views on nothing in particular and everything in general," says one of the Boston newspaper accounts, carefully clipped by Twichell and inserted in his journal.

One Twain-Twichell walk had serious repercussions for literary history. In 1874, a few weeks before the Boston attempt, Twain had a severe case of writer's block. His friend and editor, William Dean Howells, had been asking him for a story for the January issue of the Atlantic. "I find that I can't," Twain wrote him on an October morning. "We are in such a state of weary and restless confusion that my head won't 'go.' So I give it up."

Two hours later, he wrote another letter: "I take back the remark that I can't write for the Jan. number. For Twichell & I have had a long walk in the woods & I got to telling him about old Mississippi days of steamboating glory & grandeur… He said 'What a virgin subject to hurl into a magazine!' I hadn't thought of that before."

The articles ultimately became Twain's "Life on the Mississippi." Twichell writes of this same day in his journal: "Had a long walk with M.T. in the P.M."

Went on another walk to the Tower with M.T. Lots of pleasant talk.
Never thought even to allude to the great Democratic victory.
Twichell Journals, Nov. 4, 1874

It threatened rain on the October morning that we started out. It had been agreed that we would not try to make the walk round-trip. But there are no longer trains to hop in Bloomfield, so we left my car at Heublein Tower and drove to the Mark Twain House in Boyer's. As we got out, Jim Kidd, whose face always seems to me to be defined by piercing, shrewd eyes, permanent laugh lines and an absolutely defeating smile, joined us, looking a little like a power boat captain in his blue-striped shirt, white ducks and maroon cap, a bag slung over his shoulder.

Boyer's face is boyish and round, set off by a near-Victorian brown moustache, though nothing as flamboyant as Twain's (which along with his hair was red in the early days in Hartford, despite our present-day image of his mane as perpetually white.) Boyer's clothes were sporty, knit shirt, khaki shorts, fanny pack. I was more forest-rangerish, jeans, grey shirt, work boots, red backpack. None of us wore the ties and jackets, puttees, dresses and ballooning bloomers that were de rigueur among Victorian walkers who had never heard of Eastern Mountain Sports.

We walked up Woodland Street and crossed Asylum. We stopped at a bridge over the railroad tracks: This was the right-of-way to Bloomfield, and might take passengers there again if the Griffin light-rail line is ever built to Bradley airport. As Woodland approached Albany, we saw the signs of decay: empty buildings, trash-strewn lots: "What a loss, what an opportunity lost," Boyer said wistfully.

So what did they talk about? Leah Strong, a professor at Wesleyan College in Georgia, wrote the only biography of Twichell in the 1960s; she opined that their conversations on these walks were "of a light nature, not involving serious thought or decisions." Paine disagrees: "They discussed philosophies and religions and creeds, and all the range of human possibility and shortcoming, and all the phases of literature and history and politics."

The unknown 1874 Boston newspaper writer whose work Twichell pasted into his journal may have been the only one to get close to this. He asked Twain. Twain told him "that Mr. Twichell sometimes gains ideas from his companion which he embodies in his sermons and Mark Twain obtains information from his pastor which he works up into comical and humorous stories, and makes note of every joke which unconsciously falls from the clerical lips."

All we know from the journal is that on Nov. 4, 1874, they did not discuss the main news of the day: The crushing defeat of the Republican party in Congressional elections, the first sign that the populace was getting fed up with corruption of the Grant administration. Twichell, Twain and most of their Hartford friends and associates were Republicans, revering the memory of Lincoln and hating the memory of slavery, so it was a grim day for them. Their neighbor Charles Dudley Warner, editor of The Courant (who first showed Twichell the walk to the Tower) editorialized that the defeat was a judgment on their party and they had better reform it.

They didn't, and the country was on a slide that three years later led to reaction: in order to get into office, a Republican president had to make compromises with the Democrats that essentially returned black people in America to a form of slavery for the next 90 years.

Fast-forward to our walk of October 1995: It was two days before the Million-Man-March, and Kidd dubbed us "the Three-Man March." Boyer asked me what I thought about it; some things he had read in The Courant had disturbed him, seemed too uncritically approving. I told him I thought the march was a valid expression of a group of people who had been historically disenfranchised and had been facing a vicious reaction in recent years. Kidd agreed, but for Boyer, as for many, black and white, the fascistic trappings of the marches organizer, Louis Farrakhan and the dis-invitation of women stuck in the throat. (We had invited curator Johnson on our march, but she said she'd meet us near the Tower for the last leg.)

We stopped at Scott's bakery on Albany Avenue for a West Indian goat-meat pie; Boyer bought a couple of sweet buns and dangled them from his fanny pack.

The atmosphere is very hazy, and it makes the autumn tints even more soft and beautiful than usual. Mr. Twichell came for Mr. Clemens to go walking with him; they returned at dinner-time, heavily laden with autumn leaves.
Olivia Langdon Clemens, early 1870s

We passed Thomas, the boarded-up Cadillac and Jaguar dealership, moved for reasons of theft problems, Kidd said, to the North Meadows. The owner, one of his parishioners, had once let him take the wheel of a $30,000 vehicle. Kidd told us of another parishioner at the other end of the spectrum, a man with a prison record, now a tireless worker for the church. He sported a tattoo on his chest of a headsman with a bloody axe. "Great for prison showers," said Boyer.

Then we crossed the North Branch of the Park River and the urban landscape changed, as it can so quickly in Hartford, into the well-kept lawns and stately trees of Scarborough Street and environs. "I could just see Donna Reed or Katharine Hepburn stepping out of one of those houses," says Kidd, pointing to a particularly white-clapboarded one veiled with red and yellow leaves. "Isn't that the perfect New England autumn scene?"

As we headed out Bloomfield Avenue — the skies ambivalent about what they were planning for us — sidewalks dwindled as Tudor houses gave out. We were now walking along the shoulder of a road that, in Twain's day, was a well-traveled country road. But it was not populated by these overpowered metal monsters that rushed toward us as we walked among the detritus of hub cap and road kill.

On Route 185, Simsbury Avenue, we began to see old farmhouses marked with dates from the 1700s and early 1800s. Blocking off the asphalt and internal combustion to our right, we might, for the first time, be seeing something like the scene Twain and Twichell saw along the route.

And in the fall… when Twichell and I resumed the Saturday ten-mile walk to Talcott Tower and back, every Saturday, as had been our custom for years, we used to carry that letter along.
Mark Twain, Autobiography

When we were planning the walk, Boyer had said, almost first of all, "We have to bring along '1601,' " and so we did.

"1601: Conversation as it Was by the Social Fireside, in the Time of the Tudors," is a short work by Mark Twain that will probably never sit on the shelves next to "Tom Sawyer" in children's libraries. It is, to put it bluntly, a dirty book. Twain wrote it in 1876 as a letter to Twichell. He had been reading old English books while researching "The Prince and the Pauper" and was pleasantly surprised by the natural and obscene speech found in them; Twain was always interested in how other ages undercut the Victorian stuffiness of his own. He thought he'd try writing his own piece of Elizabethan bawdry.

"I thought I would practice on Twichell," Twain remembered many years later. "I have always practiced doubtful things on Twichell from the beginning."

The tryout site was on the walk to the Tower. "There was a grove of hickory trees by the roadside, six miles out, and close by it was the only place in that whole region where the fringed gentian grew. On our return from the Tower we used to gather the gentians, then lie down upon the grass upon the golden carpet of fallen hickory leaves and read it by the help of these poetical surroundings. We used to laugh ourselves lame and sore."

"1601" defies synopsis; suffice it to say that Queen Elizabeth, Shakespeare, Sir Walter Raleigh and sundry other Elizabethan characters are sitting around talking, and one of them breaks wind. Several pages of dialogue are required to determine the perpetrator; then the conversation shifts to the sexual customs of various lands and times; building to a final put-down line by the Virgin Queen herself that still can't be printed in a family newspaper.

We had gotten a little bawdy ourselves, as we made our way up the old Simsbury Road. Like Twichell, Kidd showed a fine delight in the grossly obscene. Perhaps it was nervousness at the closeness of the traffic, perhaps it was the simian stimulation of our feet prodding our cerebral storytelling centers, perhaps it was just the bonhomie of three men released from their usual Saturday rounds. We were, in a way, lighting out for the territory. Anyway, we told jokes.

Rather than in a hickory grove, it was under a maple tree in a field at the Bloomfield 4-H farm where we rested to eat our lunch. I was about to suggest reading "1601" aloud, but Boyer alerted us to the sky, which was glowering.

Soon it was pouring. Boyer had a poncho, Kidd had a windbreaker

and I had only a hat borrowed from Boyer. It was a hard uphill now.
Boyer and I puffed along behind, hugging the guard rail, as Kidd strode
farther and farther ahead. "I'm glad to see he's able to keep up with us," I
said, as we watched his receding form. Muscular Christianity indeed.

We made time. We wanted to get dry, and were wet. The metal
monsters that tickled our right elbows shone their lights in our eyes as
their startled drivers spotted this trio of lunatics on the narrow shoulder.

> *Oh wake up, wake up! wake up! Don't sleep all day!*
> *Here we are at the Tower, man! I have talked myself deaf and dumb*
> *and blind... Just look at this magnificent autumn landscape!*
> *Look at it! look at it! Feast your eyes on it!*
> The Rev. Mr. — , in Mark Twain's "A Literary Nightmare," 1876

Most of the hikers were scurrying through the rain for their cars as
we entered Talcott Mountain State Park and walked up the last portion
of the path that leads toward Heublein Tower. Suddenly, we were on the
ridge. The rain stopped: against a gray backdrop, bathed with subdued
light, what Victorian travelers called the Royal View was before us.

Where they saw steeples, fields and harvesters we saw forest and
hills, light industry and asphalt; but a few steeples poked up, and a few
tobacco barns, and we could ignore the pop, pop, pop of the state police
shooting range below the cliff. The royalty of the view was still the same,
the golds and russets receding into distant haze, the many shades of
brown, the deep greens and shadows and light.

Lisa Johnson, who had helped set us on this trail months before,
and Pat Heublein were there to meet us, and led us to a table set with
cider, hot chocolate and doughnuts. Not, perhaps, what Twain or
Twichell would have wanted to find, but it was welcome. (Kidd had said
he would bring cigars. But he had decided against it; he might start
smoking again.) We paid a visit to an iron bolt sticking from a foundation
stone a few hundred yards south of Heublein Tower — the only
remaining trace of Bartlett's Tower.

The Tower volunteers were very attentive and interested, and
pressed more doughnuts on us, and there was talk of museums and grants
and church business, so it was not until we got into my Toyota that we
could be boys again. The four of us — we had been joined by
photographer Tony Bacewicz, who had dogged our steps in his car but
joined us on foot for the last mile — listened to "1601" read aloud in turn
by Boyer, Kidd and Bascewicz. We laughed ourselves lame and sore.

— On being shown the president's house
at Trinity College, Twain observed,

*"It has a Queen Anne front,
and a Queen Anne behind."*

The Mark Twain House
Hartford, Connecticut

14
Thy, Theo

....

Jim Farrell

Only the voices are missing.

Theodate Pope Riddle died more than 50 years ago, but her beloved Hill-Stead remains intact — as though she were simply away on a trip, perhaps gone to Europe again, or off designing yet another wonderful school.

The rooms remain filled with the artwork of Manet and Monet, Degas and Whistler. The furniture — a cherry Biedermeier sofa, a Chippendale secretary — has not been moved, nor the linen replaced. Theodate's dresses hang still in the closet off her bedroom.

Hill-Stead, which Theodate helped design almost a century ago, is a museum now. Thousands visit every year. They savor the paintings of the French Impressionists. They learn about one of America's first female architects, a woman who designed Westover and Hop Brook and Avon Old Farms schools. They discover, on this hill in Farmington, a remarkable farmstead built in Colonial revival style where nothing, it seems, has changed in half a century.

Only the voices are missing. The voices of Theodate and her husband, John Wallace Riddle. The voices of Theodate's parents, Alfred Atmore Pope and Ada Brooks Pope.

It was Alfred Pope who, in 1898, purchased these acres and entrusted Theodate with the responsibility of arranging, through a distinguished New York architectural firm, construction of Hill-Stead. The president of an iron conglomerate, Alfred had amassed a good deal of wealth and in the late 1880s became a serious collector of art. He settled on Farmington as the site for the home into which he'd retire in part because Effie had attended Miss Porter's School in town. (Theodate was christened Effie, but thought the name undignified and took, when she was 20, her paternal grandmother's name.)

The extent of Theodate's influence on the design of Hill-Stead is unclear, although it was apparently significant. In any case, this "great new house on a hilltop," as Henry James, an occasional visitor, called it, was worthy of the artistic treasures inside. "An exquisite palace," James wrote in a letter to Theodate, "of peace, light and harmony."

After the completion of Hill-Stead in 1901, Theodate continued her architectural pursuits. She designed Westover School in Middlebury, where her friend Mary Hillard was the first headmistress. Theodate's work at Hop Brook in Naugatuck, completed in 1916, was significant for its separate kindergarten building with low sinks and fountains — the better to accommodate children. And in 1921 she began the design of Avon Old Farms, using as a model a small English village. This, Theodate believed, was her masterpiece — enormous chimneys, irregular eaves, roofs that appeared to sag. "A natural variation in line and surface," she felt, "was far more desirable in this work than accuracy."

Theodate's father died in 1913, her mother in 1920. Theodate herself married, in 1916 at age 49; John Wallace Riddle was a career diplomat. They had no children, but shortly after the marriage Theodate agreed to bring up two young boys in the household, and she gained enormous satisfaction from the experience.

There was so much more, of course, and the correspondence that Theodate has left behind reveals a woman of tremendous gumption and determination. She wrote, in a letter to her mother in 1915, about a trip to the State Capitol in Hartford for a hearing on the suffrage bill. "I have no idea that our conservative state will pass it, but we must all do our duty," she wrote. "I told Mrs. Hepburn [mother of Katharine, the actress] that I was sorry I could not make a speech but that I would gladly throw a brick if it would help in showing my seriousness."

In another letter to her mother, Theodate recounts a request from a publishing company for a photograph to be included in a book of prominent architects. "You will be most amused to know that I was called up by telephone by their office and a masculine voice at the other end asked incredulously if I really were Theodate Pope the architect, and when I said I truly was this voice apologetically explained that it would be impossible to use my photograph as they had just heard I was a woman. They had not believed the rumor, hence the incredulous voice over the telephone. So you see, although art has no sex, I am discriminated against, though on the merits of my work they had selected me as one of the architects whom they wished to mention."

And finally, there is the letter on the following pages. Written in the summer of 1915, it gives not only insights into Theodate's character but also a vivid and intimate account of a disaster — the sinking of the S.S. Lusitania — that is generally chronicled only in the arid text of history books.

Theodate made the crossing to meet with members of the British Society for Psychical Research. (Intensely interested in things spiritual, including psychic phenomena, she hoped to establish a similar chapter in Boston.) She traveled with Mr. Edwin Friend, who was also involved with psychical research, and a maid, Robinson. On May 7, 1915, while 10 miles off the coast of Ireland, the Lusitania was torpedoed by a German submarine.

Theodate Pope Riddle, forever resilient, was among the very few who survived.

The following is a letter sent by Theodate Pope Riddle to her mother in summer 1915, just weeks after the sinking of the Lusitania.

My Darling Mother:

I am going to try to tell you about the Lusitania. Marjorie [Edwin Friend's pregnant wife] will wish to know some day, but I really think she should not hear the details yet. Please be very careful about this. It might have such a bad effect on her and the baby, but you know that better than I, of course.

You left us when they called out "All Ashore!" but I was sorry when I realized we might have had more time together. The ship did not sail for two hours after that; we were taking on passengers from the Cameronia, I was told.

When we pulled out of dock I was in the writing-room and saw then for the first time in the morning Sun, the German threat. I said to Mr. Friend, "That means of course that they intend to get us," though the name of the ship was not given. We were a very quiet shipload of passengers. I comforted myself with the thought that we would surely be convoyed when we reached the war zone. I talked with practically no one on board except Mr. Friend and Mme. Depage, as I was tired. The Purser changed my stateroom for one on the boat deck, as there was a very noisy family next [to] me and I could not sleep.

Early Thursday morning, the day before the disaster, I was awakened by shouts and the scuffling of feet. I looked out of my porthole and watched the crew

*At Hill-Stead, with husband John Wallace Riddle and
the boys they took in, Theodate was at home.*

loosening the ship's boats and swinging them clear of the railing. In the afternoon, Mr. Friend read me parts of Bergson's "Matiere et Memoire," translating as he read. There were passages that illustrated so wonderfully some of the common difficulties in communication. They were most illuminating, and I could see the vividness of the inspiration they were to Mr. Friend; and as we sat side by side in our deck-chairs, I marveled to myself that such a man as Mr. Friend had been found to carry on the investigations. I felt very deeply the quality of my respect and admiration for him. He was endowed so richly in heart and mind. I had built so much in my future of which he and his work were to have been so very large a part.

After Father's death, I had laboriously reconstructed my life and this structure has also gone. But my agony of mind has been for Marjorie and I have wondered if she would have the strength to see me return without him. I do not think she ought to see me yet. It will be much harder for her than she realizes and it would be too cruel to give her an additional shock.

Friday morning, we came slowly through fog, blowing our fog horn. It cleared off about an hour before we went below for lunch. A young Englishman at our table had been served his ice cream and was waiting for the steward to bring him a spoon to eat it with; he looked ruefully at it and said he would hate to have a torpedo get him before he ate it. We all laughed, and then commented on how slowly we were running; we thought the engines had stopped.

Mr. Friend and I went up on deck B on the starboard side and leaned over the railing, looking at the sea which was a marvelous blue and very dazzling in the sunlight. I said, "How could the officers ever see a periscope there?" The torpedo was on its way to us at that moment, for we went a short distance farther toward the stern, turning the corner by the smoking room, when the ship was struck on the starboard side. The sound was like that of an arrow entering the canvas and straw of a target, magnified a thousand times and I imagined I heard a dull explosion follow. The water and timbers flflew past the deck. Mr. Friend struck his fist in his hand and said, "By Jove, they've got us." The ship steadied herself a few seconds and then listed heavily to starboard, throwing us against the wall of a small corridor we had quickly turned into. We then started up to the boat deck, as I had told Mr. Friend and poor Robinson that, in case of trouble, we would meet there and not try to run around the ship to find one another. The deck suddenly looked very strange, crowded with people, and I remember that two women were crying in a pitifully weak way. An officer was shouting orders to stop lowering the boats, and we were told to go down to deck B. We first looked over the rail and watched a boat filled with men and women being lowered. The stern was lowered too quickly and half the boatload were spilled backwards into the water. We looked at each other, sickened by the sight, and then made our way through the crowd for deck B on the starboard side. There we saw boats being lowered safely from above. The ship was sinking so quickly we feared she would fall on and capsize the small boats, and it seemed not a good place to jump from for the same reason.

We turned to make our way up again through the crush of people coming and going. We walked close together side by side, each with an arm around the other's waist. We passed Mme. Depage; her eyes were wide and startled, but brave. She had a man on either side of her, friends of hers, so I did not speak. It was no time for words unless one could offer help. On the port side of deck A, again we saw more boats safely lowered, and Mr. Friend wished me to join the throng of men and women crowding into one. He would not take a place in one as long as there were still women aboard and, as I would not leave him, we pushed our way towards the stern, which was now uphill work, as the bow was sinking so rapidly. Robinson appeared on my right. I could only put my hand on her shoulder and say, "Oh, Robinson." Her habitual smile appeared to be frozen on her face. Mr. Friend said, "Life belts!" and I went with him into nearby cabins, where he found three. He tied them on us in hard knots and we stood by the ropes on the outer side of the deck in the place which one of the boats had occupied. We looked up at the funnels; we could see the ship move, she was going so rapidly. I glanced at Mr. Friend — he was standing very straight, and I thought to myself, "the son of a soldier." We turned and looked down the side of the ship. We could now see the grey hull and knew it was time to jump. I asked him to go first. He stepped over the ropes, slipped down in the uprights and reached, I think, the rail of deck B, and then jumped. Robinson and I watched for him to come up, which he did in a few seconds, and he looked up at us to encourage us.

I said, "Come, Robinson," and I stepped over the ropes as he had, slipped a short distance, found a foothold on a roll of the canvas used for deck shields and then jumped. I do not know whether Robinson followed me.

The next thing I realized was that I could not reach the surface, because I was being washed and whirled up against wood. I was swallowing and breathing the salt water, but felt no special discomfort nor anguish of mind — was strangely apathetic. I opened my eyes and through the green water I could see what I was being dashed up against. (It looked like the bottom and keel of one of the ship's boats.) It was the under part of a deck. I could see the matched boarding and the angle iron over the railing. I had been swept between decks. I closed my eyes and thought, "This is of course the end of life for me," and then I thought of you, dearest mother, and knew that Gordon would be a comfort to you. I was glad

I had made another will, and I counted the buildings I had designed — the ones built and building, and hoped I had "made good." Quietly I thought of the friends I love and then committed myself to God's care in thought — a prayer without words. I must then have received the blow on the top of my head which made me unconscious. My stiff straw hat and my hair probably saved me from being killed by it. Then for perhaps half a minute I opened my eyes on a grey world; I could not see the sunlight because of the blow on my head. I was surrounded and jostled by hundreds of frantic, screaming, shouting humans in this grey and watery inferno. The ship must just have gone down.

A man insane with fright was clinging to my shoulders. I can see the panic in his eyes as he looked over my head. He had no life belt on and his weight was pulling me under again. Had I struggled against him, he would probably have clung to me, but I never even felt the inclination to. I said, "Oh please don't" and then the water closed over me and I became unconscious again. He must have left me when he found me sinking under him. I opened my eyes later on the brilliant sunlight and blue sea. I was floating on my back. The men and women were floating with wider spaces between them. A man on my right had a gash on his forehead; the back of a woman's head was near me. I saw an old man at my left, upright in the water and, as he could see the horizon, I asked him if he saw any rescue ships coming. He did not. An Italian, with his arms around a small tin tank as a float, was chanting. There were occasional shouts; I could see the crowded ship's boats far away. I wondered where Mr. Friend was. I noticed the water felt warm and saw an oar. I reached for it and pushed one end of it toward the old man on my left, and then as my heavy clothes kept dragging me down, I lifted my right foot over the blade of the oar, and held it with my left hand. This helped to save me. I tried to lift my head a little to see for myself if there was not some aid coming. Then I sank back very relieved in my mind, for I decided it was too horrible to be true and that I was dreaming, and again lost consciousness. This was about three o'clock.

The next thing I was aware of was looking into a small open grate fire. This was half past ten at night and I was in the captain's cabin on the rescue ship Julia. I decided that the opening of the grate measured about 18 by 24 inches; I did not remember the shipwreck. I saw a pair of grey trowsered legs by the fireplace and, turning my head, saw a man leaning over a table, looking at me where I lay wrapped in a blanket on the floor. I heard him say, "she's conscious" and two women came up to me and patted me and told me the doctor was coming. I thought they looked alike and asked them if they were sisters and what their names were. When I tried to talk, I found that I was shaking from head to foot in a violent chill, though there were hot stones at my feet and back. A doctor came and picked me up, calling two sailors, who made a chair with their hands and lifted me. I was too stupid to hold on to them and fell back, but the doctor caught me by the shoulders and I was carried off the ship and through the crowds on the dock, and the sailors shouting "Way, way!" They lifted me into a motor and in a few moments we stopped at what proved to be a third-rate hotel.

I told the doctor I could step out of the car myself, but in trying to, I crumpled up on the sidewalk and was picked up and carried in. I was left on a lounge in a room full of men in all sorts of strange garments, while the proprietress hurried to bring me brandy. The Englishman of our table, who had been so anxious to eat his ice cream, was in a pink dressing-gown; he came and sat by me. I asked him if he had seen Mr. Friend. He shook his head without answering. I was given brandy and with help walked up stairs and was put to bed. All night I kept expecting Mr. Friend to appear, looking for me. All night long, men kept coming into our room, snapping on the lights, bringing children for us to identify, taking telegrams, getting our names for the list of survivors, etc., etc. I kept asking of officials for news of Mr. Friend and giving a description of him.

A civil engineer who lives near Hartford and knew of me took it upon himself to look everywhere for Mr. Friend — in hotels and hospitals and private houses. He returned every two or three hours, but brought no news. I will not write more now of that night and my illness and frightful anxiety about Mr. Friend. Three days later, when I was taken to Cork by Mr. and Mrs. Haughton, I became convinced that Mr. Friend was delirious from injury and unidentified and Mr. Haughton, at my request, put notices in two papers for a week. I simply cannot write any more about it now. Write soon and often to me, my darling mother. Tell Marjorie I have written, perhaps you can judge if she would better read this. She must take no risk.

P.S. Did Mr. Haughton tell you of the way in which I was saved? Mrs. Naish, to whom in a great measure I owe my life, saw me pulled on board with boat hooks; the oar had worked up under my knee and kept me afloat. I was the last one rescued by that ship and was laid on deck with the dead. Mrs. Naish touched me and says I felt like a sack of cement, I was so stiff with salt water. She was convinced I could be saved and induced two men to work over me, which they did for two hours, after cutting my clothes off with a carving knife hastily brought from the dining saloon. They say that one suffers greatly in being restored from drowning, but I was totally unconscious of it all, owing to the effect of the blow on my head, and was unconscious for some time after breathing was restored; had also severe bruise above and below my right eye, which disfigured me by the swelling and discoloration. I seem to have escaped several separate deaths in a miraculous way and yet I truly believe there was no one on the ship who valued life as little as I do. I had told Mr. Friend one day, as we stood by the rail, that if the Germans did torpedo us, I hoped he would be saved to carry on the work we had so much at heart.

I have tried to tell it carefully, but I cannot dwell on it.

Thy,

Theo

15

Yo' Harriet!

Joan D. Hedrick

Writing a biography of Harriet Beecher Stowe gave me license to indulge in what I like best about New England: its sense of history. Even in the woods, sections of stone walls stand unperturbed from previous centuries, mute testimony of successive generations. I love handling old letters, so immediate in their concerns and yet their authors long dead, the holes in the paper and the ink blots making palpable the fingers of the letter writer. I spent much of the first year of my research at the Day House at Farmington and Forest Streets in Hartford, adjacent to the homes of Harriet Beecher Stowe and Mark Twain. In a quiet third-floor room I went over hundreds of such letters, trying to imagine the world that each assumed.

Yet Stowe as a subject was anything but calm, peaceful, and meditative. Like a good 19th-century evangelical Christian, she rooted herself in eternity and then threw all her energies into changing the present. That she is still causing trouble is evident from Robert Alexander's new version of "Uncle Tom's Cabin." An African-American playwright, Alexander has written a piece with the provocative title, "I Ain't Yo' Uncle," which the Hartford Stage read in its "Voices!" series. I was asked to participate in a panel discussion with the playwright and the audience after the reading.

On a cold December night, over 300 people filled the amphitheater-style seats of the Hartford Stage. I surveyed the racially mixed audience from the first row, noting that as a white person, I was in the minority. Then the reading began.

"I Ain't Yo' Uncle" opens with Stowe's most militant black

Harriet Beecher Stowe's "Uncle Tom" had plenty on his mind when he returned 150 years after his birth.

character, George Harris, shouting, "Bring in the accused!" Harriet Beecher Stowe is then dragged on stage and charged with creating stereotypes. Topsy, transformed into an in-your-face urban rapper, claims that Stowe reduced her to a dancing pickaninny. Stowe defends herself by saying "Dancing is wonderful, especially the way you dance. If I could dance like you, Topsy, I would dance all the time." I began to squirm. Well, yes, Stowe did say something like that in "Uncle Tom's Cabin" — but this seemed like a — well, like a stereotype.

When Stowe sees that her characters are determined to tell their own stories, radically revising her novel, she objects, "You can't re-write history!" But Tom replies, "I can change who writes it."

Harriet Beecher Stowe Center, Hartford, CT

Harriet Beecher Stowe

And that's what Alexander's play does. Characters jump out of character and behave in outrageous ways, upstaging one another, arguing with Stowe and writing their own scripts. When the moderator of the post-performance discussion turned to me and said, "Before we start, what reaction did you have to seeing this?" I was mute. Having invested 10 years of my life in trying to see from Stowe's point of view, I had about 10 seconds to decide how it felt to see Stowe's vision turned on its head. I was the only white person on the panel. The complexity of my responses defied speech. I said I had no opening comment to make and that we should proceed to the questions. What I was feeling, but couldn't articulate, was, "It feels very strange to have my white privilege challenged." I ordinarily do not have to question the privilege of seeing the world through white eyes and seeing a "reality" that is constructed around white assumptions. But it had been stripped away in that two-hour dramatic suspension of reality.

I'm still thinking through the issues that "I Ain't Yo' Uncle" raises, and writing this piece turned out to be much more difficult than I had imagined. My first impulse was to defend Stowe against oversimplification — from that flattening and distorting of perspective that results when someone outside a culture generalizes about it. But then I thought about the image of "Uncle Tom" and the power it has had to do just that.

An "Uncle Tom" is commonly understood to be a black person who has sold out to white culture, or who does the bidding of the white establishment. During the civil rights era the pejorative was so freighted that when a black newspaper in Cleveland printed a report that a local black leader in Akron had been called an "Uncle Tom," the politician (who was a woman) brought suit and won $32,000 from an all-white jury.

When Stowe published "Uncle Tom's Cabin" in 1852 it took the country by storm, selling 10,000 copies in its first week of publication, bringing white readers to tears, fueling the resistance to the recently passed Fugitive Slave Law and leading President Lincoln to remark, when he met Stowe in 1862: "So you're the little woman who wrote the book that started this great war!" Stowe had the genius of the popular writer who knew how to write to her white audience's assumptions, desires, and fears. By portraying with a mother's eye the pain that slavery wreaked on slave families routinely separated by the auction block, she aroused deep feeling in a generation that had experienced high rates of infant mortality.

Stowe's portrait of Uncle Tom, while not the shuffling Sambo one might expect, likewise appealed to a white audience. She makes him a kind of Christ figure who, rather than flee, allows himself to be sold to spare other slaves on the Shelby plantation that fate. As he is being transported by riverboat to the deep South, he saves a white child, Eva St. Clare, who has fallen overboard, and Eva persuades her rich and indulgent father to purchase Tom. While Eva is dying of tuberculosis, she makes her father promise to free Tom, but when St. Clare is killed in a tavern brawl (yes, this is a melodrama), Tom is sold again, into the cruel bondage of Simon Legree. When Tom refuses to tell Legree where his runaway slaves Cassy and Emmeline are hiding, the enraged Legree orders a beating that results in Tom's death. George Shelby, son of Tom's original owner, comes to purchase Tom's freedom, but arrives too late.

Read by millions, "Uncle Tom's Cabin" passed almost instantly into popular culture. Uncle Tom appeared in song, theater, statuary, toys, games, handkerchiefs, wallpapers, plates, spoons, candlesticks and every form of kitsch that the commercial mind could imagine. Because this novel by a white woman had such power to create the "reality" through which black culture entered the national psyche, it has remained a cultural force that African-American writers and artists continue to contend against. As African-American scholar Richard Yarborough has observed, " 'Uncle Tom's Cabin' was the epicenter of a massive cultural phenomenon, the tremors of which still affect the relationship between blacks and whites in the United States."

Uncle Tom leapt from the pages of Stowe's novel onto the stage almost as soon as the novel was published. Having the moral drama of "Uncle Tom's Cabin" on stage broke down the Puritan strictures against theater-going that lingered among the evangelical middle class. In order to soothe their fears, Purdy's National Theatre in New York added, near the box office, a large portrait of the theater manager with a Bible in one hand and a copy of "Uncle Tom's Cabin" in the other. Unfortunately, not all the stage versions of the novel were morally uplifting. One of the early stage adaptations, done by Henry C. Conway, softened the criticism of slavery and the South, introduced new and disreputable characters with names like Penetrate Partyside and even went so far as to replace the death of Uncle Tom with a happy ending. When Stowe saw this version performed in Hartford, she had trouble following the plot, and her neighbor, Charles Dudley Warner, had to explain it to her. When Penetrate Partyside came on stage and began talking in strong language, she left in disgust.

Once free of Stowe's artistic control, Uncle Tom capered and shuffled, making a fool of himself for the benefit of largely white, immigrant audiences — many of whom were Irish, like my ancestors — who paid money for the entertainment of seeing white actors in blackface giving their version of "coon songs" and black dialect. The "Tom" plays became an American institution. Borrowing freely from vaudeville and the minstrel tradition, they brought theater to the backwoods of America, while in the cities they often functioned as a foil against which the white working class established its racial and cultural identity. Vaudeville's stock in trade was the ethnic sendup. As white performers passed through their lips exaggerated neologisms, an intriguing dialect and street slang that had both color and appeal, they taught their immigrant audience what it meant to be white by playing black. In the process, they flirted with tabooed material. As white scholar Eric Lott has argued, a mixture of white fear and desire charges the stereotype of Uncle Tom. What better way to control a fear than to act it out, to put on the mask of the feared black man and reduce him to an object of hilarity? And what better way to demonstrate one's Americanness than to engage in America's racial drama?

If the image of Uncle Tom underwent radical revision, so too did cultural attitudes toward these images. Alex Haley observed in 1964 that "Tomming" used to be necessary for blacks to survive and prosper. Haley gave the example of the president of a black college soliciting funds from a white audience. Asked by a white woman in the audience to sing "Swing Low, Sweet Chariot," Haley reported, the surprised president collected himself, sang — and went home with the donation he sought. Faced with the social reality of a black man in the prestigious role of college president, what this white woman "saw" was shaped by stereotypes created by stage, film and vaudeville. Because she had the money, she could make her perception appear to be reality. But if powerful individuals can shape perceptions, social movements can transform them. The Civil Rights Movement of the 1960s would seem to have made "Tomming," Amos and Andy, and the Sambo of minstrelsy relics of the past.

I found one of these relics of the past among my family memorabilia, and as I explored its meaning, I found my own family history deeply connected to the stereotype of Uncle Tom. My grandmother's sister, Mars Whelan, ran away from home at age 16 and pursued a career in vaudeville as a piano player. Among the small parcel of letters and personal effects that survived Mars's vagabond life is a photo of a character actor for the Marie Nielson Company. In the photograph he's wearing a long calico dress with a white apron, his white face and hands blackened with burnt cork. He has a kerchief on his head and his padded chest is covered with a plaid triangle of cloth with the apex pinned to his waist. He is leaning on a broom, a jovial expression on his face. On the back of the photo, which is mounted in the form of a 19th-century carte de visite, my Aunt Mars wrote "Eugene Williams as Aunt Caroline."

Before she had ever seen black people, my aunt had seen such stage versions of them played by whites. Not only did whites play blacks, but as this photo illustrates, white men played black women. Under the pressure of these images, social reality was replaced by cultural myth, especially for farm girls who had no experience against which to test the stage stereotypes. Growing up in Yates Center, Kansas in the 1890s, a decade of economic depression, labor strife, nativism, Jim Crow laws and lynchings, Mars Whelan would have absorbed from her culture a generalized white fear of blacks. The minstrel shows and the "Tom" plays were fed by these fears even as they produced comic images of blacks. In all likelihood, my aunt witnessed one or more of these Tom plays, for they were one of the few forms of theater that would have made their way to the hinterlands of Yates Center, Kansas.

Mars's knowledge of blacks was thus distanced and highly filtered. When she was 12 she was put on a train and sent to Cairo, Illinois, where she was met at the train station by a black servant in the employ of her family. She had never before seen a black person, "except in shows." Located at the southern tip of Illinois where it dips deeply into Kentucky, Cairo was a very southern town. In her handwritten memoirs, her most vivid memory of Cairo was of the infamous 1909 lynching of a black man for the alleged rape of a white girl.

Perceptions of this event depend on who is writing history. As told through the eyes of a 13-year-old Irish girl who was soon to leave the protection of her family, it resonates with the fear of her own vulnerability.

According to her account, there were ten of these young negroes who had a list of girls they were going to take — all girls who had no father. This girl had two brothers across the river in Kentucky. They came over, formed a mob, and burned this young negro at the stake in the spot where they had found the girl's body.

My aunt lived on 29th Street, one block from that spot. The New York Times reported that Will "Frog" James, a young black man from the South who had resided in Cairo a few years, was strung up in a prominent part of town by a "rejoicing" crowd of 10,000. Five hundred bullets were fired into him, one of which cut the rope. Then he was dragged to the spot where the girl's body was found. After his body was decapitated and burned, his head was put up on a fencepost. Souvenirs, including body parts, were divided and passed around to the crowd.

Neither the barbarity nor the ritual nature of this lynching was unusual, nor was the participation of women with baby carriages; lynchings freely mixed gruesome violence with the ambiance of a church picnic. It was a white community ritual, defending against white community fears. This event was to imprint deeply on my aunt's young consciousness. How powerful must the black man be if it took such a group frenzy to contain him? The black image in the white mind painted by lynchings was the flip side of the jovial Sambo of the minstrel shows.

Stowe's Christlike Tom is a middle term between these extremes, a safe version of black manhood that little white Eva could embrace. In the 1990s, the politics of perception convoluted racial and sexual politics in the national spectacles of the Clarence Thomas-Anita Hill hearings and the trial of O. J. Simpson. The intense fascination of the press and the populace with these dramas of black manhood suggest that they tapped subterranean fears and secret satisfactions on the part of the dominant white culture, even as Thomas's charge of a "high-tech lynching" and the dramatic playing of "the race card" in the Simpson trial worked in favor of both men. More recently, the Million-Man March on Washington challenged the stereotype of Uncle Tom. When stereotypes talk back, when they assume the role of agents of history and take charge of their own destinies, they shape new perceptions of their image. This "Day of Atonement" for the abdication of black male responsibility, by assuming moral power rather than passive victimhood, is close to Stowe's Christian understanding of Tom as a moral agent — albeit a less militant one than abolitionists of the 19th century or black power activists of the 20th would have desired. In another leaf from Uncle Tom, Louis Farrakhan's controversial sponsorship of the march brought to the fore issues of racism and stereotyping.

In this highly charged cultural moment, "Uncle Tom's Cabin" returned to the stage. It is cathartic that Alexander's play allows all of us, white and black and brown, to laugh. For all the passion Stowe aroused against slavery, "Uncle Tom's Cabin" finessed the finer points of black-white relations under freedom — such as the inevitable question of interracial sexuality — by sending her black characters to Liberia. Alexander's Afrocentric version reverses this. The racially mixed audience for the reading of "I Ain't Yo' Uncle" had strong reactions, but one of the most widely shared responses was triggered by a contemporary reference to interracial sexuality — and it was uproarious laughter. One good laugh can explode cultural stereotypes that arguments cannot touch.

Alexander's revival of what has been called our "national folk play" makes awfully good theater. In addition, by loosening the grip of stereotypes on the national psyche, it opens up a space for other ways of seeing. What I learned from it can be summed up in a statement about point of view: "Where you stand depends on where you sit." As Huck Finn said, "I knowed this, but I forgot it." Alexander's "I Ain't Yo' Uncle" is the kind of drama that won't let you forget.

16

Healing Children

Sandra Wheeler

In my first career, I was a nurse. It was in the 1960s, in many ways a vanished age — our patients were in 12-bed wards, and we didn't worry about what anything cost. I loved it because I loved learning about the lives of the people I tended. Now, I am a historian, and its pleasures are not unlike those I experienced as a nurse. I still learn about people's lives, and wonder what it must be like to contend with a different set of problems and possibilities from my own. I am interested in the social history of illness. This is not quite the same as the history of medicine, which concerns technological and scientific advances. Rather, it is about changes in the experience of being ill and what it meant to families and care-givers. I want to know more about what it was like when all that could be done for the sick was to provide enough rest and nourishment to enable their bodies to cure themselves.

The new Connecticut Children's Medical Center is a dramatic expression of the difference between old and new attitudes toward illness. Nineteenth-century people would be puzzled. Their buildings were expected to reflect the importance of what went on inside them; that is why so many banks were built to look like Greek temples, and why hospitals were somber piles of brick or stone with little ornament. This new building on Washington Street, however, looks whimsical, even playful. Entrances are marked by geometric shapes: a sphere, a cone, a tilted cube. Inside, it is full of strong color and bright light. Its halls and waiting rooms are decorated by artists whose work is based on children's drawings from around the state. The designers consulted children and parents as well as medical personnel in their quest for a building that would help the hospital staff make the experiences of children as pleasant as possible. Everything about the building is intended to dispel fear and anxiety. Our 19th-century visitors would be even more mystified. Are not fear and anxiety part of illness?

The answer, of course, is yes, especially for adults caring for a sick child. Because diagnoses and treatments have changed, we don't worry about exactly the same things today; fatalities from diphtheria or whooping cough, for example, are now almost unknown. Today, we assume that something can be done for virtually every problem. Effective treatment means that most sick children will recover, or that their conditions will be improved or made more manageable. Even if the worst occurs and there is nothing to be done, pain can be controlled, discomfort eased. We complain about cost, and are concerned about the side effects of drugs or procedures. We seek advice about how best to prepare children for diagnostic tests, surgery or therapy so they will not suffer emotional damage in addition to whatever is wrong physically. We want the machines and the drugs to be sophisticated and high-tech, and the people who run or administer them to be friendly and accessible and caring. But underneath it all, we are afraid that our children will not get better, that we in the adult world will fail them.

Despite high-tech treatments, being a parent of a sick child has in some ways changed little. Like us, our 19th-century great-grandparents knew the light sleep of listening for the cough, the cry. They had to find ways to calm a fretful baby, entice an unwilling toddler to eat, entertain a listless but bored school-aged youngster. They knew how hard it is to help a child learn to cope with deficits that will not disappear. Most of all, they, too, were afraid for their children.

The microfilm marked "Hartford Vital Records, Deaths 1871–1878" whirs through the machine. There, in the pages for 1872, on line two of page 52, I find:

NAME: Clemens, Langdon. PLACE OF DEATH: Forest Street. TIME OF DEATH: June 2. AGE: one year, six months. SEX: M. BIRTHPLACE: Hartford, Conn. RESIDENCE AT DEATH: Hartford. DISEASE OR CAUSE OF DEATH: Diphtheria, COLOR: W. NAME OF PARENTS: Sam'l E. Clemens. PHYSICIAN OR PERSON CERTIFYING: C.A. Taft.

I read on through the entries for the rest of the month, and then for July. There were 147 deaths in Hartford in those bright months of early summer, and half of them, 74, were of children under the age of 6. Was this an epidemic? I forward through more film, and scan the "cause of death" column. There are seasonal rhythms. In winter, children died of pneumonia, croup, scarlet fever, whooping cough and diphtheria, while the warm months brought illness from contaminated food and water: dysentery, typhoid, and the most common entry, "cholera infantum." This last is not true cholera but a term for severe infant diarrhea. Overall, young children account for about half of all deaths.

Little Langdon's diphtheria was out of season. His parents had perhaps congratulated themselves too soon upon winter's being safely over. Summer would have been less dangerous, for their Nook Farm neighborhood was far from the dirty, crowded city districts. When the addresses at which summer deaths occurred cluster downtown or on the east side of the city, "cholera infantum" appears again and again, sometimes with rows of ditto marks under it. Front Street, Charles Street, Windsor Street, Sheldon Street, State Street, Commerce Street, Kilborne Street, Spruce Street. These were dangerous places where sewers emptied into the rivers and housing had deteriorated. Poor people lived there.

Suffering through the diseases of childhood was an experience shared by all 19th-century children, but for the illness to end in death was much more common among the poor than among middle-class families like the Clemenses. A Twain biographer writes that Langdon had never been strong; perhaps he, like malnourished children of the less fortunate, lacked the robustness necessary to survive the challenge of infection. Some families endured extraordinary losses; George Wolff, age 4, his 2-year-old brother Charles and his 7-month-old sister Louisa all died of scarlet fever in a three-week period in July 1872. Their father was a musician, and the family lived at various addresses on Front Street and State Street. Mary and Charles Turley, ages 3 and 5, died in the same week of "cholera infantum" and typhoid fever. Their Charles Street address was not far from the Wolffs.

Whether they were comfortably off or struggling, parents in the 19th century must have worried constantly. To read the "cause of death" list in the vital records is to enter a terrifying world from which we today are separated by the availability of immunizations, intravenous fluids, antibiotics and clean food and water. Back then, every time a child coughed, every time a rash appeared, every time a baby's skin felt hot and feverish, every complaint of stomach pain or evidence of a cramp was a potential early warning of a devastating illness. When a child did become sick, care was largely a matter of spooning in food or drink, keeping the bed and room clean and generally providing what comfort was possible. Physicians made house calls, but could do little to alter nature's course.

Mothers and fathers watched as babies became dehydrated from diarrhea and vomiting. Those infants at least seemed not to suffer. The so-called "diseases of childhood" were far worse. Children were ill for weeks, sometimes months. Scarlet fever was what its name describes, a red rash and very high fever. Its onset was quick; sometimes, convulsions caused by the sudden temperature elevation were the first sign that the child was ill. Diphtheria was associated with a membrane that could close off the sick child's airway, making breathing difficult or even impossible. The paroxysms of coughing that gave "whooping cough" its name were uncontrollable, and were followed by vomiting and exhaustion. Babies could literally cough to death, unable to catch their breaths.

Most children survived, but convalescence was long. Even if they had been strong and vigorous before becoming ill, they had to be "built up" again, given nourishing foods to help their bodies heal. Not the least taxing problem for worn-out parents in those days before television and radio was to keep sick and recovering children quiet, for medical wisdom said that too much activity too soon would result in relapse. And there was always the fear that the child would never recover completely, but would have long-term after-effects from the diseases. Scarlet fever was especially frightening, for it was frequently followed by rheumatic fever and heart disease.

Children with these illnesses were cared for at home. Hospitals had nothing to offer, and did not admit them, in the justified fear that the infection would only spread to other patients. Grandmothers, aunts or sisters without children were summoned to spell parents at the bedside. More well-to-do parents could also hire servants, either to care for the child or to run the household so the mother could spend most of her time in the sick room. Poor families in which the mother had to work, or those with fewer relatives or no money to pay for help, had a harder time of it. Fortunately, most churches had among their members women who felt it was their duty to God to assist the sick, and they must have been blessed by the desperate families they aided.

Hospital care was available if a child had been injured, or had a chronic illness or a condition that would not endanger others. Wealthier families could obtain most services offered by hospitals without subjecting their children to admission. Physicians routinely made house calls, and private nurses could be hired; even minor surgical procedures

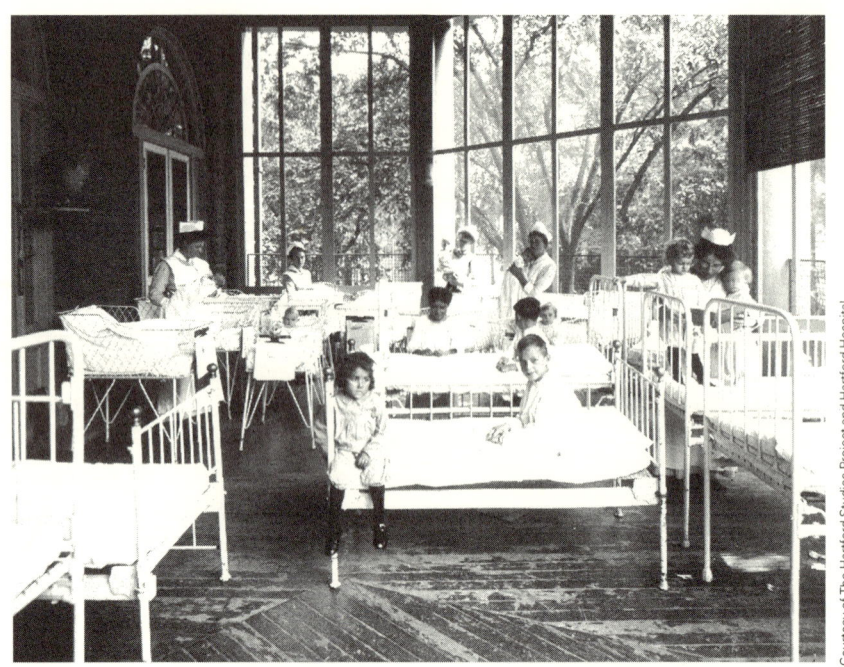

Years have passed, and technology has advanced, but never changing is the
trauma associated with sick children.

could be carried out at home. Hospital care was for the poor, and was
paid for by grants from the state, subsidies from the city and (mostly) by
money given by local people — charity. For those who could not buy
home care, hospitals offered relief for overburdened parents and real
benefits for their children, even if only in the form of adequate food and a
comfortable bed.

The ledger-like books are huge, over a foot high and almost 2
inches thick. Their bindings are worn and the pages must be turned with
great care. They hold the sketchy records of patients admitted to
Hartford Hospital in the 1870s and 1880s. Most were adults, but there
were children, too. I read for a sense of what care of sick children was
like. Today it is difficult to imagine being ill in a world before X-ray
machines and antibiotics and aspirin, when surgery was done with ether
for anesthesia and surgeons wore no gloves, and when children were
admitted to the same 20-bed open wards as adults. I have changed names
in telling the stories of these children, for the hospital insists that the

confidentiality even of people long dead must be protected. I have, however, chosen names that reflect the same ethnicity and gender of the originals.

Many children were admitted for treatment of problems that are still part of the risks of growing up. There were birth defects, such as a cleft lip or a bad birthmark, that could be repaired. There were terrible accidents: Two children were hit by railroad trains; one died. There were unfortunate adolescents who had gotten into trouble — pregnancy, venereal disease, a drunken fight with fatal injuries. There is evidence that for some young people the transition to adulthood was difficult — a 16-year-olds attempted suicide, a case of "hysteria."

It is also clear that new surgical techniques and knowledge of how to prevent infection were being successful applied. Gino Toscatti was only 4 when his parents brought him to the doctor because the child seemed unable to urinate without pain. An operation was done and two large bladder stones removed; the discharge note proudly records that he was fully recovered and urinating normally by the 14th day after surgery. Seventeen-year-old Patrick Kelly's hand was crushed under a machine at work. The physician who amputated several of Patrick's fingers was careful to note that he did so "under antiseptic spray" and that "healing was rapid and complete." Only a few years before, death from gangrene and overwhelming infection would have been a more likely outcome. This willingness to incorporate new technology into medical practice hinted at what was to come in the 20th century.

In the 1870s, however, the hospital's basic role was what it had been since antiquity, to be a place of refuge. Physicians often admitted the young for that alone. Food and shelter could preserve life, and probably did so for a group of patients about whom I can only make guesses. Each year, at the rate of two or three a month, around 30 babies were admitted under the names of their mothers ("child of..."). In each case, "infant" was written into the column for age and also in the "diagnosis" space. These babies stayed in the hospital for around three weeks; the discharge summary for almost all of them consists of one word, "recovered." An unnamed charity paid their bills. These were not infants born in the hospital, for births took place at home then. They must have been babies identified as being weak or in need of short-term care; they seem to have been admitted to be fed. Where they came from and who paid for them remains a mystery.

For others, the record leaves no doubt about why patients were admitted. The discharge summary for Flora Monroe, a 17-year-old prostitute, notes that she had "been drinking and working hard and was pretty well used up." She remained in the hospital for two weeks and was treated with strengthening "tonics." Thomas Harrison was a 16-year-old machinist who had chronic rheumatism, perhaps an after-effect of scarlet fever. The doctor recorded that the patient was "not much distressed at present but fearing an attack [of joint pain] seeks a safe harbor." He remained in the harbor granted him for a week. James Windsor was 5 when he came in to have an injured hip treated. The physician's note indicates that several treatments were attempted "without any great benefit," but that James' "general health" was not good on admission. When James was discharged after 50 weeks, he was receiving "constitutional" treatment — adequate food — and was "playing about" the ward.

Despite the healing possibilities of simple nourishment and increasingly effective surgical techniques, however, some children needed more than anyone could provide. Most poignant of these was 11-year-old Isaac Rosenthal, who was in and out of the hospital for long periods in the late 1870s with a diagnosis of "chronic diarrhea." After one of these admissions, which had lasted for 20 weeks, his physician wrote despairingly:

Patient has about three horribly smelling evacuations from the bowels a day. Very anemic. Has the look of an old man. Seems to be utterly without ambition, and simply exists. When he was here before nothing seemed to control his bowels. This seems to be case now. Many things have been tried without benefit. [Here an unintelligible list.] Left unimproved.

Isaac's father was a peddler who does not appear in city directories, probably because he was on the road much of the time. His mother is also unlisted; perhaps she was a live-in servant. Even today, malabsorption disorders like Isaac's can be difficult to manage — certainly it would not have been easy for his parents to have him with them in the 1870s. For Isaac, as for Flora and Thomas, the hospital was a haven in a harsh world.

Samuel Clemens lived at the end of an era in the care of the sick, though before he died in 1910 the beginnings of today's medicine were evident. Municipal governments began to establish Public Health Departments (Hartford's dates from 1885) to ensure clean food and water. Effective treatment for diphtheria was discovered at the turn of the century, though immunization for that and other children's diseases didn't come along until after World War I. In the first decade of the new century, hospitals began to place children in their own wards, and pediatricians cared for them there.

I am given a tour of the new Children's Medical Center, and I admire the many thoughtful details that reflect a desire to make a child's experience there as benign as possible, and to make the hospital less intimidating to parents. The sophisticated machinery is there: the monitors for the very sick, the pressure-sensitive floor in the Gait Laboratory, the isolation rooms entered through two doors with an air lock between. But this machinery is not emphasized. Instead, my attention is caught by the waiting-room furniture in many sizes and colors, and by how sections of counters in clinics are low, to make it possible for small people or those in wheelchairs to see over them. Signs identifying clinic destinations are marked with colors, numbers and shapes as well as Spanish, English and Braille texts. Children who must be admitted are placed in single rooms with windows both to the outdoors and to the interior corridor, and their parents have nearby lounge areas and kitchens. Depending upon the floor, parents can spend the night in their child's room or nearby. There are playrooms for patients, and a medical information room for family members, who will even be able to surf the Internet to learn more.

I think about Flora and Thomas and Isaac, about the babies admitted to Hartford Hospital to be fed and about Langdon Clemens. Today none of them would be admitted to the hospital, for their conditions would have been prevented or they could be treated as outpatients. Olivia and Samuel Clemens would not worry about "cholera infantum" or diphtheria or whooping cough. Milk and water are safe, and Langdon would have received a DPT immunization. Flora would receive counseling, Thomas rehabilitation services, and Isaac a special diet and medication. But there are still teenage prostitutes, still young people afraid of the next flare-up of their diseases, still children whose parents cannot care for them properly, still hungry babies.

The new hospital's decor and design are wonderful, exciting. They may help children and their parents forget, for a moment, why they are there. But a hospital is a serious place, and what goes on inside is neither whimsical nor playful. Caring for sick children is a worrisome, difficult business for everyone. It is now, and it always has been.

WHERE BABIES USED TO GO

....

The Connecticut Children's Medical Center in Hartford is not the first hospital in Hartford exclusively for children. On June 18, 1909, a large tent known as "Babies' Hospital" was erected on a lot at the corner of Mather and Vine streets. Each summer thereafter mothers from sweltering tenements brought sick infants to the hospital to escape the heat and be fed clean milk, for by then public health authorities were fully aware of the benefits of preventing diseases carried by contaminated milk. The hospital was part of a network of what today would be called out-reach clinics, then known as "milk stations" — places around the city where mothers of at-risk infants were given safe milk.

In 1917, The Courant reported that "a welcome sum of money" had been given to establish a building fund to replace the tent hospital with a permanent structure. The article carried a photograph of a bronze plaque recording the gift, which was given in memory of Dr. Oliver C. Smith. Dr. Smith was the son of Virginia Thrall Smith, who worked for the well-being of children throughout the late 19th century and was one of the founders of what would become Newington Children's Hospital.

The Red Cross took over the tent hospital in 1920, although it is not clear how many years they maintained the operation. The fate of the building fund and the whereabouts of the plaque are also unknown today.

....

17

All Our Jazz

James A. Miller

W hat kinds of civic, cultural, or for that matter political claims does a city make when it organizes a jazz festival as an emblem of its aspirations?

The mention of Newport evokes the legendary jazz festivals of the 1950s and 1960s. New York City has the JVC Festival, and jazz festivals abound in cities throughout the country, from Pittsburgh to New Orleans to Chicago to Portland, Ore. At one level, then, jazz festivals promote a vision of civic culture, boost and promote the social, cultural, and economic life of a city, and celebrate urban life without which jazz, after all, could not exist.

But jazz festivals also carry with them a certain elan, a mystique, the suggestion that people who pay attention to jazz are somehow more hip than the rest of the American populace, more advanced in their general social outlook and musical tastes, and that the cities that nurture jazz festivals are advanced outposts of the American civilization, guardians of America's original art form.

Jazz festivals, in short, help to consolidate claims for a kind of hip cosmopolitanism. So when Hartford celebrates its festival every summer there is a certain amount at stake: not just the time and energy of the board members of the festival, or the image and reputation of a city that has fallen upon hard times, but the deeper question of whether the Hartford region is hip enough to justify and sustain the effort.

The historical record is mixed on the question. Hartford seldom appears in standard accounts of jazz history, partially because of the metropolitan bias that shapes most jazz histories, which are mostly narratives of the movement from villages and small towns to the cities, rather than vice versa. However, the case could certainly be made that the recent history of jazz in the city has been considerably enriched by the migration of notable musicians from the metropolitan centers to Hartford.

But, still, there's no handy history for the popular musical life of the city that puts Hartford in the historical record, or at least on bookshelves, the way Barbara J. Kukla's "Swing City" does for Newark, N.J., or Katrina Hazzard-Gordon's "Jookin' " does for Cleveland, a fact that contributes, no doubt, to the routine bad-mouthing of Hartford cultural life that inevitably creeps into almost any conversation about the present or future prospects of the city. Take my friend Kathleen, for example. "This is a town built on actuarial tables," she maintains. "How long is it going to be before you die? That's the heart and soul of Hartford." A grim assessment, indeed, and a sobering prognosis for Hartford's future.

But what if — like reports of Mark Twain's death — accounts of Hartford's cultural demise are premature? What if an archaeological expedition through 20th-century Hartford cultural history uncovered a residue of hipness that suggested that Hartford could break out of its cultural doldrums, that jazz — with its implications of freedom, improvisation, creativity, and racial democracy — offered another way of imagining Hartford's future? Hartford can claim a rich cultural legacy spanning many years. Certainly the city entered a new phase of its history in the late 1960s, with the inauguration of bassist Paul Brown's Jazz in Bushnell Park series — still going strong in its fourth decade.

Hartford, in fact, can boast of a surfeit of riches: the Artists Collective Inc. at 35 Clark St. in the North End — it broke ground to build a new arts facility at Albany Avenue and Woodland Street. The Department of African-American Music at Hartt School — which, under the leadership of world class alto saxophonist Jackie McLean, has become, over the past 20-odd years, the hub of several generations of young musicians now making their mark on the national scene. The 880 Club on Maple Avenue, Hartford's venerable longest-running jazz club. The Hartford Jazz Society and the Hartford Festival of Jazz. Will Wilkins and Real Art Ways. Donny DePalma, Art Fine, and Harry Lichtenbaum. The Cutting Edge Jazz Series at City's Edge on Farmington Avenue. Bassist Nat Reeves, trombonist Steve Davis, pianist Mary Davis, tenor saxophonist Jimmy Greene and all of the other protégés of McLean who have been spilling out of the Hartt School like rain.

McLean, in particular, has been a force since coming to Hartford along with his wife Dollie. If this were, say, Korea, they would have been designated national cultural treasures years ago.

Actually, Hartford is widely known in offical jazz history for at least one story, told and retold by bassist Milt Hinton. It involves a spat between band leader Cab Calloway and trumpeter Dizzy Gillespie at the State Theater in 1941. The Cab Jivers, a small combo in Calloway's band, had just finished playing and the curtain was coming down when a spitball sailed across the stage in the direction of tenor saxophonist Chu Berry.

Cab Calloway, watching from the wings, saw the spitball land and was convinced that Dizzy, known for his clowning, had thrown it. After the show, Calloway called Gillespie aside to reprimand him. There was a heated exchange. Calloway slapped Gillespie in the face; Gillespie pulled a knife and nicked Calloway on the thigh and wrist before fellow band members wrestled the knife away from him.

Cab Calloway fired Dizzy Gillespie on the spot and the story, appropriately embellished, entered jazz legend, with different versions circulating in Gillespie's autobiography "To BE, or not ... to BOP," Calloway's "Of Minnie the Moocher & Me," and Milt Hinton's memoir, "Bass Line."

My friend Owen McNally, jazz critic for The Hartford Courant, knows this story (as do most Hartford jazz aficionados) but doesn't like to tell it. He fears that this particular cutting session — a term often applied to contests and displays of musical virtuosity among jazz musicians — cuts too close to the bone, so to speak, and runs the risk of perpetuating stereotypes about African Americans and jazz musicians.

Fair enough, I guess, but couldn't we at least seize upon this story to argue that Hartford was a key site for probably the most important developments in the post-World War II jazz scene: the development of bebop? That Cab Calloway's expulsion of Dizzy Gillespie from his band that night in Hartford in 1941 inevitably propelled Dizzy towards his fateful encounter with saxophonist Charlie Parker and the other architects of the modern jazz movement?

Probably not.

Most of the fans at the State Theater that night would have been there to see and hear Cab Calloway; Dizzy Gillespie would have been just a young, relatively obscure musician to an audience nurtured by the values of mainstream swing, music values that typified Hartford jazz fans in the late 1930s and early 1940s.

Looking for hipness in Hartford? Start by checking out
alto saxophonist Jackie McLean.

But, beyond the Cab Calloway-Dizzy Gillespie episode — which reveals very little about the sensibility of the city — what we know about the history of jazz in Hartford derives from a rich and sometimes contradictory body of oral testimony, shaped — as always seems to be the case in explorations of Hartford's past — by the historical fault line that inevitably separates the fabled and frequently mythologized Front Street era from the modernity and cultural sterility of Constitution Plaza.

Is there anything to be learned, are there any lessons to be retrieved by searching for patterns in Hartford cultural history between the mid-1930s and the early 1960s? That was the era when urban renewal irrevocably altered the face of Hartford, the "Hartford cultural holocaust," as one of my friends calls it.

Out of the memories and recollections of people such as McNally; of founding members of the Hartford Jazz Society Art Fine and Harry Lichtenbaum; of New England Jazz News editor Thomas D. Harris IV; of pianist Norman Macklin; and of trombonist, band leader and promoter Paul Landerman, a picture of Hartford's love affair with jazz begins to emerge and take on dimension.

Hartford's embrace of the jazz scene seems to coincide with the heyday of the Swing era during the mid-1930s, a period when jazz had become consolidated within the rubric of urban, mass-produced, mass-consumed popular culture, attracting its audience through interlocking networks of recordings, music, publishing, nightclubs, radio broadcasts, and touring band circuits.

George Malcolm Smith, a witty, flamboyant Trinity College graduate, and one of the founding members of the Hartford Jazz Society, recalled in one of his columns for The Swinger, the newsletter of the Hartford Jazz Society, a Battle of the Bands at Hartford's Foot Guard Hall in 1936. It featured the Jimmie Lunceford Orchestra — widely regarded as one of the most disciplined and showmanly African-American big bands during the Swing era and, in Smith's ironic, retrospective terms, ". . . a team of obscure upstarts recently arrived from Kansas under the leadership of a piano player named Basie."

Lunceford's orchestra won the battle hands down, Smith reported, much to his subsequent chagrin about his participation in this collective lapse in critical judgment.

Like his counterparts from elite Northeastern colleges and universities — John Hammond in New York; Marshall Stearns, then a young English professor at Yale University; George Avakian, who wrote for Down Beat Magazine; George Simon, who covered swing music for Metronome; Princeton-educated Frank Norris; Harvard graduate George Frazier, and others — George Malcolm Smith played an important role as a critic. In his capacity as the main voice for jazz on radio for Hartford audiences and in his role as elder statesman of jazz in the region, Smith helped shape the canons of production and consumption of jazz in Hartford for many years.

The connection between swing music and cultural elites in the 1930s on the national scene and in Hartford harkened to the enthusiasm for jazz that swept many college campuses during the Jazz age of the 1920s. It helps to explain, among other things, the predominantly white, middle-class configuration of the audience that crystallized around jazz in Hartford during the 1930s. And why the featured band would have been the Paul Whiteman Orchestra, featuring none other than the "King of Jazz" himself.

Ironically, two months earlier, on Jan. 16, 1938, an audience assembled at New York's Carnegie Hall for a concert by Benny Goodman and his orchestra. It was an event heralded by the New York Times and critical pundits as a watershed moment in the history of swing music. As David Stowe notes in his book "Swing Changes: Big-Band Jazz in New Deal America," it was the first major cultural opportunity since the failure of Paul Whiteman's symphonic jazz in the late 1920s.

The Goodman concert was a smashing success. Right after the concert, Benny Goodman and most of his musicians headed uptown to Harlem to a significantly less publicized but equally important cultural moment: the battle of the bands between the Chick Webb and Count Basie orchestras at the Savoy Ballroom. This was a meeting between two of the hottest black bands in the country, and a battle whose outcome was far from clear-cut.

Meanwhile, back in Hartford, Paul Whiteman — widely regarded as passe on the national scene — received such an enthusiastic welcome in Hartford that a Courant reporter filed the following tongue-in-cheek casualty report after the concert: "[Bushnell] management reported 234 seats damaged by those who Suzy-Q-ed in their chairs, 345 first-aid cases of barked shins, and a two-foot rift in the front hall of the balcony… shivered by a blast from a hot trumpet."

Just as the triumphant Paul Whiteman concert at the Bushnell hinted at a time warp between Hartford and the city from which it took many of its cultural cues, so did the Benny Goodman concert at Carnegie Hall, juxtaposed next to the battle of the bands at Harlem's Savoy Ballroom, hint at some of the cultural rifts, fissures, and contradictions in the jazz scene.

In the national arena and in Hartford, this would shape the social and cultural dynamics of jazz for many years to come. Between high culture and popular culture. Between highly visible cultural events eagerly embraced by established cultural institutions and gatekeepers, and events relegated to the cultural margins. Between an official jazz culture and an unofficial one where many of the creative ideas and trends were generated. Between white and black musicians, their audiences, and their respective relationships to the reward system of the music industry, and American society.

These fault lines, however subtly, shaped the production and consumption of jazz in Hartford, too. If you talk to long-time participant-observers of the Hartford jazz scene of the 1930s, '40s, or '50s, within minutes you will be regaled with stories of the legendary Bond Hotel on Asylum Street in downtown Hartford.

You will be reminded of trombonist and band-leader Paul Landerman, who held sway there from 1939 to 1950, and who was also the trombonist for the pit band at the Old State Theater on Village Street. You'll hear about the stage shows at the State, memories and artifacts of which are still lovingly preserved by Lichtenbaum, who virtually lived there every Saturday during its heyday. You'll hear about the impresario and producer Norman Granz's Jazz at the Philharmonic Concert at the Bushnell, beginning with its first Hartford appearance in 1949, when Granz decided that it was a good idea to open his traveling concert series there. Most of all, you will hear fond memories of an era of bi-racial harmony and cooperation. This was itself an ideological creation of the Swing era, even when the ideals of racial equality and harmony were out of sync with the hard facts of Hartford social and political life.

One of the most prominent cultural vehicles for promoting a vision of interracial solidarity during the post-World War II era was Granz's philharmonic series. Born and reared in Los Angeles, Granz had presented, in the early years of World War II, racially integrated jam sessions that broke the color barrier in Los Angeles night clubs. His first philharmonic concert in 1944 was organized as a benefit for 21 Mexicans convicted in the aftermath of the Los Angeles zoot-suit riots of the preceding year.

He later organized benefits to support the Fair Employment Practices Commission and anti-lynching legislation. In addition, he led a national drive encouraging band-leaders to adopt an anti-discrimination clause in their contracts, urging them to refuse to play in racially segregated establishments. It pledged them to struggle against Jim Crow statutes. Granz, in short, made an explicit connection between jazz and the struggle for racial equality, and you could not attend a Granz concert without being greeted with the announcement that was standard for all of his shows:

"Jazz is America's own. It is the music which grew out of a young and vigorous melting-pot nation. It is a product of all America, deriving much of its inspiration and creation from the negro people....It is played and listened to by all peoples in harmony, together...Pigmentation differences have no place in jazz. As in genuine democracy, only performance counts. Jazz is truly the music of democratic America. It is an ideal medium for bringing about a better understanding among all peoples."

Swing music, in short, provided the basis for an ideology, a vocabulary and widely shared set of assumptions about music and social relationships. If you attended a Granz concert, you bought the whole package and, presumably, were swept up in the world of possibilities it represented. From this perspective, the philharmonic concert at Bushnell Memorial Hall in May 1953, featuring trumpeters Roy Eldridge and Charlie Shavers, tenor saxophonists Ben Webster and Flip Phillips, the Oscar Peterson Quartet, and the Lester Young Quintet, among others, has to be seen as a watershed moment in Hartford cultural life. It signalled a level of acceptance of jazz and, in Norman Granz's terms, of social tolerance that bode well for Hartford's future.

Outside the Bushnell, however, and the State Theater, the Bond Hotel and the Heublein Hotel (where the jazz aficionados who formed the nucleus of the Hartford Jazz Society gathered), the official ideology of jazz culture gave way in the face of hard facts, to a racially divided and deeply segregated city.

Pianist Norman Macklin remembers that African-American musicians often found housing in Hartford's North End when they performed in the city in the 1940s and '50s. It was a sober reflection of the inhospitable social conditions that black musicians and ordinary citizens often encountered in the city. But it also was a boon of sorts for the major venues for black music in Hartford: the Colored Elks Club on Canton Street, The Subway Restaurant on Main Street, and the fabled Club Sundown.

By most accounts the North End is where you would go in the 1950s if you wanted to hear the real music — somewhat akin to white folks going to Harlem in the 1920s. And certainly the North End was a mecca for black music in Hartford. It attracted talented musicians such as alto saxophonist Harold Holt, pianist Gene Nelson, drummer Walter Bolden, pianist Horace Silver, and numerous others. The second-best-known story about Hartford in official jazz histories tells how tenor saxophonist Stan Getz, hired by the Club Sundown as its featured attraction in 1950, fell in love with its rhythm section — Joe Calloway, Walter Bolden, and Horace Silver. Getz invited the three to join him, thereby indirectly helping to launch Silver's career.

Looking back at the different accounts of the jazz scene in Hartford, especially during the late 1940s and 1950s, it is difficult not to be captivated by the legends of a golden age of jazz in an earlier moment of Hartford's history. Certainly in the years after urban renewal in the early 1960s, the dynamic jazz scene entered into a period of sharp decline.

When the fledgling Hartford Jazz Society booked a major concert headlining vocalist Joe Williams and featuring the Junior Mance Trio at the Bushnell Memorial in 1963, only 78 people showed up. This left nearly 2,500 vacant seats in the hall where thousands had rocked to the music of Jazz at the Philharmonic only 20 years earlier. Joe Williams peeped out of the curtain from backstage, surveyed the near-empty auditorium, and asked for his money before he went on the stage to perform. Art Fine, the president of the Jazz society, paid up out of his own pocket. The members of the Jazz society paid him back over the next three years.

In 1963, Joe Williams was at the peak of his form following his triumphant performances with the Count Basie Orchestra at Newport; the Hartford audience was clearly lagging behind. The lesson of the Joe Williams episode may be that Hartford cultural promoters, taste-makers, and audiences have historically seemed to be behind time a great deal of the time, on time some of the time, but very seldom ahead of the time. It's easy enough to aspire to hipness by embracing well-established jazz musicians; it's even hipper to embrace those musicians whose fame is still ahead of them.

The jazz scene in Hartford has always fluctuated between safe, comfortable, mainstream choices — lullaby music for the capital city of the Land of Steady Habits — and more adventurous styles. As Hartford enters its next cycle of jazz festivals, jazz listeners have the opportunity again to decide what time it is.

18

Preserving Sam Colt's Legacy

Lary Bloom

In August of 1986, Tracy Atkinson, then the director of the Wadsworth Atheneum, summoned Bill Hosley, his young curator of American Decorative Arts, from his basement office to discuss an "urgent concern." Hosley's curiosity was aroused — his relationship with the boss was not one characterized by urgency.

That morning Atkinson reviewed with Hosley details of what appeared to be a scandal of historic proportions. Over on Capitol Avenue, the Museum of Connecticut History, relying on the advice of a consultant, had delivered to private collectors nearly 300 of its rare guns designed and manufactured in Hartford by Samuel Colt. In return, it received a few Colt weapons deemed to be of equal value. There was dispute about the value, and about the museum's authorization to make a trade that sent Hartford treasures worldwide — even, it was believed, to the collection of King Hussein of Jordan. And now, The Hartford Courant was snooping about looking for another smoking gun. Could the Atheneum, which had its own collection of rare Colt weapons, account for everything, or had it been swapping Colt's pieces, too?

Hosley gulped. The Colt collection was under his wing, but only technically. He always said, with a smile, that he is "the curator of everything except painting and sculpture — of whatever they don't want: the furniture, the guns, the pottery." He knew of the existence of the weapons, and of a few other items, including the Charter Oak chair, the elaborate piece with bas-relief, crafted from the remains of Hartford's legendary tree. It was the chair for which Sam Colt, in a fit of typical urban pride and one-upsmanship, outbid the city in 1857.

None of the Colt collection was on display, and so Hosley went digging, reviewing old reference cards and inspecting the vault and every corner of the place where works are stored that for reasons of space and judgment seldom, or never, make it to the walls or display cases. He not only accounted for the chair and all the guns the museum was supposed to possess but he also came across other Colt-related buried treasure: textiles, hundreds of paintings, prints, metalwork, historical ephemeral, international travel souvenirs and letters to Sam and his wife Elizabeth from Brigham Young, Jefferson Davis, Stephen Douglas, the Sultan of Turkey, the Czar of Russia.

Hosley's training and natural interests had always led him into dark corners of the past. "My main thrust was always history, art, and what is now called cultural heritage to preserve things so they don't get trashed. This was always my motivation."And now he had come across a cache of evidence that was not just guns but "a big civic story to tell, involving a lot of funky people, and a lot of really neat stuff. I've always believed one of the most exciting things the Atheneum can do is tell its great patronage stories: Daniel Wadsworth [founder of the museum], Chick Austin [its flamboyant director from 1927 to 1945], Frederick Church [the great painter born and buried in Hartford], J.P. Morgan [the financier]. These are people in whose stories the community has a big stake."

And so this discovery focused Hosley's curiosity about Sam Colt. He questioned why it was that such a legendary figure, one whom Hosley himself would eventually promote as a pioneer inventor and manufacturer and the creator in Hartford of "the Silicon Valley of the 19th century," was such an ill-defined and largely ignored character in his own community. To be sure, Colt has been part of Hartford's official history for a long time, has had his named attached to an Atheneum wing, and has been written about as a Hartford citizen (most significantly by Ellsworth Grant in his book, "The Colt Legacy"). But if Mark Twain had never been suitably celebrated in the town where he did much of his greatest work, Sam Colt — his name "more widely known throughout the world than that of any other living American inventor," said publisher and politician William Hamersley in 1856 — had hardly been celebrated at all.

The more he researched it, the more Hosley was fascinated by the Colt story, the more he pressed his own vision of resurrecting the legend and making it a permanent force in Hartford.

Hosley was fascinated, not only by what Colt accomplished but also by the methods he used. "Colt was one of the original masters of spin. He shaped his own reputation. He became synonymous with his product. He was charismatic, outspoken, an in-your-face kind of guy."

Nowadays, Hosley points out, we have a Department of Economic Development and other public authorities that offer incentives to those who entertain grand, or even modest, plans as employers. But when Sam Colt introduced the idea of such incentives nearly a century and a half ago, arguing that the city, in return, would benefit greatly from the taxes imposed on the

Samuel Colt

residents of his factory village, he found a jury of unsympathetic faces. It was an argument he eventually won, but his patience for the city fathers often expired, and vice versa. When he offered to build a large technical college (it might have been Hartford's version of MIT) on the condition that the new state Capitol be built in his neighborhood, those in power decided he had crossed too many lines.

They were only too happy to put Sam, the shameless promoter, in his place. It was Sam, after all, who with Elizabeth had built Armsmear, an ostentatious home in the South End. Hosley says, "Colt was not playing by the rules of Hartford society, which encouraged a more Calvinist approach. New Englanders were ambivalent about flaunting wealth, if not downright hostile to it."

And there were, of course, questions and scandals befitting any prominent family. There was the matter of Sam and Elizabeth's only child to survive to adulthood, Caldwell, who never took a profession, a compassionate way of saying he was a disappointment (he died in mysterious circumstances in Florida at the age of 35). There was also the issue of a woman named Caroline Henshaw, and her child said to have been fathered by Sam's brother John, or perhaps by Sam himself. This is not to mention the murder — John was found guilty of killing a printer but before he could be hanged, he killed himself in jail with a knife smuggled in by — Sam? These events were the O.J. Simpson trials of the era, but in lore survived a shorter time than even the locally undervalued Colt manufacturing story.

That story does have its followers — else valuable guns would not have been sought worldwide from the Museum of Connecticut History (the practice of selling them off, in the wake of the investigation, ceased). In the end Colt's factory produced weapons that were crucial in the Mexican War and Civil War, and, eventually, guns that won the West; but in Hosley's estimation, his greatest contribution was not guns at all, but mass production, interchangeable parts made by machine. It was an achievement in the art of manufacturing that became legendary around the world, with the clear exception of the city in which it was pioneered.

Next fall marks the 10th anniversary of Hosley's accidental discoveries. It will have been a decade full of devotion to the Colt story, and of notable triumph. For in the fall of 1996, the Wadsworth Atheneum will open Hosley's longtime dream — its longest-running show in modern times (five months) displaying 350 pieces from the Colt collection. At the same time, a new book is scheduled to be released, written by Hosley and published by the University of Massachusetts Press, tentatively titled "Crossfire: The Legend and Legacy of Sam and Elizabeth Colt."

To a very clear extent, Hosley's message about the Colts has been embraced. Patrick McCaughey, the director of the Atheneum, says, "Bill has been persuasive in his argument that Hartford's past is Hartford's future."

The Atheneum's marketing department has offered its support by helping to produce for the fall of 1996 something rare for the city: a package for group tours that includes other star-quality Hartford landmarks, including the Mark Twain and Harriet Beecher Stowe houses, the state Capitol, and The Old State House. It is supported by grant money from the state Department of Economic Development, which apparently sees the wisdom of such cultural cross-pollination. McCaughey says Hosley "is terribly keen to keep pointing out to people if you revive a great part of Hartford's past you must not make it a solo deal. You should not do it for narrow and selfish institutional interests."

What we have here is an opportunity for Hartford to receive fleets of buses from Schenectady and Springfield and Providence, and, yes, even Boston and New York.

But to suggest that all is well in the Colt kingdom, or in Hosley's pursuit, is to ignore the realities of the city and of the shaky "business" of culture. Raising money for the exhibit has been difficult. A lot of the collection needed repair and cleaning. Hosley says it took $6,000 just to address the woodwork and upholstery on one chair. Frames and furniture

Sam Colt's enterprise and vision deserve to be recognized and celebrated, and Bill Hosley is a man with that very plan.

were dirty or had some damage. And so the exhibit itself is a great economic and cultural risk. Hosley hopes it becomes a blockbuster — something that even exceeds the enormous success he had in the mid-'80s with another show that offered a sense of place, "Great River." He says the idea of resurrecting Colt in Hartford will end "if we get creamed financially." Because, beyond the exhibit itself, Hosley wants a Colt permanence — he wants the community to retain, promote and benefit from the legacy.

He has seen so many other communities prosper from such treasures of the past. He and his wife Christine Ermenc, director of education at the Connecticut Historical Society, take their two small children, Abigail and Benjamin, on businessmen's holidays — about 30 weekend trips a year to historical sites and small museums, because this stuff is in their blood. And they sense it in Hartford's blood, even if Hartford itself doesn't seem to.

He tries to inspire businesspeople who find it hard to grasp what he is selling — the notion that the past is something to be honored, and is marketable, and that we have to bring together what Hosley calls the stakeholders in the Colt story — the many institutions in town that have a clear benefit in getting the word out.

The establishment, he points out, finds it easy to be impressed by tall buildings and to overlook the possibilities of historic preservation. He argues about misplaced values. "Had one-quarter of the money used in the effort to mimic New York-style architecture been invested in adaptive reuse of some of Hartford's historic treasures, we would have something more valuable, and something to be proud of."

He tells these people that tourism is money, and the Colt story, properly adored and disseminated, means big-time tourism, particularly in that the city has such an impressive cast of characters in the Colts, the Clemenses, the Stowes, etc.

He once wrote me, in support of the Twain's World project (which promotes the same tourism idea, but with Colt in the supporting cast), that "history and personalities are the one thing we have that is specifically ours. If you can help make something of it, we'll all be richer and wiser." In that letter, he also argued that, in his view, the economic benefits of the Colt heritage may be more promising than those from Twain's.

This pursuit has become so important to him that it may on occasion have encouraged a straining of credibility. Patrick McCaughey says, "It's hard for Bill to say anything negative about Sam or Elizabeth — visible pain crosses his face — even when he talks about their son Caldwell, who was a worthless rake."

Hosley can be excused. He knows the frustration of selling history. It was Hosley and a group of other visionaries who created the Victorian Trail, a promising concept of connecting Hartford's historical dots, but one which has not engendered much in the way of tourism. "We were unable to achieve consensus about where it was going, and we ran out of juice."

And now Hosley worries, too, that in this politically correct era that those who see the Colt legacy as representing a glorification of guns will have undue influence. Indeed, the National Endowment for the Humanities rejected the Atheneum's first request for support of the Colt exhibit because, Hosley believes, of the guns. And how do you raise funds in a city where guns are perceived as a major issue?

So, slide show in hand, he pleads his case to all who will listen. "It's not about guns," he says. "It's about enterprise and vision." There have been many other arguments on the gun-maker's behalf, going back to spiritualist A.J. Davis's 1854 view (that a century later would be mirrored by atomic bomb defenders) that Colt "is doing more than a thousand clergymen to bring peace on earth... by multiplying weapons of defense so extremely deadly that they will frighten the war-spirit out of the most courageous warrior." For a gentler defense, and a commentary on Hartford's role as a center of American prosperity, we can turn to Isabella Beecher Hooker, women's rights advocate and member of a distinguished literary family, who said, "I for one feel thankful that if pistols must be made, they are to be made in Hartford since they bring so many pleasant accessories."

Hosley's own fervor to represent the importance of the Colt story — "It's where the Twain story was 30 years ago, underfunded and underappreciated" — eventually produced impressive support.

In late September, the underfunding was addressed in a big way. Hosley had planted a seed with Fleet Bank, impressing its executives with his own enthusiasm for the Colt story and arguing that they should sponsor the Atheneum exhibit. And then McCaughey tried to close the deal. The director was asked by Richard Higginbotham, the CEO of Fleet Bank of Connecticut, to appear before the contribution committee to make his pitch. Ten minutes had been set aside, but just before showtime McCaughey was asked, "Could you do it in seven?"

McCaughey was his persuasive self and, at the 6 1/2-minute mark, he introduced the exclamation point to his case when he produced from its case a Colt presentation pistol worth $500,000. The committee was wowed.

Shortly thereafter, it voted to donate $75,000 so that Fleet could become the major corporate sponsor of Hosley's dream. It was a landmark moment, and not only for cultural heritage. It was likely the first time in American banking history that such an institution was thrilled to fork over huge sums at the point of a gun.

One day in late summer, Bill Hosley led me on a tour of the Colt Trail. We started in a cemetery (Old North, where we walked through the weeds) and we ended in one (Cedar Hill, where we marveled at the beauty). We toured Armsmear, where I met a real countess, and where we climbed the tower where Sam Colt took his dinner guests so they could marvel at his empire. We offered opinions on the old Colt armory, which Hosley worries about. I watched as he proudly announced the work to clean up the elaborate tribute in bas-relief and sculpture on the edge of Colt Park that Elizabeth commissioned in honor of Sam. I sensed his joy at the story he told — a young girl of Puerto Rican ancestry rode her bike up to him one day while he was working at the site (picking up broken bottles and condoms) and said: "This is the coolest thing in Hartford. This is Sam Colt — he built the armory." I felt his despair when he spotted yet another new effort at defacement on the monument — a fresh coat of white paint applied to certain critical points, including the face of young Sam Colt. "Sometimes I want to sit out here with a gun and wait. It makes me cry." We spent some time there, and just before we left, he read the inscription on the back of the monument aloud: "His wife in faithful affection dedicated this memorial." He said, "Faithful affection is not what killed this city."

At Cedar Hill cemetery, he inspected the huge monument in marble he has seen dozens of times, and saw details and inscriptions he hadn't noticed before. He climbed as high as he could, with a child's delight, to read small words, and as he descended he lost his footing, fell to the ground, and skinned his knee.

When he rolled up his pant leg, I noticed a gaping wound, and blood running down his leg. But Hosley continued marveling at his heroes buried in that ground, and did not attend his own injury. Instead, he surveyed the glorious landscape of Cedar Hill and rattled on about Sam — Sam the visionary, Sam who could see things where others could not see them, Sam who would stop at nothing to tell his story.

19

Front Street

Susan D. Pennybaker

The faces that greet us in these photographs are those of the immigrants who came to Hartford at the end of the last century. Some proudly declare their trades, shops, wares and pastimes. Their children play in unpaved streets; the hawkers hustle chickens, flowers, produce and meat. Mothers and daughters mind their infants. These same streets shield prostitutes and house servants and politicians, tiny restaurants and sweatshops. They are home to booksellers and laundresses and rabbis, small hotels, gambling joints and pool rooms. Vaudeville acts, melodrama, Wild West pageants and minstrel shows thrill the idle. The police keep watch on foot, on cycle and on horseback. The wealthy come to do their daily shopping, side-by-side with Hartford's growing working population. The Connecticut River forever threatens to overflow its nearby banks and when it does, rot follows, while the fears of floods of biblical proportions linger and fester. Insurance companies, forges, small textile manufacturers, ironmongers, livery stables and wharf owners in the adjacent parts of city, bear witness — hovering, watching and making a buck.

Though Hartford Hospital, the Orphans Asylum, schools, places of worship and union halls are within walking distance, many residents do not survive into old age in this Front Street neighborhood before the First World War. Italians and Irish, blacks and Jews, Poles and Russians, migrants from Georgia and the Carolinas, from China, Germany and Sweden, overcrowd the precarious housing stock. The first war brings prosperity for some but others labor under the weight of continuing racial and religious discrimination and the absence of an adequate family wage. Medical care and schooling are fleeting, elusive.

The pictures do not tell us of the fates of those depicted in them. Many coveted the chance to move out of Front Street and took it if it came. Others stayed as shop owners and businessmen but fled to more secure ground after hours. They took their income with them. The inducements to comfort offered by less-congested living drew many in the white population of the area — some to Blue Hills, to Grandview Terrace and the South End; some to the suburbs to West Hartford, to Windsor, to Wethersfield. A torrent of outmigrants made the journey along the trolley lines between the wars — they formed enclaves of people like themselves. At times they mingled with others whose ways and speech and politics were very different. Lingering pockets of the descendants of former slaves and of free blacks survived outside the city limits. Tobacco workers crowded unsanitary barracks in the adjoining fields, but in Hartford neighborhoods and in the surrounding region the down payments for homes, the brokers' assent, and the credit to buy were advanced cautiously and with prejudice. Still, folks moved on if money and opportunity and the color line permitted. If the fortunate looked back wistfully, they looked forward even more resolutely.

On a Saturday or for an evening, one might stroll again through Front Street; one might visit a butcher, a baker or a saloon; one might greet an elderly relative who still paid a low rent. When World War II delivered the GI benefits and "individual" homeownership within reach for some under the FHA, thousands of couples moved out of Hartford. Front Street and other Hartford districts gradually became for them pieces of living history — museums of the 19th century, emporiums of pastrami and antique books and a way to glance at the tenement past without having to live in it. This was so except for those who stayed, perhaps out of sentiment or even out of poverty especially if there was nowhere to move to or if Front Street was simply a better place than where some people had come from. The apparent unity of the old center of the city with its now increasingly segregated racial and ethnic neighborhoods, and its bucolic, suburban fringes, was unstable; it did not ensure the city's future life or well-being. The movie houses and department stores did not foretell an enduring, robust economy despite the buzz of Main Street in the 1940s and the 1950s. Still, in anticipation of continuing prosperity, Front Street became enshrined as a mecca of the city's reconstructed past — the unpredicted portion of Thomas Hooker's legacy, a terrain of the picturesque.

When the planners of the 1960s sought new monies through an enhancement of the city's Grand List, and elements of the business and political community saw gold beneath the bricks, this district of the old central city as it then was loomed as an albatross, as an eyesore, as a failing risk — as ultimately uninhabitable and unprofitable unless transformed. Windsor Street beckoned as meat-cutting joints and dilapidated housing signalled an eligibility for federal subsidies. Both Italians and blacks could be moved, if some more easily than others. The taxes and commercial presence of the large companies were so sorely

needed. Profit margins might easily result from redevelopment. "Modernity" had fostered urban schemes of dubious success elsewhere in the country, schemes of tall buildings and shortsightedness. Likewise, Hartford's experiment in new-myth making, its plaza named for the document that Connecticut claimed as her own, floundered, alienated, provoked and finally prevailed as a concrete and steel ghost. (No fragment of a post-war welfare state was this; no European-style reconstruction after the devastating second war.)

There is now talk in quiet tones that some powerful voices had demanded apartment buildings instead of office blocks. And what of compensation for the businesses, for the landlords? And what of re-housing? Have the taxes from the geometric girders and the shimmering,

Courtesy of The Hartford Studies Project and the Connecticut State Library Collection

lonely glass structures kept the city more alive than it would have been otherwise? Were the planners unwitting demons whose new kingdom gleefully eradicated the nostalgic turf of others' childhoods, childhoods of their parents' stories, their grandparents' makeshift playgrounds?

Do we recapture the walkaday, workaday feeling of the old East Side in Upper Albany or at Park and Broad? Has the possibility of moving in and out of the city widened for our residents over time? What happened to the bright-eyed, fervent urban renewers as fortunes changed? Can we get the Front Street story straight, or will it always represent a chimera — a symbol, a notion — so emphatic in its racial and religious and ethnic overtones as to defy the planners and the historians and the journalists who seek objectivity and truth? Are these the photographs of a lost community that sought to preserve itself in the face of inhumane and profit-seeking developers, or are these the faces of past poverty, of hard work and of short lives? Or photographs of what we still seek ultimately to demolish ... or to restore as artifacts, as sanctuaries of memory? For whom? Who shares the memory? Who will frame the future?

Above: *Yes, it had its problems and limitations, but the bustle found on Front Street is something the city wants to reclaim.*

20

Defining Noah Webster

Rob Kyff

Who was Noah Webster?

He stares down at us from portraits like a judgmental uncle, a persnickety, persimmon of a man who seems about to correct our spelling of "persnickety" and our pronunciation of "persimmon." Even his adulatory moniker "Schoolmaster to America" evokes images of a crusty, chalky pedagogue dispensing canings and dunce caps.

OK. So the guy wasn't Mr. Personality.

But once you get past that stern image — and anyone who wants to understand Noah Webster must — you discover our nation's most underappreciated Founding Father: one who stitched the fabric of American national identity together, not with laws or guns or roads — but with words. His blue-backed speller and his dictionary, toted across America in knapsacks, Conestoga wagons and railroad cars, helped unify and standardize American language. Thanks to him, people from Maine to Mississippi to Montana can communicate with each other, even if they don't always agree with each other.

You also discover something else: a complex, often troubled man who in his 85-year lifespan trembled with powerful passions, bitter disappointments and repeated humiliations. It took him many years to find his life's work. He suffered deep depressions. He never achieved real economic prosperity. He died embittered and disillusioned with the democratic experiment he had helped launch. And yet he enjoyed a loving and harmonious family life.

The long road of Noah Webster was not an easy or simple one. Beneath that severe demeanor lay a very human soul, someone very much like us.

The good old spelling book of Noah Webster

As you drive along South Main Street in West Hartford, the Noah Webster House is easy to miss. Set back from the road behind leafy maple branches, the copper-red New England saltbox might be mistaken for a private family residence, which indeed it was before being purchased by the Town of West Hartford and restored by the Noah Webster Foundation in the mid-1960s.

Volunteer historical interpreter Jim Hostetter, a tall, energetic Travelers Corp. retiree who wears an 18th-century homespun linen waistcoat, jack shirt and breeches, tells visitors how hard life was for middle class farm families like Noah's. "Everything about this house is hard work," he says.

To the right of the front door is the parlor, the best room of the house, where guests were entertained, books were read, and letters were written — and, almost certainly, the room where Webster was born.

In 1758 this was the West Division of Hartford, an area of family farms. From the front step of this farmhouse on a ridge south of the village, young Noah could look east across pastures and fields to the distant city. There, in the 1600s, his Puritan ancestor, John Webster, had helped found the colony of Connecticut and served briefly as its governor.

Noah was not meant to be a farmer. Boys who planned to be farmers didn't carry a Latin grammar book to the fields. Boys who planned to be farmers didn't complain about being in a school where the day was wasted "in idleness, in cutting the tables and benches to pieces."

So, in 1774, inspired by the tutelage of Congregational minister Nathan Perkins and financed by his father, Webster headed to Yale, then a hotbed of Enlightenment thought and revolutionary fervor. During the war with Britain, he suspended his studies twice to serve with the Colonial militia.

After his graduation in 1778, Webster returned to his father's home. Now 6 feet tall, with auburn hair, he was the Revolutionary-era version of today's "boomerang kid" — he had no idea of what profession to pursue and nowhere else to live. His father gave the new graduate a sorely depreciated $8 Continental bill and blunt advice: "Take this; you must now seek your own living; I can do no more for you."

Noah floundered. For four years, he moved from place to place with no goals, no marketable skills and few friends. He taught school in

Hartford and Glastonbury, but found he detested teaching. He earned a law degree in Litchfield only to find the legal field overcrowded with other ambitious young lawyers.

In the summer of 1783, he returned to teaching and set up a school in Sharon. His school was a success, but his love life wasn't. One Sharon woman described the charms of the nerdy pedagogue this way: "In conversation he is even duller than in writing, if that be possible." But she added a telling remark, "He is a painstaking man and a hard student. Papa says he will make his mark."

Both the woman and her papa were right.

Rejected in love by two women and exhausted from teaching, Webster left Sharon and wandered through northwestern Connecticut and across the state border, ending up in the little town of Goshen, N.Y. He had 75 cents in his pocket, and for several months he suffered what he described as "extreme depression and gloomy foreboding."

But from this period of despondency and hopelessness emerged Webster's greatest achievement. After opening a classical school in Goshen, Webster finally conceived a way that would foster both education and nationalism. He would write an elementary spelling book providing school children of the newly founded United States with thoroughly American standards of pronunciation, spelling and usage.

His wish, he said, was "to diffuse a uniformity and purity of language in America, to destroy the provincial prejudices that originate in the trifling differences of dialect and produce reciprocal ridicule ... a national language is a bond of a national union." Everywhere in Europe, he argued, social classes and geographical regions were separated by local accents and dialects. The Frenchmen of Brittany could not understand the Frenchmen of Languedoc; nor could the Englishmen of East Anglia comprehend the Englishmen of Devonshire. He didn't want this to happen in the United States.

Webster's "A Grammatical Institute of the English Language," later renamed "The American Spelling Book" but always known as "the blue-backed speller," eventually comprised three volumes. It was not what we think of as a spelling book today. It was really a primer — a book that taught children how to read, the "Dick, Jane and Sally" of its day. The speller included not only didactic moral stories set in America, but patriotic speeches, history poems and passages extolling American heroes. On the title page of Part III, Webster inscribed, "Begin with the infant in his cradle; let the first word he lisps be 'Washington.' " So through his speller, Webster not only gave Americans a common language but a common heritage as well.

Webster's book found a ready audience across the new nation. It became the standard primer in classrooms, selling an estimated 75 million copies by 1900, second only in sales to the Bible, providing Webster with a stable, if meager, income for life. Students reciting the book's lettery litany — "amiable, accuracy, admiralty, adversary" — could be heard in classrooms from Toledo to Tacoma. After the Civil War, when newly emancipated slaves wanted to learn to read, the first book they asked for was Webster's speller.

Thanks to the speller's benign guidance, wrote historian Henry Steele Commager, "generations of young Americans learned the same words, the same spellings, the same pronunciations; read the same stories; absorbed the same moral lessons." In its time, the speller was "Sesame Street" and "The Lion King" rolled into one. More than any other single publication, it forged a national language and culture.

Forrest Grump

Between 1785 and 1800, Webster roamed the Eastern seaboard, vigorously promoting his speller, befriending political leaders, lecturing, editing and writing. During this period he wrote "Sketches of American Policy," which argued for a strong federal government, penned tracts supporting the Constitution, wrote a two-volume history of epidemics (still respected for its statistical methodology, if not for its medical conclusions), edited one of New York City's first daily newspapers, The American Minerva, lobbied for copyright laws (largely to protect his own writings), and drew plans for a canal between Hartford and Boston.

He crusaded for free public education, a more practical curriculum and education for females. (Feminists, hold your cheers; he felt well-educated women would make better mothers.) He was an ardent abolitionist and, in a book for children, "The Little Reader's Assistant," he described the atrocities of slavery, writing "vengeance must fall upon the heads of men who commit this outrage."

The ultimate networker, Webster became an 18th-century Forrest Gump. He seemed to pop up everywhere. He played whist with George Washington at Mount Vernon, reportedly making Washington laugh when he refused maple syrup with the laconic Yankee remark, "we get enough of that where I come from." He talked spelling reform with Ben Franklin. He attended sessions of the Constitutional Convention. He

Noah Webster will forever be known as a man of words and letters,
but look deeper and you'll find more.

was aboard John Fitch's newly invented steamboat on its maiden voyage.
He engaged in a full-fledged shouting match with the Frenchman
Citizen Genet when Genet suggested America was still a puppet of
Britain.

He counted among his friends and acquaintances such political and
scientific lights as James Madison, Thomas Paine, Aaron Burr, Roger
Sherman, Benjamin Rush, David Rittenhouse, John Dickinson and
Edmund Randolph. Indeed, the Schoolmaster to America had become
part of the "national class" of men to which he had always aspired.

But why, then, didn't Webster achieve a status equal to those of the
Founding Fathers? After all, he was as prolific as Jefferson, as versatile as
Franklin, and as incendiary as Paine. Part of the problem was, yes, that
old bugaboo, his personality. Webster was a nudger, a climber, a cultural

busybody. He was also an overachiever. Webster's versatility, noted Commager, was not so much a product of natural curiosity and intellect but of nagging ambition, grim determination, and indefatigable officiousness, and perhaps of vanity as well... For all his wide and varied interests he did not have a richly stored mind; for all his vitality he did not have an open mind; narrow, cold, almost passionless, he was wholly lacking in those grace notes his contemporaries added to their scores with such ease.

Webster's bumptious personality made him the perpetual wannabe, the outsider with his nose pressed closely on the window. Despite all his diverse crusades and hortatory tracts, in the eyes of the nation's luminaries, and, more important, in his own, he just didn't measure up.

Webster clearly recognized his inability to fit in. "I suspect I am not formed for society," he wrote in 1788, "and wait only to be convinced that people wish to get rid of my company, and I would instantly leave them for better companions: the reflections of my own mind."

Paralleling Webster's personal rejection was his increasing disillusionment with the principles of the American Revolution: equality, freedom and democracy. While during the 1770s and '80s he had championed these doctrines, the rising spirit of faction in American politics, the horrors of the French Revolution, and uprisings such as Shays' Rebellion shook his faith in the common man. By the end of his life, he would become an embittered elitist and near monarchist, proposing the voting age be raised to 45, denouncing the rabble, and condemning Jacksonian Democracy.

Disillusioned with mankind, Webster turned to God. In 1808, he experienced a profound fundamentalist conversion. The answers to American's problems, he came to believe, lay in complete submission to the absolute sovereignty of God and His Bible. If all Americans would simply abide by evangelical Christianity, he believed, the nation's political divisiveness, economic chaos and social upheaval would disappear. He helped found Amherst College to train ministers who would travel west and civilize the frontier, and wrote a sanitized version of the Bible, in which "testicles" became "peculiar members," "teats" became "breasts" and "wombs" were not mentioned at all. His new-found religious fundamentalism relegated him even further to the sidelines of American political discourse.

Yet, here's perhaps the most enchanting and moving aspect of Webster's life: Despite all his public turmoil and disappointment, he savored a loving and joyful relationship with his wife and children.

He married Rebecca Greenleaf of Boston in 1788, and his beloved "Becca" would provide a sanctuary of comfort and support for the rest of his life. In a charming discovery made in 1996, Sally Whipple, director of the Noah Webster House, discovered a long-lost ring Noah apparently gave to Becca to commemorate one of their later anniversaries. In its setting lay the intertwined strands of Noah's and Becca's hair, an apt metaphor for their lifelong bond.

The couple had eight children, one of whom died in infancy. Webster delighted in his six daughters and one son, spending hours playing, singing, reading and laughing with them. He carried raisins in his pocket to dispense to them as treats. When one of his daughters died giving birth, Noah and Becca were despondent for months and reared the new grandchild as their own. After his children grew up and left the house, Webster could often be found staring lovingly at their portraits in the drawing room. As Webster biographer Richard Rollins wrote, "It almost appears that there were two Noah Websters. The cold, cantankerous, authoritative, and self-righteous public man shielded a private, sensitive, warm and loving family man."

The Dictionary

It was no coincidence that Webster began working on his life's masterpiece, his American Dictionary of the English language, around 1800, the same time he became disenchanted with American democracy. For, as much as his dictionary was intended to affirm America's nationalism and its cultural and linguistic independence from Britain, it was also intended to restore the sense of order and authority he saw disappearing from American social and political life.

For more than 25 years he labored by hand on the dictionary's 70,000 entries, his effort producing constant pain and soreness in his hands. Here was a project perfectly suited to his ambition, precision, and persistence. Published in 1828, Webster's dictionary was an achievement of monumental proportions.

There are many myths about why the dictionary was so pre-eminent: that it included many invented words (in fact, only a handful were Webster coinages); that it simplified many spellings (actually, only a few of Webster's new spellings — "honor" for "honour," "music" for "musick" and "plow" for "plough" — caught on while many others didn't — "groop," "medicin," "fantom);" that it was filled with Americanisms (actually, only about 50).

But what made the dictionary a milestone in the history of American English were its two, whole-hearted assertions: that American English was the equal of British English, and that English is a living language, capable of change and improvement. "The process of a living language," Webster wrote, "is like the motion of a broad river which flows with a slow, silent, irresistible current." Reflecting this mutability, he accepted new grammatical constructions and included about 12,000 words that had never appeared in any other dictionary.

Webster's definitions, which were actually short essays, were remarkable in their clarity and conciseness. Webster may have lacked the gracenotes of his contemporaries, but his definitions were clean, lyrical tunes, some even containing a dash of — dare we say it? — humor, for example: "Dandy — a male of the human species who dresses like a doll and who carries his character on his back."

His dictionary, which like his speller promoted America's national identity, would become the most famous of his achievements, even exceeding the speller in its enduring influence. By the time of his death in 1843, the name "Webster" had become synonymous with "dictionary."

Noah's Arc

Noah Webster's life was a broad arc that stretched from the Revolution to the Age of Jackson, from the idealistic optimism of his youth to the bitter disillusionment of his old age, from the blissful husband and father to the ornery curmudgeon.

Sometimes it's tempting to ignore Webster's human flaws and focus only on his prodigious accomplishments. Commager seemed to suggest this approach when he wrote, "It is not what Webster was that is important, but what Webster did."

But Webster's complexity defies such a sharp division between man and deeds. What Webster was is important. For, buried in those 70,000 definitions, those repetitive spelling drills, those hundreds of hectoring tracts on government, abolition and religion, even in that expurgated Bible, lies something of the loving man who kept raisins in his pocket for his children.

For, in his cranky manifestos and precise definitions Webster was fathering and nurturing something he cherished as much as his own family: a land linked by language, lore and love. From the varied voices of America singing, he fashioned a melody clear and true.

The Mark Twain House
Hartford, Connecticut

— Of the State Capitol, Twain said,

"I think I can say, and say with pride, that we have legislatures that bring higher prices than any in the world."

21

Arch Madness

....

Lary Bloom

I f you climb the 95 winding stairs, you may find children already at the top who made it there without wheezing and complaining. The irony is that these kids (perhaps dragged along on a field trip) may not be as compelled to be there as you. They must be told that the Civil War had an enormous local impact — this Soldiers and Sailors Memorial Arch was dedicated in 1886 to the 4,000 Hartford citizens who fought on the Union side, 400 of whom perished. The children, bouncing around up there, noting without a sense of awe the glorious views of Bushnell Park and the carousel and Hartford's downtown, may lack proper reverence for what it took to create this remarkable memorial. It took boatloads of brownstone from Portland, Conn.; the epic work of sculptors and masons to make a monument 116 feet high with twin towers watched over by angels named Gabriel and Raphael; a fortune for the time for construction, more than $50,000, and $1.5 million a century later for refurbishing; and the contribution of an architect so dedicated to the project that George Keller and his wife Mary consigned their ashes to the memorial's thick walls.

Yuck, a child might say. But Madeleine Zaehringer, 8, of Watuaga, Texas, did not say yuck. She said "cool." Other kids on this particular Thursday noontime figured, "How special could Hartford be?" But Madeleine, the little Texas tourist, there with her father, Henry, was awestruck. From the towers, she looked out over the vista and pointed to big buildings and fountains and the train station and then to the dome of the state Capitol. "They said it is 23 carat gold up there."

Those are some of the reasons her dad brought her here "while the wife is at a teaching seminar in Storrs." Back home in Texas, Henry had looked over the brochures and decided to take Madeleine to Hartford. Madeleine was dressed for the occasion, wearing a pink T-shirt that says "Connecticut" that had been purchased in Fort Worth. Henry and his daughter, it was clear, were walking Hartford advertisements.

"This town is great," he said. "We went to Boston earlier. It was terrible. Dirty, rusting, crowded." Hartford was an unexpected pleasure ("Even your freeways are beautiful"). His daughter could now report to her new third-grade class that she had toured Connecticut's capitol city, and from what Madeleine could survey from the peak of one of its historic and hallowed places, it had been heavenly.

Michael McAndrews, The Hartford Courant

In the center of Hartford, 95 steps up,
is a special view from an extraordinary perch.

22

City Hallmarks

Lary Bloom

They don't tend to look upward, these citizens of Hartford who scurry to the tax office to pay a bill, or who eagerly arrive here to secure, where licenses are issued, the necessary forms to get married, or who intend to visit the Office of Weights and Measures to seek, we presume, an ounce or a centimeter of assistance. If they did look upward, if they did pause for just a moment before entering the City Hall, known by purists as the Municipal Building (for reasons too tedious to go into), they would see something residents in other cities don't get to see.

They would see one of the finest architectural examples of Beaux Arts Revival, municipally speaking, in America. They would see arched windows and two varieties of grand columns, Tuscan and Corinthian (if you don't remember your Introduction to Fine Arts, the former has simple capitals, the latter stylized leaves). They would see, staring out at them, the sculpted deer, a symbol for Hartford, for — don't you see? — hart is another name for deer, and ford, well, you know what a deer does at a creek.

Those on the way to Mayor Mike's office seldom pause to note the fluted bronze doors or, once inside the lobby, gaze upward to see the vaulted ceiling. If they were to examine that lovely ceiling, they might picture in their minds the archaeological work of architect Nic Ferzacca of Design Group One of Chester, who, during the effort to restore it, stood on a scaffolding and slowly sandpapered through several layers of paint to discover the original color ("historic green").

Do those who bring their petitions and their gripes to council chambers take note of the ambitious and beautiful bas-reliefs at either end of the atrium, or the trompe l'oeil tribute to a native son, financier J.P. Morgan (who donated much of the land for the building)? Do they pause in the light? For whatever else you may say about City Hall, it is a place in this gray world where there is light. During the eight-year restoration (the dream and triumph of Frank Vernile, the facilities manager), perhaps the most religious moment was when the skylight-cleaning was completed and the beams from above lit the marble floors and everyone's souls. Right down to the floor below ground level. For, indeed, this place is so special the sunlight shines where it shouldn't. An empty political promise? No, an architectural miracle, from a year (1915) when they really knew how to design and construct a gorgeous, thousand-year building, of which ordinary citizens were justifiably proud.

Hartford Courant file photo

They enter City Hall, people do, preoccupied with taxes and transactions. But oh, if they would only look up!

23

Mail Call

···

Lary Bloom

We know where he was standing (Gillett Street). We know his route (the rich vicinity of Hartford's Nook Farm). We know how much money he made, or at least the neighborhood (between \$600 and \$850 a year). We know that his uniform, under an act of Congress in 1888, should have been a little spiffier ("A single-breasted Sack Coat of 'Cadet Gray'). We know what sort of mail he delivered daily, on foot, to the house of Sam and Livy Clemens and their three daughters (there is, for example, the letter from editor and friend William Dean Howells, who argued that the new Twain book, "Life on the Mississippi," would do better if entitled "Piloting on the Mississippi in Old Times.") We know the sort of mail he carried from the Clemenses (Sam Clemens to his mother-in-law: "Mother Dear … The shaving-stand you got for me is just the thing needed … It compels the morning shave. Consequently, I have not missed shaving on any morning since I have possessed it. I thank you very much — you may easily believe Livy does also …") What we don't know about this postman is his name. That is, we do know what his name might have been — one of 37 in the records. Is he Julius Herzfeld? Charles Jackson? John O'Farrell?

On the other hand, we know for certain the name of Jimmy Jerome, who carries mail to the Mark Twain House in modern times, although not by foot. He grew up in the North End of Hartford, and before he started delivering here six years ago, "I didn't even know this place existed." Now, it's his best stop. "Sometimes I use the restroom and, going through the house, I get a sense of history. Mark Twain is a part of American history, and we need that, especially nowadays." Jimmy has started to read Twain, and he can now converse on the subject with his son, Jamie, 16, a huge Twain fan. The kind of mail he has delivered to the house is much different than what arrived a century ago, but still star-quality. There were, for example, letters from Arthur Miller, William Styron, and Garry Trudeau brimming with enthusiasm over their participation in various Twain House projects. There was Russell Baker's invitation to John Boyer, the director, to come to Virginia. And there was the letter from Stephen King, who begged off because of his schedule. The novelist wrote, "I'm busier than a one-legged man in an ass-kicking contest." Just the sort of direct and insensitive response Twain would have admired.

The Mark Twain House, Hartford, CT

Decades before Jimmy Jerome, this letter carrier's mission included missives to and from Sam Clemens.

24

Landscape Artistry

Lary Bloom

Sometime this fall, perhaps even today, the two ancient and stately ginkgo trees on the grounds of the Institute of Living will drop their yellowed leaves in a giant hurry. By the myth, legend, and eyewitness accounts of some who have labored many seasons at Hartford's famous mental health facility, when one leaf of the ginkgo tumbles, all do, immediately. And there is another legend about these trees — in Asia, where the species originated, the sap was once prescribed as treatment for mental illness.

Was this belief central to the trees' planting 145 years ago, when Fredrick Law Olmsted, the designer of New York's Central Park, was asked to produce a suitable landscape for one of his hometown's most noted institutions?

There was no record, but we know something of Olmsted's motivations. When he was a boy, his father took him on horseback rides in the Connecticut River valley, where he formed a lasting sense of peace and beauty that shaped his career. Olmsted believed that the integration of nature was necessary to any functional design. And when it came time to create this design, he wanted a feeling of gardens and of lavish yards. He wanted, he said, to "kill out the Lunatic Hospital and develop the Home!"

As explained by Charles E. Beveridge, author of a new book, "Fredrick Law Olmsted: Designing the American Landscape," the great landscape architect was interested in common ground. "He was trying," Beveridge says, "to make the place as homelike as possible," where those who sought treatment would be reminded of life beyond, and where the public could drive their carriages on a pleasant afternoon.

Much has changed over the last century and a half. The "lunatic asylum" called the Hartford Retreat became the Institute of Living. It changed from a longterm treatment facility, where sons and daughters of the rich stayed for years, or for life, in cottages built by their parents, to a place where nowadays the stay is short, often less than a week. It is a "mental health center" (in the new lingo of the times) trying to deinstitutionalize those who need care for drug dependency, or schizophrenia, or depression, or many other common ills. And it mightily plays down the reputation it earned in mid-century, when Hollywood stars considered it a worthy place to dry out.

One thing that hasn't changed (but perhaps people think it has) is that the circular carriage path is still open to the public, only now it is a

Hartford Courant file photo

On the grounds of the Institute of Living,
signs of tranquility can be obvious or elusive.

walking path. In short, the public is invited in, if discreetly. No cameras are allowed, and, if you see your neighbor strolling what is commonly called "the campus," it would not do to shout, "Hey, Joe, what are you here for?" You may see more than your neighbor — occasionally celebrities still show up. And so do people who've gained notoriety.

The Institute has worked hard to demystify mental illness, to remove the stigma, but obviously privacy still matters.

So when you take your Sunday drive now, come into the front gate, get a map from the guard and hear the rules, but then park your car and tour 35 acres of the most peaceful acres you will ever see (and so campuslike it is often mistaken for the Trinity College campus, which is a few blocks west). Walk past the golf house, where famous "guests" used to sit by the pool. And do examine those ginkgos, and the pecan tree, and the white ash that lightning hollowed out but miraculously still grows. Spend a few lovely moments with all the still-growing children of one of the world's greatest landscape architects. And savor a singular sanctuary where peace of mind means everything.

25

Planting Seeds and Ideas

··

Steve Courtney

Charles Dudley Warner — the friend of Mark Twain, the editor and part-owner of The Courant, the best-selling author of travel books and quietly humorous meditations on life — was tilling the soil in the kitchen garden of his house on Hawthorn Street in 1869 when he got the idea that the readers of The Courant might be interested in his thoughts. In 1870 his growing season's-worth of newspaper columns became his first book, "My Summer in a Garden."

A garden, of course, begins with seed catalogues.

> *How fascinating have the catalogues of the nursery- men become!*
> *Can I raise all those beautiful varieties, each one of which is*
> *preferable to the other? Shall I try all the kinds of grapes,*
> *and all the sorts of pears? …Oh, for the good old days when*
> *a strawberry was a strawberry, and there was no perplexity about it!*

Then, gardeners know, comes an intimate relationship with dirt.

> *The love of dirt is among the earliest of passions, as it is the latest.*
> *Mud-pies gratify one of our first and best instincts. So long as we*
> *are dirty we are pure… The love of digging on the ground (or of*
> *looking on while he pays another to dig) is as sure to come back to him*
> *as he is sure, at last, to go under the ground, and stay there.*

Clearly, this is not a step-by-step gardening guide; Warner means to instruct. "He was erudite and very genteel, very intelligent and compassionate for his time," says Richard Conroy of Portland, who did his Trinity College master's thesis on Warner.

*"My Summer in a Garden" is rich with the insights
and meditations of Charles Dudley Warner.*

Warner noticed, for example, that his Doolittle raspberry canes had sprawled all over his beds of Colfax strawberries. Two men named Dolittle and Colfax were well-known political opponents. "Politics makes strange bedfellows," Warner wrote, and a bon mot germinated.

> *The bean is a vulgar vegetable, without culture, or any flavor*
> *of high society among vegetables. Then there is the cool cucumber,*
> *like so many people — good for nothing when it is ripe and the wildness*
> *has gone out of it.... Lettuce is like conversation: it must be fresh*
> *and crisp, so sparkling that you scarcely notice the bitter in it.*
> *Lettuce, like most talkers, is, however, apt to run rapidly to seed.*

Warner went on to publish enough books and novels to fill 14 volumes of collected works before he died in 1900. But "My Summer in a Garden" remained his most popular book.

In the end, it is a garden of disappointments, teaching what Nook Farm historian Kenneth L. Andrews called "the higher virtues, hope deferred and expectations blighted." Birds devastate Warner's peas, snakegrass spreads in his strawberry patch, caterpillars wilt his melon vines. Warner has spent years cultivating a pear tree. It finally bears pears; then a boy steals them all.

> *... boy the destroyer, whose office is the preserver*
> *as well; though he removes the fruit from your sight, it re- mains in*
> *your memory immortally ripe and desirable. The gardener*
> *needs all these consolations of a high philosophy.*

26

Bushnell's Places

Steve Courtney

"There has been much speculation of late" wrote Dr. Horace Bushnell, after whom Bushnell Park, Bushnell Memorial Hall and various other Hartford-area Bushnellisms are named, "as to whether a child is born in depravity, or whether the depraved character is superinduced afterward."

A logical question for any parent, then or now. Presumably, Samuel and Olivia Clemens wanted the answer when they were newlyweds in 1870 and Livy was three months pregnant; Mark Twain sent away to Charles Scribner & Co. in New York for a copy of the book in which that statement appeared, Bushnell's "Christian Nurture."

Who was this beparked and beconcert-halled Bushnell? The histories call him a liberal Congregationalist theologian — a sobriquet guaranteed to glaze the eyes of most moderns. Theologians these days, unless they do something really outrageous like advocate wild sex, are pretty well ignored. But in 19th-century Hartford, ministers had clout, and what they thought about the doctrines of their faith was a matter of vital interest to the still largely Protestant population. Their trials — and Bushnell was nearly tried for heresy — were the O.J. trials of the day.

It was originally published as "Discourses on Christian Nurture" in 1847, by the 45-year-old pastor of Hartford's North Congregational Church. It was a bombshell in the spare, Calvinist world of Connecticut. Old-time ministers believed that an infant could not enter the church until adulthood — after an explosive, born-again, hellfire-and-brimstone conversion as an adult.

Nonsense, said Bushnell. A child has to absorb religion gradually, and the process has a lot to do with how the parents behaved. "The child,

The concert hall and park make the Bushnell name recognizable,
but Horace himself was an enigmatic sort.

after birth, is still within the matrix of the parental life... and the parental life will be flowing into him all at that time, just as naturally, and by a law just as truly organic, as when the sap of a trunk flows into a limb."

Such heretical thoughts, and a later work in which Bushnell said the Bible was great poetry, but not itself a direct apprehension of God, got him into big trouble in 1850 Hartford when traditional ministers charged him with heresy. But his congregation at the North Church stood by him, as did other liberal religious leaders, and a trial was avoided.

Soon Bushnell was involved in elections, the slavery debate, and civic affairs — campaigning to get an unpromising patch of land near the stagnant Hog River and the railroad tracks designated a park. In 1853 Hartford became the first city in the nation to set aside funds for a public park; it was then know as City Park.

By the time the Clemenses moved to town in 1871 with their newborn son Langdon, Bushnell was spending his retirement in writing, in campaigning to get the new state Capitol built next to City Park and in riding his gig like the devil down Farmington Avenue. Twain gave him, after Bushnell dropped a heavy hint, a copy of "Roughing It."

While he was on his deathbed, the city hurriedly renamed the park in his honor. When he died in February 1876, the Rev. Joseph Twichell preached at his funeral. God had granted Bushnell a great favor, Twichell said: "He spared his life till almost all men were at peace with him. This is a favor not often granted to men who are so much involved in controversy as he was, but it was granted to him."

27

Signatures on the Wall

....

Lary Bloom

The new hall — designed by the same team that would later design Radio City Music Hall — was Hartford's monument to culture. And soon after it was finished in 1930, the giants came to the Bushnell Memorial. Toscanini, Stokowski, Robeson.

But these were in the days before on-location recordings and videotapes and so, to keep a permanent record of who came to Hartford to play music or star in a play or to tell funny stories, the theater's electricians got an idea: a public autograph book. They would ask the stars to sign the walls of their little room. One of the first to do so was Helen Hayes, whose four-night stint in "Victoria Regina" sold out in a matter of hours. And so for more than six decades, stars great and not-so-great have left behind their signatures, and made this little room of electrical fixtures luminous, and a highlight of the hall's public tours.

There are hundreds of names. We selected only a relative few, and offer a way to categorize them:

Gone But Hardly Forgotten:

Ethel Merman, Benny Goodman, Helen O'Connell, Maurice Chevalier, Helen Hayes, Vincent Price, Pearl Bailey, Mitch Miller, Johnny Ray, Rick Nelson, Hal Roach, Tiny Tim, Meredith Willson, Henry Mancini, Patsy Cline, Harry James, Vaughn Monroe, Richard Tucker, Arthur Fiedler, Marvin Gaye.

Extra Added Attractions:

Katharine Hepburn (signed, next to her name, "Local Girl"), Bette

Midler ("The one and only divine Miss M"); Tommy Tune (a staff with a sixteenth note), Seiji Ozawa (top to bottom, in Japanese).

Faded Signatures:

Allen Ludden, Garry Puckett and The Union Gap, Chubby Checker, Vaughan Meador, Tony Orlando, Rod McKuen, Bobby Vee.

Still Vivid After All These Years:

Mel Torme, Tony Bennett, Bob Hope, Carol Channing, Johnny Mathis, Tony Randall, Phyllis Diller, Carole King, Joan Baez.

Couples Still Together Only on the Walls of the Bushnell:

Robert Goulet and Carol Lawrence, Jose Ferrer and Rosemary Clooney, Carly Simon and James Taylor.

Funny Business:

Bill Cosby, Corbett Monica, Jackie Mason, Tom Poston, Victor Borge, Mort Sahl, and with his signature message about getting no respect buried under an electrical box, Rodney Dangerfield.

Handicap Access:

Jose Feliciano, Ray Charles, Itzhak Perlman.

Stars of Today:

Jerry Seinfeld, Anita Baker, Whitney Houston, Garrison Keillor, David Copperfield.

Hartford's Own:

Sophie Tucker, Charles Nelson Reilly, Jackie McLean. (Norman Lear and Louis Nye played the Bushnell — but only at their high school graduations.)

All in the Family:

Nat King Cole with Natalie Cole; Judy Garland with Lorna Luft and Liza Minnelli; and Bonnie Raitt with John Raitt (When he returned to the Bushnell nearly 50 years after his first appearance there, he found next to his own signature his daughter's, from 1992, and a very public personal note: "Hi, Dad").

The many stars who've played the Bushnell are remembered for their performances, and often for a little something else.

28

Amistad

....

Steve Courtney

In 1901, 60 years after he first saw the Africans in Farmington, Charles Ledyard Norton could still remember the wonder he felt. "In my childish eyes" — he was 3 — "they seemed to me a mighty host." The Africans' leader, Sengbeh Pieh, "used to toss me up and seat me on his broad shoulders while he executed a barbaric dance on the lawn for my entertainment."

The idea of Farmington abolitionists raising a home for freed slaves is an appealing one, one that, for me, merited a visit to that town, now a catchword for suburban exclusivity. For the 35 black men and three black women who had arrived in town in the spring of 1839 were the "mutineers" of the Spanish schooner Amistad.

They were Mende people from Sierra Leone in West Africa, kidnapped into slavery. They commandeered the ship in 1839, killed the captain, and ended up off the shore of Connecticut. Steven Spielberg has given us his version of the story in the movie "Amistad."

It's not giving too much away to reveal that the courts set the Mende free to return to Sierra Leone. While they waited for their abolitionist supporters to raise money for the trip, they lodged in Farmington, where antislavery sentiment was strong.

Their supporters had built a dormitory for them on property belonging to abolitionist Austin F. Williams. The dormitory is a nondescript, brown clapboard building next to the far grander Classical revival Williams house, whose widow's walk can be spied on the left as you drive south from Farmington on Route 10.

In February, a few years ago, I struggled through the snow to get into the smaller building; inside, the air was cold and musty. The stairs to

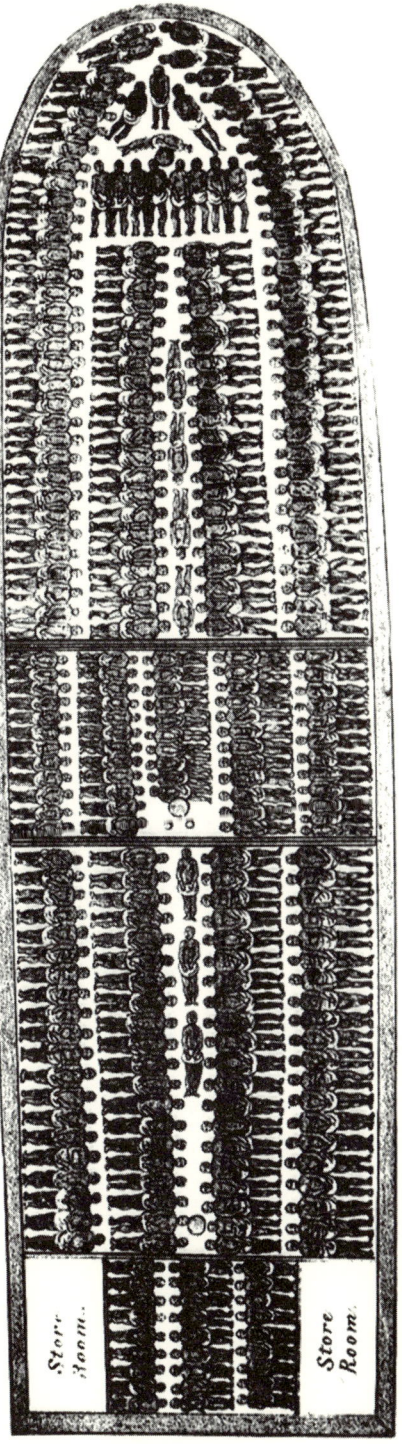

This lithograph
of a slave ship,
from 1836,
is a disturbing
reminder of a
shameful time.

the second floor, where Sengbeh Pieh and the men lived, had a decided list to the left as I climbed them.

Sengbeh had a private room. It was now oddly painted, with a different primary color on each wall. When I visited, it was filled with mildewing cartons of old New Yorker magazines, picture frames and model railroad tracks. One window would have given Singbeh a view west; the other south. There was no view east, toward Africa.

The men lived in a larger space next to their leader's room. The women boarded with other village sympathizers. The Mende studied, were taken on fund-raising tours of American cities, and amused the children of the village. They swam in the Farmington canal; one, named Foone, took a cramp and drowned, and is buried in the village. (In 1992, the present leader of Sierra Leone took part in a rededication ceremony at the grave.)

They performed athletic feats for the villagers. "A broad flight of steps then led down from the southern piazza of my father's house," Norton wrote, "and I distinctly remember seeing the athletic Cinquez turn a somersault from these steps and then go down the sloping lawn in a succession of hand springs heels over head, to the wonderment and admiration of my big brothers and myself."

Cinquez is Norton's spelling of Sengbeh; he is most often referred to as Cinque. As his English improved, he wrote letters, such as one to President James Tyler: "You have done a great deal for us. Now we want to go home, very much, very soon. As soon as you can send us." And to Adams, in Biblical terms: "Our soul is escaped as a bird out of the snare of the fowler — the snare is broken and we are escaped."

But it was the thought of Sengbeh in his second-floor room, feeling the approach of winter, that stayed in the mind on that wintry visit. "They say we are like dogs without any home," he wrote to Tyler in October 1841. "But if you will send us home you will see whether we be dogs or not. We want to see no more snow." In November Sengbeh was on a boat home.

29

The View from Church

Steve Kemper

rederic Edwin Church, born into an old Hartford family in 1826, was the most famous and affluent painter in America in the decade before the Civil War. In huge landscapes — some of them 10 feet wide — Church portrayed the New World as grand, pristine and sublime, a place of spectacular natural details, endless horizons and unlimited potential. He painted an energetic young country's vision of itself and its future, and America took him to its heart — until the Civil War showed the nation a different image.

One painting, "Heart of the Andes," pulled in $3,000 in three weeks in New York City and then went on tour. In St. Louis a young man named Samuel Clemens plunked down two bits several times to see it, and wrote his brother, "Your third visit will find your brain gasping and straining with futile efforts to take all the wonder in." (The painting is now in the Metropolitan Museum of Art in New York.) Years later Clemens met the painter in Hartford, where Church occasionally visited family and friends.

By the time he was famous, Church had long since left Hartford for New York City and the Hudson Valley, but his roots ultimately claimed him. When he died in 1900, virtually forgotten, he was buried alongside his parents, siblings, wife and children in Spring Grove Cemetery, off Main Street in Hartford's North End.

Church and his reputation rested in obscurity until the rediscovery of American landscape painting in the 1960s and 1970s, when critics almost unanimously declared him our finest 19th-century landscape artist for his meticulous rendering of flora, his superlative treatment of water, light and clouds, and his sweeping sense of drama. In 1979, his

Frederic Edwin Church's spectacular landscape paintings captured the pulse of a nation.

Wadsworth Atheneum, Hartford. Bequest of Mrs. Clara Hinton Gould.

Wadsworth Atheneum, Hartford. Bequest of Mrs. Clara Hinton Gould.

"Coast Scene, Mount Desert (Sunrise off the Maine Coast)."

painting "Icebergs" sold for $2.5 million, more than twice the previous record for an American painting. A few years ago one of his works brought $9 million.

But as his reputation rose from the ashes, his gravesite in Hartford was lying toppled and thrashed by vandals. When Hartford Courant columnist Tom Condon wrote about this disgrace in 1989, the cemetery's administrative manager, a retiree named Caleb H. O'Connor, didn't even know who Church was, but he soon had the site cleaned up. Last summer he restored the gravesite and protected it with a locked wrought-iron fence, thanks to a grant from a group associated with Olana, Church's dazzling Hudson Valley home, which makes Twain's house look dowdy and is now a museum. This painter of magnificent vistas now rests amid urban density, his grave not quite shaded by a few hemlocks.

In 1846 the Wadsworth Atheneum became Church's first paying customer when the 2-year-old museum bought his portrayal of the Hooker party — which included one of Church's ancestors — traveling through a benign wilderness to found Hartford. The Atheneum now owns nine Churches, including several major works, most notably "The Vale of St. Thomas, Jamaica."

For me, one of most moving paintings in the Atheneum is "A View in Cuernavaca, Mexico," painted a year or two before his death. "Cuernavaca" is small, perhaps 9 by 12 inches. The view in it is almost blocked, first by a man-made stone arch and then by a crumbling stone building. Far beyond these things, almost beyond view, mountains rise in the distance, pale and vague. It's as if the grand unbounded future, the new Eden envisioned by the young Church and his young country, has dimmed and retreated beyond reach, blocked by experience and approaching death.

In the end, Church decided that he belonged not near his spectacular house with its wide views of the Hudson River Valley, but in a crowded plot hallowed by personal history, beneath a few hemlocks, near the people he loved.

30

In Good Hands

Steve Courtney

Barbara Lapins is a quiet, self-effacing woman — not a woman, you would think, who would stare down traffic day and night, in fair weather and foul, from the tiny triangle of park where Asylum and Farmington avenues come together.

But Barbara does — or rather her eyes and chin do, cast in bronze. Barbara was a model for the figure of Alice Cogswell in the statue that commemorates the foundation of the American School for the Deaf. It portrays a girl in early 19th-century costume, surrounded by a pair of giant hands.

It all seems very long ago to Barbara, and some things are hazy. She was 12 in 1952, when Frances Wadsworth, a sculptress with Mamie Eisenhower bangs, came peeking into the classrooms at Granby Elementary School to find the face she wanted. Interested in Barbara's clear chin and widely spaced eyes, she called Barbara's mother for permission.

So Barbara put on her Sunday-best dress, nylons and flats one Saturday and went to the studio on Day Street. Wadsworth gently told her she didn't have to dress up; a sculptor's studio is a dusty place. Barbara was mortified. But every Saturday for several weeks she came back: "It was a quiet time," she says.

Another girl served as the model for Alice Cogswell's body, in its high-waisted Empire dress. The girl's father, Barbara recalls, supplied the large hands that surround the girl's figure.

It's a protective gesture. It was seeing deaf Alice Cogswell unable to to play with other children that led Thomas Hopkins Gallaudet of Hartford, in 1815, to begin the first movement for the education of the

*You will find, at the intersection of Asylum and Farmington,
the intersection of Barbara Lapins and Alice Cogswell.*

deaf in America. Before his effort, it was believed the deaf were
ineducable. The hands' gesture also has less obvious meaning. To sign
the work "light," you put your hands together in that way, then extend
your arms out and upward.

A group of Hartford worthies, including Cogswell's father (and
Wadsworth's husband's ancestor, museum founder Daniel Wadsworth)
sent Gallaudet to Europe. In France, the deaf were learning the language
of signing from the Abbe Sicard in a Catholic charity organization.
Gallaudet learned what he could, then, when funds ran out, returned to
Hartford — but brought Sicar's assistant, Laurent Clerc, with him.

They started their school in a downtown hotel, then moved to a
house on Prospect Street, then to a new building on Asylum Hill, and the
street in front of it, Asylum Avenue, because the Asylum for the Deaf and
Dumb was there. (Both "Asylum" in the sense of a protected place and
"dumb" in the sense of being unable to speak have taken on new and
unpleasant meanings since.) A century later, in 1921, the school moved to
West Hartford.

There it serves what has come to be called, proudly, the deaf
community. They are not a quiet group. The lunchroom at the school is
a noisy place — even if much of the "noise" is silent to us, the rapid
movements of arms and hands in signs and gestures.

Of Alice Cogswell, who was deafened at age 2 by spinal meningitis,
no picture remains, only a silhouette, a common way of portraying family
members in the early 1800's. So in 1952, when Frances Wadsworth was
commissioned to sculpt the monument, the sculptress had the shape of a
nose to work with, but little else. Hence her foray into the Granby school
for a chin and eyes.

On Asylum Avenue recently, Barbara Lapins, now a senior
executive secretary at the Institute of Living, held two fingers up so she
couldn't see the statue's nose. "Yes," she said, "those eyes are definitely
my family's." She hadn't been that close to the statue since April 18, 1953,
the rainy Saturday that the statue was dedicated. A shy group, she and her
mother, brother and sister had stood behind the statue and can't be seen
in photos of the event. But her eyes and chin can be seen there every day.

31

A Highway Runs Through It

Tom Condon

Peple who passed by the house in the early 1970s sometimes saw one or the other of the sisters, standing impassively at a window. The ladies were in their 90s then, and could no longer travel even the couple of blocks to their hairdresser at Sage-Allen. They might not have left if they were able to; the city around them had changed beyond comprehension.

Soon, Julia Isham, then Charlotte, no longer came to the window. Now the house itself has become a lonely spinster.

You may not know the name, but you know the Isham-Terry House. It's the three-story Italianate villa that stands just north of downtown next to I-84 west — so close, in fact, that part of the property was taken when the highway was built.

The house is fascinating for its eclectic 19th-century architecture, its period furnishings and family curios, and for the tableau it preserves almost perfectly of upper-middle class Hartford life in the first years of the 20th century.

The challenge is how to lure people to a grimy, inelegant part of town to enjoy the experience.

The house is testimony that the near North End wasn't always on the skids. When Ebenezer Roberts, a prosperous merchant, built the house in 1854, the neighborhood was becoming home to the carriage trade. So it was in 1896 when Dr. Oliver Isham, a bachelor, bought the house. His teenage sisters, Julia and Charlotte, moved in to care for him and serve as his receptionists.

And so they lived, friendly with the city's best families, active in their church, sometimes going for a spin in their 1902 Oldsmobile,

Hartford Courant file photo

Behind the doors of Julia and Charlotte Isham's home
is evidence of the way life used to be.

almost always entering their cat in the Hartford Cat Show. Somehow they endured the highway construction in the 1950s, the urban riots of the '60s, the decline of their neighborhood thereafter.

The sisters lived until 1976 and 1979, and did almost nothing to the house after about 1920. That's both bad and good. The Antiquarian and Landmarks Society, which inherited the building in 1980, has had to attack structural neglect: a leaking roof and a collapsed cellar wall.

On the other hand, except for the later addition of a hideous shag carpet that belongs in a frat house, the building is so flawlessly preserved that it seems as if the sisters are merely out for an afternoon during the Taft Administration.

Enter through the stained-glass doorway on High Street. On the right is the doctor's office, with the sign still resting on the chair. Behind this is a darkly impressive dining room, with a stupendous built-in buffet, right out of Henry James.

The parlor fills the whole south side of the building, and is dominated by an Egyptian Revival pier mirror. The library, with carved wood ceiling, tall windows and remarkable carved rocking chair, is compelling.

The house has a hundred other fascinating touches: Hartford's most perfectly preserved 19th-century bathroom, the sisters' framed Mayflower Descendants certificates, Terry clocks (their mother was a Terry).

Unfortunately, only 200 to 300 people a year get to see the house. It was once open on Sundays, but now is shown by appointment, so a staff member can provide security. Sadly, if no one watches the visitors' cars, their marketable components are sometimes removed.

The Antiquarian Society is trying to broaden the visitor base, said Vivian Zoe, director of development. She's negotiating for secure parking, trying to bring meetings to the house, trying to start a program with nearby Quirk Middle School.

"It's a struggle, but were here," said Karin E. Peterson, the house's hugely energetic curator. "We've spent money on it every year, we're preserving it as best we can and we want to share it."

32

Portal to the Past

....

Anne Farrow

A woman in a yellow slicker, her glasses foggy with rain, leaned on her cane and peered, smiling, into the deep garden behind the Main Street landmark. Inside the house, a group of about 30 toasted, with plastic cups of white wine and modest hors d'oeuvres, the dedication of the gate on which the woman rested her hand.

It was a happy moment.

The tall new gate being celebrated late on a drenching and humid Thursday afternoon will provide access to one of the oldest gardens in Hartford, a garden designed during the last year of the Civil War for what is now the very oldest house in Hartford, the Butler-McCook Homestead.

Not only an important example of Victorian horticultural design, the garden is also an emotional statement about a family that cherished its own unity and history, even as the world around them changed utterly.

The people who are passionate about this house, including but not limited to its conservator, the Antiquarian & Landmarks Society, simply call it Butler-McCook: Butler for the man who built it in 1782, and McCook, for the family who long ago intermarried with the Butlers and left the elephantine white house to the landmarks society 30 years ago.

Since the house and its remarkable collections — there are pieces of furniture that have not been moved in 200 years — opened to the public in 1973, the garden Jacob Weidenmann designed in 1865 also has been open. But to *get* to the garden, which now enjoys the attentions of the West Hartford Garden Club, you had to enter from a block away, or during hours the historic house was open.

Arthur Simoes Photography

*A gate to a garden, on Hartford's busy Main Street, is the product
of passion and a designer's childhood memory.*

With help from a charitable trust, the society put on a design
competition and invited the public to submit designs for a gate, so that
the garden — which the McCooks described as their oasis — would be
constantly accessible.

They also sought a plan to improve the walkway leading from the
bustle of Main Street back to the garden, so that whether you can walk or
whether you cannot walk, it's easy to navigate the distance back to
Weidenmann's Victorian beds of boxwood and roses and the flowering
trees the family added to his designs. It is a property of nearly three acres,
and once you get behind the house, the sounds of late-day traffic
rumbling toward the interstate fall away.

For the designer who won the competition, announced a year ago in the spring, the garden gate represents a gateway that is also personal. Paulo Vicente was a small boy when his family moved to Connecticut from Portugal, but he remembers Butler-McCook from visits to the immigration offices next door in the Federal Building, a tall taupe edifice. Delayed by rain and heavy traffic on the highway north from Southport, where he works at an architectural firm, he missed the celebratory words about his gate, which he designed to feel like a foyer to a room.

Indeed, the gate is tall and wide and makes you feel as if you have arrived somewhere. It is painted a sage green, and manages at once to suggest something homelike, which the garden is, and something important, which it also is. Of all of Jacob Weidenmann's domestic designs — he was a major landscape architect of the mid-19th century and created the designs for Bushnell Park and Cedar Hill Cemetery — only this garden survives.

"This is the past *preserved*," said Bill Hosley, who reserves for history the kind of enthusiasm people exhibit for a favorite team, or a stamp collection, or rock 'n' roll. "This is the *only* house on Main Street that a person visiting from 1900 would recognize inside and out," said Hosley, a former Wadsworth Atheneum curator who is now the landmarks society's executive director.

The plan for the dedication had been to gather around the gate, but the deluge at rush hour moved the event inside, where the centerpiece was a sandwich board in the shape of the gate, painted by Vivian Zoe to wear a few days earlier in the Hooker Day Parade. Zoe is the development director of the landmarks society and has been, to use a word that would not appear on any flow chart, the angel for this project.

She hugged people coming in from the rain, and took their wet coats. The room got crowded, and because it was steamy for October, the windows were wide open. If you sat on the radiator by the window, you could see the new gate, which seemed to vanish into the trees bordering the property.

Behind the house, the garden was a deep rectangle filling with darkness and a white rose as tall as a man glowed in the falling light.

33

Seminary Moments

Tom Condon

Duncan Black MacDonald left the University of Edinburgh in 1892 with the radical idea of teaching Islam at the Hartford Seminary. No other American seminary offered such a course. What was the point? Islam was the stuff that Christian missionaries were trying to convert the heathens away from.

MacDonald thought otherwise. He saw no reason to look down on Islam; its followers were descendants of Abraham and people of The Book, as were Christians and Jews, and devout Muslims believed the Koran to be the final fulfilment of the prophecies of the Bible. MacDonald convinced the seminary's directors that missionaries stood a better chance of success if they understood the culture of the countries they were to visit.

Old photos show MacDonald with curly hair, bushy beard and wire-rimmed glasses, intently lecturing his students in their Eton collars. Other professors began teaching about about Buddhism and Hinduism, and the seminary became a leading center for the study of non-Christian religions.

It still is, and is getting more attention than ever, thanks in no small measure to its Duncan Black MacDonald Center for the Study of Islam. With growing interest in cults and other religious topics, in this country and abroad, the seminary's experts are quoted regularly by the national media. Enrollment is up to 250, a 25-year high. Local residents have discovered the seminary's lectures, workshops, fims, bookstore and library. "We're on a roll," said Seminary president Dr. Barbara Brown Zikmund, with succinct enthusiasm.

This couldn't have been foreseen by those at the founding of the seminary in 1833. It was started by strict Congregationalist ministers who felt the theology coming from the state's only divinity school, Yale, was getting far too liberal.

The debate focused on the nature of man. The orthodox Calvinist position had man born with a sinful, depraved nature. Enlightenment-crazed Yale men such as Nathaniel Taylor began to preach that depravity was a matter of free choice; man could choose good or evil. Ministers headed by Bennett Tyler shook their heads and founded their own seminary in East Windsor.

But by the late 19th Century the school had moved to Hartford and become a center of liberal Protestantism. In addition to courses in Islam and Arabic, the seminary was the first in the country to prepare women for ordination.

So it continues. The seminary has seen difficult times. In the 1970s, faced with declining demand for ministers, its directors made a wrenching decision to stop training for the ministry and focus on graduate training for ordained clergy and lay people. They sold the Gothic campus on Elizabeth Street to the state — it's now UConn Law School — and commissioned a new home. Architect Richard Meier's striking white-enamel building hints at what God would do with Legos. It is a living metaphor for inquiry; light comes in at all angles.

The seminary is still a Christian-oriented institution studying other religions — not to convert them any longer, but to learn to live with them, and become enriched by them.

So when the faculty and students gather in the chapel for a Christmas service, they'll read about Mary and the Christ child — from the Koran.

A leading center for the study of non-Christian religions, Hartford Seminary celebrates the spirit of inquiry.

34

Twain on the Talk Shows

Andrew Marlatt

Press Release

Hartford, Conn. — Samuel Langhorne Clemens, a.k.a. Mark Twain (1835-1910), one of America's greatest authors, has returned after 85 years of death to discuss his works, comment on modern society and find a good cigar. "Can't smoke in Heaven," says the legendary humorist. "Granted, it's a terrible habit, but the truth is, they don't allow habits in Heaven, good or bad. It's a stiff bunch up there. If it weren't for the Baptists, the place would be dead."

After spending a month catching up on the news since his death, Mr. Clemens will commence a national tour on July 30. He will appear on Crossfire, Rush Limbaugh, Late Night with David Letterman, Geraldo and Charlie Rose on PBS, among others.

As for Mr. Clemens' afterlife and the means of his return, the author wishes it made clear that, as a condition of his return, he cannot answer queries on the subject. He has, however, provided this list of answers to likely questions:

1) I did not meet God.

2) I did not meet Jesus.

3) I did not meet Buddha, Mohammed, Vishnu, or any of that ilk.

4) I did meet St. Peter.

5) He doesn't like all those jokes about people having to get past him before entering heaven.

6) Except the one about the HMO executive who's only allowed a three-day stay; that one lays him out cold.

Crossfire

Voice-over: On the left, Michael Kinsley. On the right, Pat Buchanan. In the Crossfire, author Samuel Clemens.

Kinsley: Mr. Clemens, you've no doubt heard how some people are pulling your "Adventures of Huckleberry Finn" from library shelves because it repeatedly contains a word disparaging to blacks. Because of that, people say you are a racist. Are you, or were you, Mr. Clemens?

Clemens: I was, and am, Mr. Clemens.

Kinsley: Ha, ha. No, I mean are you, or were you, a racist?

Clemens (pauses): The question of color is, well, let me tell you about Old Joe and Old Sam, who every day for 40 years …

Buchanan: Hold that thought. We'll be back after this.

(Commercial)

Kinsley: We're back. Mr. Clemens, you were going to answer the racist charge.

Clemens: I don't suppose time allows me a story.

Buchanan: You could …

Kinsley: But it wouldn't leave us time to argue.

Clemens (shakes head): I see the lay of it. All right, I'll put it plainly. In my books, some of my characters commit murder and adultery, but that doesn't mean I advocate murder and adultery. Some of my characters are happily married, have four children and don't drink, but that doesn't mean I advocate such a lifestyle.

Kinsley (laughs, raises eyebrows): Was that an answer?

Buchanan: So some of your characters might be racist, but you, personally, are not.

Clemens: If by that you mean, Do I make it a practice to disparage any one race more than any other?, the answer is no. I have been asked this question before, and I give the same reply: To me, a human being is a human being. He can't be any worse.

Kinsley: Mr. Clemens, with all due respect, that's a very cagey answer. But tell me, are you aware that some of your supporters, in defending you against the racist charge, claim that based on his speech, Huck Finn was actually African American? Was he, in fact, African American?

Buchanan: Here we go. More revisionist history —

Kinsley: Pat, Pat, let him answer. Was Huck African American?

Clemens: Yes.

Buchanan: He wha— ?

Kinsley (smiles at camera, severe spectacle glare): You heard it here first, folks.

(To Clemens) That would make Huck the greatest black hero in American literature.

Clemens (frowns): I don't believe I said that. I said he was African American, as you put it.

Kinsley: But—

Clemens: Since my return, gentlemen, I've had the opportunity to read an encyclopedia or two, and from what I read, it would seem the entire human race has been shown to stem from somewhere in Africa.

Buchanan: That means we're all—

Clemens: African American, sir. 'Cept you have to account for different nations, so you'd have your African Irish, your African Russian, and so on.

Kinsley (grinning): Can't you see Jefferson Davis turning over in his grave?

Clemens: Not unless you're buried next to him.

Kinsley (smiles): So we're all the same. Well that's a pretty liberal doctrine, Mr. Clemens.

Buchanan: Ah! So now the PC-liberal elite defends Mark Twain!

Kinsley: Oh Pat, go build an orphanage or something.

Buchanan: So, Mr. Clemens, the fact is that your writings supported minorities.

Clemens: As I recall, my writings supported my family.

Kinsley (laughs, throws up arms): Does this man ever give a straight answer?

Clemens: I have yet to find that profitable, or, frankly, preferred.

Buchanan: We're out of time. Michael and I will be right back to have one last go at each other.

(Break)

Kinsley: Well, Pat, I'm inclined to believe Sam Clemens really was an advocate for the disenfranchised of his time. I guess that makes him one of us, Pat — a liberal.

Buchanan: A liberal in his time is a conservative in ours.

Kinsley: Ha, ha. That's deep, Pat, but doesn't that make you a future neanderthal?

Buchanan: I take solace in that fact that it also means someday your socialist left-wing offspring will detest you.

Late Night with David Letterman

Letterman: My next guest is — and this is very, very exciting; you people will be selling your ticket stubs for cold hard cash after this show — my next guest is, to my mind, the greatest author in the history of this country, right up there with the guy who wrote "Sharky's Machine"... hee, hee, who was that guy, Paul?

Paul Schaffer: I, I don't know. Crazy guy. Crazy movie.

Dave: Ladies and gentlemen, his mother knew him as Samuel Clemens. You know him as Mark Twain.

(Applause. Clemens walks on stage, shakes hands, nods to crowd, sits. Demi Moore, previous guest, sits to his right.)

Dave: Mr. Clemens, or can I call you Sam? Or Mark? Do you prefer one or the other, or is it a mood thing?

Clemens: I seldom let my mood get in the way of—

Dave: Watch out kids, here it comes!

Clemens: Pardon?

Dave: Oh, um, sorry. It's just that, I don't know, I expected you to be so witty that ... hey (big smile), I just thought you were gonna say something witty. I mean, you were, like, the wittiest man alive, weren't you?

Paul (singing): Man, witty man, crazy witty man

Dave (leaning over, hand on Clemens' chair arm): Have you ever looked in Bartlett's? You know, that familiar quotations book thing. Man! It's like, you and Shakespeare wrote it or something. You're all over it! Did you know Shakespeare? He wrote "Sharky's Machine," I think.

Clemens: I don't imagine—

Dave: You know, Mr. Clemens, you're like, I don't know, 100 years old or something

Clemens: One hundred and sixty.

Dave (open-mouthed): One-sixty! And I thought I didn't have a shot at Demi Moore!

Demi: I think he's cute.

Audience: Awwww

Dave: Well, of course, we all do, don't we? (Forced smile. Frown.) Now, seriously, you're 160 and, you know, the world's changed a lot in that time, and don't you just find it incredible that right here, in this city, you still can't get a cab at rush hour?

(Clemens pulls cigar from breast pocket, lights it, puffs.)

Dave: Hey, hey there! Those things'll kill ya! Hee, hee.

Clemens: Forgive me. (Offers Dave cigar and light)

Audience: Ooooo

Dave: Hee, hee. You know I was thinking. Here you are, the most famous author in the world. You're probably richer than (turns to audience) — well, not me, of course — most people, and yet here you are, doing this two-bit show for $500 and a year's supply of Jimmy Dean pork sausage, or whatever we give guests these days. What I'm sayin' is, Sam, Mr. Clemens, are book sales sagging that bad? I can loan you some money. I think I've got an old check from NBC layin' around here somewhere.

Clemens (standing): Of all the gentlemen I have met on my return, you make death the most tolerable.

Audience: Ooooo

Dave: Paul, call Bartlett's!

Commercial

Voice-over: Mark Twain, you just came back from the dead. What're you gonna do next?

Clemens: I'm goin' to Washington, D.C.!

Director: Cut! No, it's Disneyland! Disneyland!

Clemens: Well confound it, what is this Disneyland?

Director. A theme park. It's got a castle and cartoon characters and funny shows and —

Clemens: Call it Disneyland if you like, but I've been to Washington and you just described it.

Charlie Rose

Rose (leans forward, eyes half-closed): Is it uncomfortable to find yourself, like your character in "A Connecticut Yankee in King Arthur's Court," in another age?

Clemens: Not at all. Things are pretty much as bad as I left them.

Rose: How so?

Clemens: France is still on the map.

Rose: Ha, ha. Yes. But seriously, don't you believe the human race has made some advances since your death?

Clemens: Has it? Still got no third eye; always thought that would be an advancement. And an extra stomach, for long trips.

Rose: No, no, I don't mean humans literally, but some of the things we've accomplished. Technology, for instance.

Clemens: You have made great strides in that arena, unfortunately.

Rose: Unfortunately?

Clemens: I didn't make any money off it.

Rose (smiles): Yes, I understand you invested in a failed technology or two in your day.

Clemens: Don't speak ill of the dead, son.

Rose (smiles): Of course. And that reminds me of something you once wrote. In Pudd'nhead Wilson's New Calendar, which is just packed with wonderful phrases, you wrote that "Pity is for the living, envy for the dead." You also wrote, "Be good and you will be lonesome," and, "Man is the only animal that blushes, or needs to." (Rose pauses, opens mouth, raises one brow, half-shuts eyes, cocks head, leans in, pats tabletop). In essence, you had a very dark outlook.

Clemens: We're all in the dark. When someone says they have seen the light, they're in the dark when they see it. And when someone goes to the light, that's another way of saying they're dead, or about to be.

Rose (pauses): Mr. Clemens, did you suffer from depression?

Clemens: I suffered from life. Of course, most people can't accept that, so they call it depression. It's like the time —

Rose: Um, um, I'm sorry, Mr. Clemens, we're out of time.

Clemens: We bein' interrupted by one of those infernal commercials?

Rose: Well, this is public television, so, eventually, yes.

Oprah!

Oprah: Sam, you died 85 years ago, and now you're back, but I understand you have no place to live, is that right?

Clemens: That's the case so far. My Hartford home is now a museum, and they've offered to let me a room, but I turned it down. It was the place Livy—

Oprah: Your wife, Olivia

Clemens: Yes. The place Livy and I shared. I couldn't go back. My former home in Elmira, N.Y., is also off limits. My last home, in Redding, Conn., no longer exists. But I'm no stranger to adverse conditions; why, one time out in Nevada, I, I, madam, I've made you cry.

Oprah (sobbing): It's all right. It's just that, I know your homelessness.

Don't touch that dial! Mark Twain grants Geraldo, Rush, Oprah, David Letterman and others a series of exclusive interviews.

Geraldo

Geraldo: Ladies and gentlemen, I'd like you to meet arguably the greatest author in American history, Samuel Langhorne Clemens. (Applause. Clemens, already seated, nods.) Of course, he's also known by his pen name, Mark Twain, the author of "Tom Sawyer," "Life on the Mississippi" and one story that gets to the heart of the matter today, a story called "Those Extraordinary Twins." For those who haven't read it, it's about Siamese twins, Angelo and Luigi, who are Italian royalty. They wind up in this small Missouri town where a local girl, Rowena, falls in love with one of the heads, Angelo. Now, yes, we have a question from the audience.

(Geraldo sprints up aisle, holds microphone before a woman, 45.)

Woman: Yes, Mr. Twain, I was wondering, did Rowena and Angelo make love? How did that make Luigi feel?

Clemens (pauses): Madam, I confess I've never been quite able to discuss my work in an intelligent manner, and some would argue that it's only because there's no intelligence in it to discuss, but nonetheless, I was told this meeting was called to attempt such a discussion. That story you mention, I suppose it's too much to expect that you actually read it.

Woman: I, um—

Geraldo: My staff provided a synopsis. In fact, before you came out, our stage manager gave the audience a quick overview.

Clemens: Well, then, you overviewed it wrong. Rowena's affection for Angelo was a minor point. The nut of the story—

Geraldo: Minor point? In the audience today we have six women who've fallen in love with Siamese twins. Stand up, where are you?

(Several women in front row stand up)

Geraldo: Their love was hardly minor. For example, Louise here — Louise, step up here a minute — Louise here lost her love when her mother ran off with the other twin, isn't that right, Louise? (Louise hangs head, sniffles) It's all right, Louise, let it out. (Louise and Geraldo hug)

Clemens: Never should have left the Mississippi.(Stands to leave)

Geraldo: Wait! You can't go! There's some questions you have to answer. For instance, in "Adventures of Huckleberry Finn," young Huck and Jim spend weeks together, alone, on a raft. Tell us, tell the world, was this the first instance of an interracial gay couple in literary history?

Clemens: Son, I may be 160, but I'm not too old to—

Geraldo: Okay then, tell us about the story "A Medieval Romance." For our viewers, it's the story of a woman, Lady Constance, who falls in love with her cousin, Conrad, only she doesn't know it, but Conrad is really a woman. Conrad spurns her, then Constance gets pregnant by another man, and tells everyone Conrad is the father. Great stuff. Yes, a question. (Gives microphone to man, 32)

Man: I'm not against lesbians, but doesn't your story promote out-of-wedlock parenthood?

Clemens (reddening): This is the damnedest interpretation I ever—

Geraldo (holds up hand): Please, please. I sense your anger. (Turns to audience, raises voice) What do you think? Do you sense his anger?

Audience: Yes!

Geraldo: Sam, it's all right to talk about these things now. It's the 1990s. I think you need a hug.

(Geraldo, arms wide, steps toward Clemens, who punches Geraldo in the nose and stalks off set)

Geraldo (on floor, holding nose): Wait! Have you met Elvis? How does he look?!

Rush Limbaugh

Rush: Mr. Clemens, you wrote so many great books: "Innocents Abroad," "The Prince and the Pauper," and "Tom Sawyer," which, if memory serves, included that femi nazi Becky Thatcher.

Clemens: Femi-nazi?

Rush: Just a little term I use. It only offends the guilty. Now, Mr. Clemens, one of the most remarkable things about your works, to me, is the timeless aspect. In "To the Person Sitting in Darkness," you spoke out against American intervention abroad. In "The Gilded Age," you wrote against bloated government. By Jove, we have the same problems. We could use you today.

Clemens: Who is we?

Rush: Americans, Mr. Clemens. Americans who want to take back their country.

Clemens: Was there an invasion? I hadn't heard.

Rush: Invasion? For decades, the liberal media elite had a stranglehold on this country. Our pride, our industry, our family values suffered as in no other time in our history.

Clemens: Values? When I was born, Mr. Limbaugh, men could openly, shamelessly buy other men.

Rush: Well, yes, slavery was—

Clemens: I was referring to Congress. But now that you bring it up, we had slavery as well. Are you sayin' our values have got worse than that?

Rush: No, sir. But after Mr. Lincoln — a Republican president — we had a spate of Democrats in control of the White House and Congress. They're the ones who sent this country into the fiery pit, a pit we are only now climbing out of. For that we can thank good, hard-working Americans like, who's on the line? Cal. Cal from Port St. Lucie, Fla. You're on the air.

Cal: Megadittos, Rush.

Rush: Thank you.

Cal: Megadittos, Mr. Clemens.

Clemens: Megadittos. That some sort of Indo-Germanic?

Rush: Ha, ha, ho. No, it's just a right-thinking American's way of thanking me for doing the Lord's work.

Clemens: Ah, Anglo-Bombastic.

Rush (Long pause. Lowers eyebrows and voice): You're a tiny little liberal, aren't ya? Be warned: I eat liberals for breakfast, lunch and dinner.

Clemens: From the look of you, I'll wager you've managed a snack between meals, as well.

Press Conference

(for which Clemens requested all questions be submitted in writing beforehand.)

Clemens: I have asked for this press conference, if that is the term, to announce that this is my last public appearance for the foreseeable future. The explanation is not complicated. Like the horse who enters a race only to find himself up against automobiles, the times have simply outrun me. I don't mean intellectually, of course. I've still got more sense than any 10 of you. But by trade I'm a storyteller, maybe not the best storyteller, but it's what I do, or did — I'll let you folks change the tense as you see fit. In my day, storytellin' was a fine art, maybe the highest art form. I'm not very objective on the subject. But it was the popular form of entertainment. A man could tell a story and people would wait and listen for him to finish, unless it was a particularly bad story. Then they might hang 'im, which, in some cases, was warranted. But today, the modern person doesn't take the time to listen; doesn't seem to want to listen. Everything has to be quick. Everything has to be done in 30 seconds. I imagine the sexual act has suffered quite a bit under this system.

This tendency toward immediacy is the reason I have asked you to submit questions in writing. I would like to have time to answer. I don't need you chattering away and interruptin' me just when I get goin'. And don't groan so. I've learned a little about the modern attention span, and will be brief.

(Picks up first card)

What are your plans for the future?

The life of a lecturer holds some attraction for me, but for the present I'm inclined to be a truck pilot, or truck driver, as you say. An honest profession, all in all. From what I see, these colossal belching beasts that drag their metal carcasses across the country are the closest thing I'll find to piloting a riverboat.

What do you think of television?

I haven't seen enough of it to know what to think, though I see it is the popular thing to criticize this device; to say that it separates us, keeps us locked up in our homes and prevents us from speaking to one another. But I may have misunderstood. These may be the arguments in favor of television.

What's the greatest threat to America?

Same as it is for the rest of this world, same as it's always been: irrational thinking. Unfortunately, it is the stuff of which we are made. Take those who claim God is on their side. And that's most of you. Where I was these past 85 years, I met people from all races, from all nations, from all religions and from no religion. To me, that says God doesn't take sides. Now, I read where, fairly recently, a man, a humble man of modest means, won a bass fishing tournament. It was a big tournament, biggest there is, and he hooked the most bass, or the heaviest, or a combination. I'm not sure which. For this, the man won loads of money, enough to make him rich. And almost overnight, he became famous. Got invited to all the biggest fish tournaments. Got paid good money to say he used all kinds of supplies that would help people catch more and more fish. And then, not long after this upswing in his fortunes, he died in an aeroplane crash. Now I ask you, whose side was God on, the fisherman, or the fish?

(Much media befuddlement. Sam Donaldson bets Tom Brokaw $5 it's the fish. Clemens reads the next card.)

Who would you like to meet the most?

I can jump on that directly: this author, Salman Rushdie — if I pronounced that right. I figure any man who can so upset the religious community is plain worth knowing.

Many have called you the greatest American writer. How would you like to be remembered?

It seems to me that half of you have sat me on a pedestal, and the other half would like to bury me under it. But if you're the type to praise me, say only that I was a thinking man; that, in itself, would put me above most. And if you're the type to condemn me, say only that I was a thinking man; that, in itself, should be offensive enough to you.

Do you think the races will ever be equal?

I believe the races are equal; we just pig-headedly refuse to acknowledge it. But that's human nature. Makes no difference if it's race, politics, business or love, offer a human being equality and the first thing he'll do is try to get more of it than the next fella. Like Old Sam and Old Joe, who sat down one day to play a game of checkers. They had been playing together every morning for 40 years, and on each of those mornings, three things never changed. Sam always played with the red checkers. Joe always played with the black ones. And Sam always won. But on this morning, Joe showed up with red checkers. He laid them out opposite of Sam's red checkers and silently, as he did every other day, Joe made the first move. Right off, Sam was indignant.

"What you think you doin', Joe? he said. We cain't both be the same color!"

"Why not?" Joe asked.

"Cause we cain't, that's all! If thar ain't no difference 'tween us, then no one can win over t'other. Thar's no advantage."

Joe slowly stroked his chin and stared at the board. Finally, he looked up at his gray-haired friend. "Sam," Joe said, "you been playin' red for 40 years, and for 40 years you been winnin'. I just wanted to see if it was you, or your color, what keeps you ahead."

"That's the most nimble-brained theory I ever heard!" said Sam, whose face puffed up red as his checkers. It was easy to see why Sam was so agitated. He was a naturally cantankerous fellow, and nothing in the world could upset him so as taking part in a parable, and that's exactly what he sensed coming. But as he was just a fictional creature, he had no option but to sigh and shake his head. He snatched up one of his pieces, moved it a space, and plunked it down loudly. "Fine," he muttered. "Your turn."

As the game wore on, Sam tried with all his mental might to keep track of which checkers belonged to whom, but after two dozen moves, it was clear they were lost and beyond hope. Exasperated, Sam folded his arms and sat back with a scowl.

Joe looked up. "You quittin', Sam?"

"Quittin'? Hell Joe, it's a useless draw. It's all a jumble. There's no winner when we're the same color."

"Not so," said Joe, failing to hold back a grin. "See, you been red for near on 40 years. I only been red one day and we already draw'd."

What do you see as man's greatest achievements since your death?

Hmmmm. I know people call me a cynic, and for that I thank them, but I confess that humans have done some extraordinary things since I left. You've cured diseases. You've invented the jet aeroplane and the computer, a curious machine which I may well never fully comprehend. In addition, I read where you actually sent human beings into space. This is a feat I find doubly remarkable, both for the fact that it was done, and for the fact that those who went up wanted to come back.

Oh, yes. I should add that there is a further remarkable development. I understand that you've made a weapon, a damnable weapon, capable of blowing this entire planet back to God. You haven't done it yet, which just goes to show that, once again, mankind has made something he doesn't know how to use correctly.

Now, does anybody have a match for an old man's cigar?

About the Contributors

Barbara Beeching: A native of Gary, Indiana, and a graduate of the University of Missouri School of Journalism, Barbara Beeching has lived in Connecticut since 1963. She spent 18 years with the state Department of Economic Development before retiring in 1992. She has a master's degree in American Studies from Trinity College and is pursuing a Ph.D. in American History at the University of Connecticut.

Lary Bloom: Editor of Northeast, the Sunday magazine of the Hartford Courant, Lary Bloom has also written a column in the magazine since its inception in 1982. He initiated the Twain's World project in 1995, and he is the author of "The Writer Within" and "Something Personal." A graduate of Ohio University, he was also editor The Miami Herald's Tropic magazine and the Akron Beacon Journal's Beacon magazine.

Garret Condon: A staff writer who specializes in health coverage, Garret Condon has been at the Courant since 1982. He has also worked at two other Connecticut newspapers, The Day of New London and the Middletown Press. A graduate of Boston College, he earned a master's degree in English from Trinity College.

Tom Condon: Tom Condon is a columnist for the Courant. He is a native of New London, Conn., a graduate of the University of Notre Dame and the University of Connecticut School of Law, and a Vietnam veteran. He has held a variety of reporting and writing jobs since joining the Courant in 1971, and has also written several books, most recently "School Rights: A Parent's Legal Handbook and Action Guide" (Macmillan 1996) with Patricia Wolff.

Steve Courtney: A journalist for 22 years, Steve Courtney is deputy editor of Northeast magazine. A graduate of Charter Oak State College, he has been a bureau chief, copy editor, science writer and magazine writer for the Courant. He is a student of history and is working on a biography of the Rev. Joseph Hopkins Twichell.

Jim Farrell: After 15 years as a journalist with the Concord (N.H.) Monitor, the Miami Herald and the Courant, Jim Farrell switched careers and is now an eighth-grade language arts teacher at Bennet Middle School in Manchester, Conn. A graduate of Holy Cross College, he still serves as a contributing editor to Northeast.

ANNE FARROW: Anne Farrow studied medieval poetry in the graduate program at the University of New Hampshire, and has worked in New England newspapers for 23 years. She joined the staff of the Courant in the summer of 1988, and has been special features editor at Northeast since 1992, where her abiding interest in literature has found expression in many of the magazine's public projects, including The Sunken Garden Poetry Festival and Connecticut Voices.

BRENDAN GILL: Brendan Gill was a New Yorker writer for 61 years and wrote a 1975 best-seller about the magazine, "Here at the New Yorker." A Hartford native, he was hired by editor Harold Ross in 1936 and wrote short stories, book reviews, film reviews, architectural criticism and "Talk of the Town" pieces. A man with a passionate love for architecture, his prime victory was the preservation of Grand Central Terminal.

JOAN D. HEDRICK: The author of "Harriet Beecher Stowe: A Life," Joan D. Hedrick received a Pulitzer Prize and a Christopher Stone Award for that landmark 1994 biography, which was published by Oxford University Press. A graduate of Vassar College who received a Ph.D. in American Civilization from Brown University, she has taught history at Trinity College since 1980.

STEVE KEMPER: Steve Kemper is a long-time contributor to Northeast, having written the magazine's "Conversations" column since 1986 as well as numerous other stories. He has also written for many national magazines, including Smithsonian, National Geographic, Outside and Yankee.

ROB KYFF: Rob Kyff is the language columnist for the Courant whose syndicated work also appears regularly in newspapers around the country. A native of Armonk, N.Y., Kyff has degrees from Amherst College and the University of Minnesota. He has taught English and history at Kingswood-Oxford School in West Hartford, Conn., since 1977.

ANDREW MARLATT: A freelance journalist, Andrew Marlatt's work has appeared in Northeast, New York, Yankee, Internet World, FamilyFun and many other magazines. He is a graduate of the University of Georgia and a product of the metro-Atlanta public school system, where he won the Presidential Physical Fitness Award in sixth grade.

COLIN MCENROE: Hartford-born and Yale-educated, Colin McEnroe is a freelance writer and radio talk-show host. A contributing editor for Mademoiselle and Men's Health, his work has also appeared in dozens of other magazines. He also writes for the Courant, where he worked full-time for two decades. McEnroe is the author of two books, both published by Doubleday.

JAMES A. MILLER: James A. Miller is professor of English and American Studies and directs the Africana Studies Program at the George Washington University. His publications include "Harlem: The Vision of Morgan and Marvin Smith" and "Approaches To Teaching Wright's 'Native Son.' " He was formerly a professor of English and American Studies at Trinity College and a trustee of the Mark Twain House.

SUSAN D. PENNYBACKER: An associate professor of history at Trinity College, Susan D. Pennybacker has written extensively for numerous publications. She has degrees from Columbia University, the University of Pennsylvania and the University of Cambridge, England. Pennybacker has been involved with the Hartford Studies Project since 1991.

SANDRA L. WHEELER: Sandra Wheeler, who received a certificate from the Modern Archives Institute in Washington, D.C., is a partner in an archival consulting business and the archivist at Hill-Stead Museum in Farmington. She is also part of the Hartford Studies Project at Trinity College.